Anita —

It's an honor & pleasure to have you as a friend & colleague.

Neal Z.   12/17/04

Treatment Planning for Person-Centered Care: The Road to Mental Health and Addiction Recovery

Treatment Planning for Person-Centered Care: The Road to Mental Health and Addiction Recovery

Mapping the Journey for Individuals, Families, and Providers

Neal Adams, MD, MPH
Diane Grieder, MEd

ELSEVIER
ACADEMIC
PRESS

AMSTERDAM • BOSTON • HEIDELBERG • LONDON
NEW YORK • OXFORD • PARIS • SAN DIEGO
SAN FRANCISCO • SINGAPORE • SYDNEY • TOKYO

Elsevier Academic Press
30 Corporate Drive, Suite 400, Burlington, MA 01803, USA
525 B Street, Suite 1900, San Diego, California 92101-4495, USA
84 Theobald's Road, London WC1X 8RR, UK

This book is printed on acid-free paper. ∞

Library of Congress Cataloging-in-Publication Data
Application submitted.

British Library Cataloguing in Publication Data
A catalogue record for this book is available from the British Library.

ISBN: 0-12-044155-1

For information on all Elsevier Academic Press publications
visit our Web site at www.books.elsevier.com

Printed in the United States of America
04 05 06 07 08 09 9 8 7 6 5 4 3 2 1

Acknowledgments

As all authors note, this book could not have been written without the assistance and support of many people. Similar to the team assisting the individual to achieve his or her goals in the person-centered approach, we have also had a team accompanying us on our first book-writing journey. Sincere thanks to our editor, Nikki Levy, who warned us, "writing a book will be the hardest thing you ever do," and she was right!

Many thanks to our colleagues who were willing to read, offer comments and support, and even edit portions of the book as it evolved: Ed Diksa, Wilma Townsend, Nirbay Singh, John Morris, Lesa Yawn, Nikki Migas, Wendy Graddison, Yana Jacobs, Penny Knapp, Sherry Kimbrough, and James W. Baxter.

Thanks are also due to the many individuals receiving services we have met in our professional careers, who have been a source of inspiration to us. They have taught us how to listen, to have hope, and to believe in them.

Most importantly, thanks to our respective families, who joined us on this road trip—sometimes willingly, sometimes not—and were the fountains of support, encouragement, understanding, and forgiveness that made writing this book possible. To our spouses, Lucy and Marion, and to our children, Alyssa, Caleb, Parris, and Zachary, we will be forever grateful.

Contents

SECTION I

Planning the Trip

SECTION II

Getting Started

SECTION III

On the Road

SECTION IV

Journey's End: The Destination

APPENDICES

Learning by Example

Prologue

Providers should consider this book one of the most important instructional tools in the field of mental health and addictive disorders. As an individual who began her professional life as a case manager, who later moved into administration and management, and who now works as a consumer advocate and consultant, I know that there has traditionally been little practical teaching about how to develop a treatment plan, or why it is important beyond its role in financial reimbursement. The value of a plan as a road map to assist the individual in their treatment process was never considered. There is a real need for a book that can assist all participants in mental health and addiction recovery to master the skills of a person-centered approach to developing individual plans.

Later, in my capacity as the chief of the Office of Consumer Services within the Ohio Department of Mental Health, the importance of an individual plan was immediately germane to our discussions about "what is recovery?" This in part led to the development of the booklet *Emerging Best Practices in Mental Health Recovery*[1]. That book was the result of work by consumers, families, clinicians, and researchers who studied the consumer's recovery process and the role of providers and the community in assisting them. *Emerging Best Practices* also led to the development of a curriculum on "Clinicians Facilitating a Consumers Recovery Process," which supported the development of a recovery management plan (RMP)/treatment plan. We found that language is crucial in the recovery process; changing the

---

[1] Ohio Department of Mental Health, 1999.

name of the document put the focus on the individual instead of putting the focus on the illness, as the term treatment plan seemed to do.

I have since left the Department of Mental Health and have been working with behavioral health systems on the implementation of the Emerging Best Practices in Mental Health model. This includes a very specific structure to assist providers and consumers in implementing person-centered care. I have trained providers and consumers, sometimes together, on this structure. I have also guided them in the journey of putting this process and form into practice. The journey is the individual's journey, so the individual must be the one who makes the final choices. In making these decisions, it is important that there is a structure to promote a dialogue between the individual and the provider about possibilities and choices. The creation of a person-centered plan can provide that structure and help the individual, in partnership with the provider, to identify long- and short-term goals for the consumer to work towards with their caregivers.

An RMP is a person-centered plan. In an RMP, all goals are written in both clinical terms as well as layperson language so that both the consumer and provider can relate to aspects of the RMP from their own perspective. Using the individual's own words, the RMP helps to identify the skills, knowledge, and action steps/interventions necessary to meet the goals. It also provides an opportunity for the individual to identify activities in the community that they want to pursue or organizations in the community can assist them in accomplishing their goals. The individual and the provider then decide how the provider can best assist them in accomplishing their goal. Oftentimes the RMP is actually completed by the individual, who is then given a copy to take home.

This process is all about helping the individual make decisions rather than the provider being the decision-making authority. It is about the individuals taking on more responsibility in their own recovery processes. Over time the individual will better understand that his or her illness is just one dynamic in their life. It is about enabling both the provider and the individual to recognize that in order to live, work, and have a meaningful life in the community, individuals must learn to make decisions for themselves and not rely forever on 24/7 supports. It is the individual's life to be lived.

In attempting to introduce these new approaches to established practice settings, many providers typically respond by saying: " . . . but we are already doing this" (i.e., person-centered planning). It is only after being trained and practicing this process that they realize it is really quite different. They realize that in the past they have not used a structure that truly enabled the individual to express and fulfill his or her partnership role in treatment and recovery. Providers come to realize that the individual needs to more actively exercise options and choices, make decisions, and be accountable for his or her actions. Providers see, in contrast, how they have been unwittingly making decisions and directing care.

After several years of experience in many different sites and settings, it is clear to me and others that a person-centered approach can and does make a real difference for individuals and supports their growth and recovery (see the epilogue for a collection of individual recovery stories). Providers who have developed skills in person-centered planning appreciate the importance of treatment plans beyond reimbursement and administrative requirements. The real goal of person-centered planning is for the provider and individual, in partnership, to create a road map for reaching the individual's goals—and at the same time documenting medical necessity and supporting billing.

Not only am I a provider and trainer, I am also a person who has received services within the behavioral health care field and whose provider used a person-centered approach to planning and creating my personal road map to recovery. Because of this, I felt like I was a part of the process, that the process was about my recovery and me, and I was able to truly benefit from services.

It is very important and necessary for individuals pursuing mental health and addiction recovery to design their own road map. This book will assist providers in understanding their role in the journey of developing and facilitating an individual's road map through person-centered planning.

Wilma Townsend

Foreword

This book offers an exciting, dynamic, and fresh approach to the challenges of developing individual plans for mental health and addiction services. Our goal is to help make planning a manageable task for providers, a meaningful process for individuals receiving services, and a resource tool to assure person-centered care and optimal outcomes.

It should be clearly stated at the outset that this book is not a how-to manual for completing forms. Rather, the focus should be on the *process* of using the service plan to build effective and collaborative healing partnerships with individuals and families in pursuit of resilience, wellness and recovery.

This book was written with a focus towards relevance for all providers and settings, ranging from traditional one-to-one approaches in private practice to multidisciplinary teams in community care organizations or residential and inpatient facilities. Using a practical approach, rich with examples adapted to a wide range of adult learning styles, it is intended to be suitable and valuable for an independent reader or classroom learning. The book is intended to help students and experienced providers improve their ability to develop person-centered plans that enhance the value and efficacy of services. In this way, providers will be better able to develop an individual plan that optimizes outcomes for the individual as well as meet the requirements of payers, accreditation standards, regulatory bodies, and so on.

We believe that there is also a need for this kind of text for students in pre-degree training programs as well as for established professionals who want to respond to important changes and trends sweeping through all of health care. Service recipients, families, advocates, policy makers, and others should all find useful information and resources in these chapters.

A recovery-oriented system or program can be defined as having values of a *person orientation* (a focus on the individual who has strengths, talents, and interests, rather than the person as a case or a diagnostic label), *person* involvement (the individual's right to participate in all aspects of the service, including designing the individual plan, and implementing and evaluating services), *self-determination/choice* (a person's right to make decisions and choices about all aspects of their treatment, such as desired outcomes and preferred services), and *growth potential* (given the opportunity and necessary resources, the inherent capacity of any individual to recover, grow, and change).

It is becoming increasingly clear that a person-centered approach to care, in which the recipient of services is the driving force in the development of his or her individual plan, is a de facto standard of quality. The importance of choice, empowerment, and engagement are recognized as keys to effective care and positive outcomes, not only in mental health and substance abuse but in general health care as well.

This book attempts to blend a commitment to recovery, resiliency, and wellness with a practical, simple, and straightforward approach so that all readers—from students to providers—will develop the skills that they need to write effective plans. The various sections include strategies, tips, and sample plans and forms, as well as illustrative examples to help practitioners succeed in the ever-evolving health care delivery system.

To help the reader more easily access the information in this book, there are several layers of content focus, with the chapters organized into four sections. Each section describes the various phases of a trip; seeing the pursuit of wellness and recovery as a journey is a useful way of thinking about the steps and processes that need to be considered in developing a person-centered plan.

With this metaphor in mind, an individual plan can easily be thought of as a map. Few people begin a journey without some sense of destination and at least a preliminary route. Together, the individual seeking services and the provider develop the individual plan (map) that will hopefully lead to the recovery goal or outcome (destination) the individual wants to achieve. The intermediate steps are the objectives of the individualized plan (sites to visit along the trip). The services/interventions (route) help assure that each intermediate step is reached.

In addition, each chapter is organized into three parts:

- *Stating the Case*
- *Creating the Solution*
- *Making It Happen*

Stating the Case is a look at the *status quo* as well as emerging trends in both theory and practice. *Creating the Solution* presents the essentials of a person-centered approach to preparing and implementing individual plans. *Making It Happen* includes examples of plans as well as strategies for changing systems and practices.

As all travelers know, a map is an indispensable tool to help guide the journey. Thinking about individual planning as a trip to be mapped helps us to better explore and understand the process. Ultimately, creating a plan is about helping an individual to envision their own journey (creating a map that directs their trip). At the same time, our ability to be helpful and stay on track is enhanced by having the course laid out and the destination identified.

Bon voyage!

Neal Adams, MD, MPH
Diane Grieder, MEd

Preface

The use of language is often anchored in history, tradition, assumptions, and values. Words communicate ideas that go beyond the terms and phrases themselves. But this is by no means static; there are trends and periodic shifts that impact how we think and understand the world around us and help to shape the work that we do. Accordingly, a few comments about language must precede the text that follows.

Our desire is to make this book as useful and relevant as possible to the needs of the broadest audience without being limited to any particular practice model, philosophy, or professional discipline beyond a commitment to person-centered care. This requires the thoughtful use of language and an attempt at neutrality. While there are those who decry as well as those who celebrate political correctness, there is no question that the use of language can either engage, distract, or even repel a reader. After considerable discussion, we elected the following lexicon to use in discussing the principles and practice of developing plans to meet the needs of individuals and families receiving services.

For the focus of this book itself, the *plan* is often referred to as an individual treatment plan, an individual services plan (ISP), a consumer services plan (CSP), an individual recovery management plan (RMP), an integrated plan, a service coordination plan, and so forth. For our purposes, we have settled on the simple term *individual plan*, which stresses the notion of person-centeredness.

We use the term *individual* to refer to patients, clients, residents, members, users, consumers, and persons served. Some words imply passivity, while others connote participation. Language that respects the dignity as well as unique attributes and needs of all people is critically important. Oftentimes throughout the book, references to the individual are tied to the *family*. For children and adolescents, it should be a given that is always implied, if not explicitly stated, that family is essential to understanding and responding to the needs of the individual. For adults, it is recognition of the important role that family plays in all of our lives—for better or for worse. Family may be defined in traditional terms or may be a constellation of relatives and friends determined by the individual. Regardless, that essential support network commonly referred to as family should almost always be considered in planning mental health and addiction services.

We have chosen the term *services* to refer to what in some settings might be called treatment, care, support, therapy, rehabilitation, and so forth. Recognizing that there are different models, different philosophies and attitudes, and a range of professional disciplines and clinical traditions (including both licensed and degreed as well as paraprofessional and peer providers), we felt that *services* was the most neutral and inclusive term to use at this time.

The term *narrative summary* is used within this book to describe what might be called an interpretive summary, diagnostic summary, or clinical formulation. It is an essential but often overlooked part of assessment and planning which attempts to create meaning and relevance from the factual database of the assessment. Understanding each individual and their unique circumstances and needs should be clearly articulated and documented.

Additionally, we settled on the term *provider* to describe people frequently referred to as doctor, clinician, counselor, therapist, psychologist, case manager, nurse, aide, caregiver, treatment team, self-help peer, and so forth, working in a wide range of settings. All of these roles and titles hold in common their service to people in need of assistance and support.

Alternatively referred to as a chart, medical record, documentation, client or patient record, electronic record, health information, and so forth, we felt that the simple term *record* was sufficient. Regardless of format or organization—from 19th century pen and paper to 21st century data systems—creating and maintaining a record of our assessments, our understanding, the plan of action, and services provided remains a key part of our job.

The idea of *recovery* is referenced throughout the book. This is an emerging concept in mental health and reflects a new way of thinking about the impact of services and the importance of individual goals and outcomes. Wellness, resiliency, and rehabilitation are among many other terms often used interchangeably. At the same time, the term recovery has had long-standing use in the addiction treatment field where it conveys a lifelong process of facing one's challenges and vulnerabilities. We believe that the idea of recovery should be a central theme and shared universal goal for all of mental health and addiction services.

We recognize that not everyone will necessarily agree with our choices. At the same time, we hope that no one will find them off-putting or offensive. We trust that each reader can translate these terms into those words and phrases that best fit their own perspective, philosophy, setting, and work. Hopefully the values and principles that follow will prove durable and transcend the limitations and constraints of language.

We have written this book based upon our collective years of study and practical experience in the field as providers, trainers, administrators, surveyors, and consultants. Too often we have seen quality programs and top-notch providers fall short of their potential to succeed and excel because of problems in individual planning. Too often we have witnessed individuals in need of help disappointed and frustrated at not receiving the services and benefits they need and deserve. Our belief is that effective and meaningful planning for service delivery does make a difference.

We have had the satisfaction of seeing providers, along with individuals receiving services, celebrate their shared satisfaction and success when lives are changed and people achieve their own vision of wellness, resilience, and recovery. This book is dedicated to and reflective of our commitment to the spirit that makes us each uniquely human. Its inspiration lies in understanding the power of one person's care for another, and the value of thoughtful planning as we work to help those who ask for our assistance.

Planning the Trip

The essential task in planning this journey of discovery and learning is to fully understand the relevance and importance of individual plans in contemporary mental health and addiction recovery practice, regardless of the setting or population served. Similar to the earlier stages of considering a trip, this section provides both history and background along with an overview of current trends and issues in assessment, individual planning, and documentation.

The notion of person-centered care was once a defining feature of rehabilitation approaches. Now it is no longer isolated to rehabilitation practice. The importance of person-centered approaches to care is reshaping practice throughout health care. Understanding what is meant by person-centered care, and clarifying the role of both the provider and the person served, are crucial to successful planning and outcomes.

At the end of this section, the importance, value, and relevance of undertaking this trip should be clear. Then, knowing the destination, the traveler can make the necessary plans and prepare for the beginning of the journey.

## CHAPTER 1

Introduction: Planning the Trip

When you're finished changing—you're finished.

Benjamin Franklin

I. STATING THE CASE

What does it mean to be person-centered? What are recovery and resiliency? What is the role of the individual plan? These are critical questions challenging all health care providers at the dawn of the 21st century, and they are especially important for both providers and individuals seeking mental health and addictive disorders services. There is a growing consensus that current service delivery systems are failing to meet the needs of society as well as of individuals and families. Changing current practices in service planning can be a powerful strategy for effecting overall systems change. Ensuring that individuals and families are at the center of the process and directing their own plans and care should be an essential component of transformation in health care delivery. The challenges of daily work and the experience of providers in mental health and addictions stand in contrast to those concepts. Across all of the disciplines, providers frequently complain about feeling overwhelmed by a host of demands that keep them from their primary task of providing services. Consistently, the task of developing individual service plans is identified as the most clinically irrelevant, meaningless, frustrating, and mandatory administrative burden providers face. Training in this necessary task is often minimal and skill levels are low. Most direct care providers would likely groan in protest at the mention of attending training on individual planning, or the necessity of having up-to-par clinical documentation.

How can the individual plan simultaneously be viewed as a key element of systems transformation and be so disdained by providers? Why was reform of current planning practice identified as a major goal in the President's New Freedom Commission on Mental Health report?[1] Is there any evidence that person-centered planning really improves the individual and family experience of care, promotes effectiveness, and enhances outcomes?

The History

The requirements and expectations for individual planning are long-standing and well established in regulation, payer requirements, and clinical standards. Despite this, auditors for licensure and certification, accreditation surveyors, and quality improvement staff consistently find that individual planning practices fall short of expectations. For example, CARF...The Rehabilitation Accreditation Commission, a leading standards-setting organization in the mental health and addictive disorders fields, has found that accreditation standards related to assessment and individual planning are cited in over 40% of accreditation surveys. Frequently identified problems include the lack of adequate assessment data, limited analysis or integration of information, uncertainty about goals and objectives, confusion about the differences between objectives and services, and inconsistent participation by the individual and the family receiving services.

While there is a general lack of study and evidence on the impact and value of individual planning, the practice may be so well accepted and expected simply because it has compelling face validity. In many sectors of our society, planning is a routine activity and a prerequisite for action. The quality of outcomes is often understood as a reflection of the integrity of the planning process and the quality of the plan itself. In general, the greater the complexity of a task that is undertaken, the greater the attention that is applied to the planning process.

Architecture is an example of a profession in which planning activities are essential to the practice, and the central role of the client is understood. Although the client may lack the professional and technical ability to design and construct a building, the architect understands that it is his or her role to make sure that the client's needs, wishes, and dreams are included in the planning process. It is a given that the client's expectations will be clearly visible in the final outcome.

It is not clear why the culture of the mental health and addictive disorders field has evolved so differently, but we can easily speculate. The tradition of psychiatry and mental health treatment derives from psychoanalytic practice, in which the emphasis was chiefly on process rather than outcome. As planning implies movement to an identified end point or goal, a process-driven approach did not necessitate nor lend itself well to planning. However, as systems of care became more organized, and as payers and oversight organizations began to demand more accountability for services and outcomes, there were increased expectations for coherent and visible planning. Yet some of the implicit values and expectations of the field and the traditions of practice were antithetical to the idea of planning. Moreover, the skill and motivation to teach and practice a planned approach to services did not exist.

In the addictive disorders field, the emphasis has been on personal and peer experience as a primary therapeutic tool and on sobriety as an outcome. The focus on proscribed group treatment and organized programs is not easily adapted to unique individual needs or concerns, and it diminishes the relevance of individual plans. Why emphasize individual planning when the goals and interventions have been effectively predetermined?

There is some limited research evidence that suggests that person-centered approaches to individual planning can make a difference. In a recent Arkansas study,[2] the outcomes of a demonstration program involving Medicaid recipients with a range of disabilities were examined. The evaluation revealed that individuals receiving "consumer-directed" services reported higher levels of satisfaction and reported that an increased number of needs were fulfilled. These data are quite promising and strongly support the value and importance of actively involving individuals and families in decisions about services.

Although there is no strong evidence base demonstrating the value of a person-centered approach to individual planning, there is some "practice-based evidence" supporting the idea that planning is more than just a burdensome requirement. Liberman et al.,[3] for example, have put forward the notion that individual planning is the essential ingredient of care:

> *A key element in achieving favorable outcomes is the active involvement of clients, together with their families and other natural supporters, in the process of treatment planning, intervention, and evaluation of progress. To motivate clients to engage in treatment and adhere to comprehensive treatment regimens, the multidisciplinary team must help them identify personally meaningful goals*

and demonstrate that collaborating with treatment providers can help them attain their goals. Because treatment and rehabilitation must be individualized, evidence-based interventions cannot be taken directly from controlled clinical trials and applied to all clients in the same way. Standardized treatments, both psychosocial and pharmacological, not only must be tailored to the individual client but also must be integrated with other services into a coherent package that changes as necessary with the phase of the disorder and the client's goals as treatment proceeds.

In spite of this, experience shows that providers continue to see creation and utilization of an individual plan as an administrative and clinical burden, an unnecessary paperwork demand that takes time away from their "real work"—responding to the needs of individuals seeking services. The commonly held view is that there is little value in planning. In day-to-day practice, it is not uncommon to find that the plan is, in fact, not used to guide services. As a result, there is little evidence that an individual plan does, in fact, lead to better outcomes rather than simply waste time and paper.

Evidence-Based Practice

Evidence-based practice (EBP) is quickly becoming the *de facto* standard of care throughout all of health care. At the same time, there are special concerns about its application and use in the mental health and addictive disorders services field. Drake et al.[4] have identified three principles of EBP as it applies to mental health and addictive disorders services. They suggest that EBP involves the following:

1. using the best available scientific evidence
2. individualizing the evidence for the unique needs and preferences of each person
3. a commitment to the ongoing expansion of evidence and clinical expertise

However, Drake et al. go on to say that "the movement toward fully informing patients and families about the evidence, engaging them in a process of informed, shared decision-making, and protecting their rights to self-determination has generally lagged in mental health and addictive disorders treatment. Accurate information regarding illness, treatment options, effectiveness, and risks is rarely offered; patients are often considered incompetent to make such decisions and subjected to involuntary treatments; and providers operate from an outmoded paternalistic model."

The gap between the Liberman et al.[3] and Drake et al.[4] insights, experience, and common practice in the field today is nothing short of troubling. Why does it seem necessary to convince providers—individual practitioners or large organizations—that planning can be an efficient, useful, and beneficial, if not essential, part of the service delivery process?

It is worthwhile to note that many of the values and principles now invoked in general health care, as well as the mental health and addictive disorders field, have their roots in the tradition of rehabilitation sciences and practice. For example, the developmental disabilities field has been undergoing a quiet revolution over the past 10 to 15 years in which the role of the individual receiving services—along with the roles of the provider and family—has been radically transformed. Similar changes have also occurred in the provision of services to children with severe emotional disturbances (SED) and their families. Long ago it was understood that focusing on strengths, fostering independence, and promoting self-determination could help people to realize their hopes and dreams even in the face of substantial challenges. The critical change occurred with a shift in the relationship between the individual and the provider from a provider-driven focus on services to a person-centered emphasis on recovery, wellness, resilience, and community integration.

The Future

Regardless of how we might try to understand the past, the vision for the future is clear. The 2003 President's New Freedom Commission on Mental Health report[1] stated the following:

> *Nearly every consumer of mental health services . . . expressed the need to fully participate in his or her plan for recovery.*

Although not stated explicitly, the report strongly implied that this has not always been the case in service delivery systems. Instead, "consumers" have often suffered the results of fragmented and complex systems that have not provided hope or the opportunity for recovery and control of their own lives. Yet self-determination is vitally important to mental health and well-being. The need for improvement in the development of individual plans as a key element in system reform points to the shortcomings of current practice. Success in creating person-centered individual plans is essential if we are to succeed in creating the service-delivery systems that people want and deserve for mental health and addictive disorders.

The President's Commission created a new vision of the experience of receiving services. The roles of the individual and family must be made explicit: an individual plan should describe the services and supports an individual and family need in order to enhance resilience and achieve recovery.

> *Consumers' needs and preferences should drive the type and mix of services provided, and should take into account the development, gender, and linguistic or cultural aspects of providing and receiving services. Providers should develop these customized plans in full partnership with consumers, while understanding changes in individual needs across the lifespan and the obligation to review treatment plans regularly.*

Always a dynamic endeavor, the mental health and addictive disorders field is moving into a new era; there is growing awareness of the paradigm shift impacting all of health care. Interest in—if not demand for—quality and accountability, and the expectation that services are person-centered and based upon the current best evidence of effectiveness, continues to increase. At the same time, the language of recovery, and a new hopefulness about the value and effectiveness of services, is spreading among both providers and individuals receiving services. The importance of ensuring that services are customized and responsive to the unique needs and attributes of each individual and family is more critical than ever. This is consistent with the crucial need to be culturally competent in all phases of assessment and service provision. The development of individual plans creates an opportunity to group these sometimes competing demands and expectations. A well-crafted plan is the key to success in providing services.

The psychoanalytic/psychodynamic tradition of mental health practice placed an emphasis on issues of transference and power differentials in the relationship between the individual and the provider. The new emerging model for the mental health and addictions field clearly calls for re-examination and re-alignment of the treatment relationship; a cooperative partnership and effective alliance between the person served and the provider must prevail. Individuals and families present their unique strengths and resources, while the provider serves as a consultant who offers expertise with full respect for the dignity of the individual and family and recognition of the importance of their choices and preferences. The emphasis is not on exploration of the subterranean unconscious or on covert fault-finding, but rather on the clear articulation of the individual's hopes and dreams coupled with an understanding of the challenges and barriers that must be overcome. The provider is transformed from a dominant and controlling figure to a coach and facilitator helping people to develop skills and grow. This must be reflected in all phases of the process, especially in assessment and planning.

Person-Centeredness

Past practice can be understood, in part, as a result of basic assumptions or rules that structure the relationship between providers and individuals receiving services. Individual planning has typically followed a medical model or tradition with an emphasis on the problems and deficits of the individual. Treatment goals and objectives have been driven mostly by provider attitudes and assumptions. The focus has been on symptom reduction and the management of disability instead of life success. While there has been, at least in theory, some acknowledgment of the importance of input from the individual receiving services, development of individual plans, for the most part, have not been truly person-centered. Rather, the tendency has been to emphasize problems or diagnoses and to use pre-scribed responses in lieu of individualized goals, objectives, and service interventions.

The Institute of Medicine (IOM)'s 2001 landmark report, *Crossing the Quality Chasm: A New Health Care System for the 21st Century*,[5] cited *person-centeredness* as one of the six primary aims of a transformed quality health care delivery system. Not only does the report identify core goals or domains, it also identifies 10 rules or principles that should guide and shape provider behavior. The report also contrasts the implicit and explicit rules that have guided and governed current practice with a proposed new set of guidelines. With its emphasis on person-centered care, the IOM provides a framework to support quality improvement strategies that help shift theory and policy into practice.

Sadly, good examples of person-centered approaches to individual planning in everyday mental health and addictive disorders practice are difficult to find. Many providers are at a loss as to how to achieve this vision. Given that individual planning is often viewed as an administrative requirement of limited clinical value, there is little appreciation of individual planning as an acquired skill, if not a clinical art. Although individual planning should be viewed as an essential clinical activity that is given high regard and supported with the necessary resources, all too frequently it is not. In some settings it is frankly devalued, and the connection between individual planning and outcomes has been lost. Frequently, the time allotted to assessment and plan development is too limited. Merely filling in the blanks on an individual plan form does not satisfy the requirements for proper individual planning. Rather, an accurate understanding of the individual's needs, strengths, and goals, as discovered through the relationship with the provider, should shape and form both the process and the product. The plan format should support rather than define the process. The development of the plan must be a learning experience for the individual as well as the provider and must act as the basic foundation of an effective helping relationship. In this notion of planning, creation of the plan is in itself a meaningful and valuable (and billable) service provided, not just another bureaucratic hurdle to be cleared.

Education and Training

A review of the literature on individual planning reveals, for the most part, a gap between emerging concepts of best practice and the training and education of the workforce: there seems to be little, if any, emphasis or focus on person-centered approaches. Individual planning is not often taught in either pre-degree education or professional training programs. Moreover, it is not at all uncommon for non-degree paraprofessionals to be given primary responsibility for the creation of individual plans. Typically, on-the-job training is limited at best. To the extent to which planning is taught, the emphasis is on didactic review of the formal elements of a plan. There is little if any focus on actually developing and practicing the skills in service settings. Feedback is provided only on rare occasions. This is not only a reflection of how individual planning is undervalued, it is also an explanation as to why practice is so slow to change.

This is but one example of many ways in which today's education and training programs fail to adequately prepare the workforce for the real demands of providing services.[6] Training and skill development must keep pace with changing expectations and demands. Resources to support these changes are clearly needed. If the vision of a recovery-oriented system is to be realized, individual planning needs to assume its rightful place in the curriculum and training experience for providers in the mental health and addictive disorders field.

II. CREATING THE SOLUTION

The relationship and interactions between individuals and providers must change if the aim of person-centered care is to be achieved. Without such changes, the substantial gap between theory and practice, the difference between what should be and what is, will continue to grow. The solution lies in a commitment at all levels of the mental health and addiction service systems to assure that individual planning succeeds. Individual planning needs to become an essential, valued, and meaningful clinical activity, rather than an administrative requirement.

A New Framework

A new framework and perspective are needed to understand the import-ance of the individual plan. A person-centered approach offers an exciting, dynamic, and fresh response to the challenges of individual planning for mental health and addictive disorders services; the recipient of services must be the driving force in the development of a plan that articulates a vision of recovery and wellness for each individual and family. Ideally, individual planning should be the following:

- an opportunity for creative thinking
- a successful strategy for managing complexity
- an opportunity to build an alliance with the individual receiving services
- a mechanism for acknowledging the hopes and dreams as well as the strengths and resources of each individual and family
- a means for assuring the provision of person-centered effective (and, whenever possible, evidence-based) services
- a process for creating a guide for the journey to recovery of each individual and family

Such a framework creates a positive alternative to current practice that is about more than just changing procedures, forms, or requirements. Ultim-ately, it is about changing the very model by which we understand the needs of persons seeking help and the response of providers. Individual planning must be a manageable task for providers, a meaningful process for individuals receiving services, and a resource tool to ensure optimal out-comes, while satisfying the expectations and requirements for payers and oversight authorities.

According to the 2003 President's Commission report,[1] individual plans are viewed as

> . . . *a genuine opportunity to construct and maintain meaningful, productive, and healing partnerships. The goals of these partnerships include:*

- *improving service coordination*
- *making informed choices that will lead to improved individual outcomes*
- *ultimately achieving and sustaining recovery*

The Map

An individual plan has been compared to a road map that displays the path or direction of the journey for each individual and family. Using this metaphor, the goal of services can be considered the destination consistent with their vision of recovery. But, as with most journeys, there are many possible routes, barriers, and obstacles that must be overcome or avoided, unanticipated detours and side trips to distract or deter, and mid-course corrections to be made. In a long journey, we often make stops along the way. The longer the journey, the more likely the route to be indirect and filled with detours and midpoints.

All too often the journey is initiated without a clear destination or route. This is similar to stating that we need to get there without ever really saying where *there* is. We frequently get behind the wheel simply because it seems important to get going but without knowing what direction to head in or the next point along the way. Providing mental health and addictive disorders service is not as simple as going to the convenience store around the corner—a trip that is routine and admittedly needs little planning. Rather it is created anew for each individual and family based upon their unique needs and preferences. It is surprising how often services are initiated without this kind of understanding or plan.

Like a road map, a plan displays the course. Figure 1.1 provides a simple yet effective image of this idea. Sometimes the final destination seems to be remote and unattainable. By division into a plan or itinerary with a series of intermediate destinations, a potentially overwhelming journey is broken into manageable steps. This is helpful for the traveler—the individual receiving services—and for the provider serving as "coachman" or pilot.

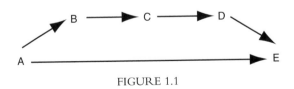

FIGURE 1.1

In this diagram, A is the starting point—derived from the assessment and based upon an understanding of the individual's needs; E is the end point—the goal of the person in seeking services, the end of the journey. The important question to ask and understand is this: why is the individual not able to simply move directly from A to E? Those reasons are oftentimes identified as barriers or challenges and become the focus of service interventions. In an individual plan, points $B, C,$ and D are the equivalent of objectives that work to remove or resolve the barriers. The arrows from A to B to C and so on represent the services and activities that help the individual move along in his or her journey.

This diagram should not be taken too literally—it does not mean to imply that the process is always sequential and linear. Sometimes several objectives may be addressed simultaneously; at other times there is doubling back; and there are occasions when a change in plans or route will require mid-course corrections. But this kind of map makes the process of recovery and meeting goals very clear to all those involved. Instead of being a mysterious and obscure process, it will be one that is apparent and clear to the provider as well as the individual and family seeking services.

Developing the skill and discipline to create these kinds of maps—either figuratively or literally—can do a tremendous amount to change current practice, the experience of individuals, and the outcome of services. This is a very practical and easy way to approach individual planning. With a shared understanding and clarity, both the planning process and recovery itself proceed more rapidly and with greater efficacy.

III. MAKING IT HAPPEN

A simple, straightforward, and practical approach to translating the concepts of person-centered care and individual planning into routine practice is clearly needed. This approach should apply to all providers responsible for planning and providing services, ranging from solo practitioners to multi-disciplinary teams. It involves a learnable set of skills and techniques that can substantially change both the experience of care and the outcome when applied to the needs of individuals and families. This book is intended to help providers gain the knowledge and skills required to make necessary changes in their practice. It is also intended to inform policymakers and administrators of systems changes that should occur to support providers in their efforts.

Systems Change

The importance of changing the world one individual and one provider at a time cannot be underestimated. As demonstrated by Gladwell in *The Tipping Point*,[7] small changes can often have large effects. System transformation can, and oftentimes does, occur in small ways—the whole can become greater than the sum of its parts. Ensuring that providers have the necessary knowledge, skills, and abilities to succeed in a person-centered approach is crucial to changing service-delivery systems, changing the experience of individuals and families, and making a vision of recovery and resilience real. Each reader, each student, and each provider has the potential to change practice. This is reflective of the hope, promise, and power that a person-centered model provides for individuals. Changes in treatment models, assessment practices, and the relationships between providers and individuals and families seeking services *will* make a difference.

Attention must also be paid to the larger practice environment. It would be disingenuous not to acknowledge that the changes required to truly succeed in person-centered planning often go far beyond clinical routines and individual care. Changes in systems of care are ultimately part of changing the individual planning process. It is not about merely changing administrative requirements, creating new forms, or successfully passing an audit or survey; it is about the clear articulation of values and fundamental changes in practice and the experience of providers, individuals, and families.

The burden of service systems change is often disproportionately borne by direct-care staff. However, to truly succeed, change strategies require endorsement and support from all levels of a service organization—especially administration and leadership, who need to ensure that the resources and time necessary to affect a changeover are, in fact, available.

Moving Forward

As a practical step, all those involved in providing services should conduct a fearless inventory of current practices, clinical as well as administrative. Being honest about current practice is an essential first step in identifying needs and strategies for change. It is an often-observed irony that a field dedicated to helping others make change so often finds itself bound by the past and unable to move forward.

A useful approach can be a SWOT analysis—a careful evaluation of

- **S**trengths
- **W**eaknesses
- **O**pportunities
- **T**hreats

Strengths should include recognition of current practices that should be preserved. *Weaknesses* should identify those elements of current practice that keep planning and services from being person-centered. *Opportunities* are those circumstances that allow for and foster necessary change. *Threats* are the resistances and barriers—both internal and external—that must be overcome.

Ultimately, we are left with a series of questions. How can the principles of person-centered care be adopted within the realities of the current system? What are the barriers and impediments to making necessary changes? How can each provider change his or her own practice and the larger system in which he or she works?

There will be times when the wisdom of the Serenity Prayer needs to prevail:

> *God, give me the serenity to accept things that cannot be changed; the courage to change things that must be changed; and the wisdom to distinguish one from the other.*

Hopefully the following chapters will provide the information required to promote the new attitudes, skills, knowledge, and abilities needed to support all those who travel down the pathway of change.

REFERENCES

1. New Freedom Commission on Mental Health. *Achieving the Promise: Transforming Mental Health Care in America*, 2003.
2. Foster, L., et al. *Improving the Quality of Medicaid Personal Assistance Through Consumer Direction*. Health Affairs, available at http://www.healthaffairs.org/WebExclusives/2203Foster.pdf.
3. Liberman, R.P., et al. Requirements for multidisciplinary teamwork in psychiatric rehabilitation. *Psychiatric Services*, 52(10):1331–1342, 2001.
4. Drake, R.M., et al. Fundamental principles of evidence-based medicine applied to mental health care. In press for *Psychiatric Clinics of America*.

5. Institute of Medicine. *Crossing the Quality Chasm: A New Health Care System for the 21st Century.* Washington, DC: National Academy Press, 2001.

6. Hoge, M. The Training Gap: An Acute Crisis in Behavioral Health Education. *Administration and Policy in Mental Health*, 29:4/5, 305–317, 2002.

7. Gladwell, M. *The Tipping Point: How Little Things Can Make a Big Difference.* New York, NY: Back Bay Books, 2002.

## CHAPTER 2

Person-Centered Care

> . . . everything can be taken from a man but one thing: the last of the
> human freedoms—to choose one's attitude in any given set of
> circumstances, to choose one's one way.
>
> Viktor E. Frankl
>
> Live your life, not your diagnoses.
>
> Anonymous

I. STATING THE CASE

Multiple reports in the last 5 years have stressed the need to rethink how
mental health and addictive disorders services are planned for and provided
to individuals and families. These include the *Report of the US Surgeon
General on Mental Health,* the Institute of Medicine's (IOM's) *Crossing the
Quality Chasm: A New Health System for the 21st Century,* the Center for
Substance Abuse Treatment's *Changing the Conversation: The National Treatment Plan Initiative,* the IOM's report on *Unequal Treatment: Confronting
Racial and Ethnic Disparities in Health Care,* the World Health Organization's
2001 *Report on Mental Health,* and the 2003 report of the President's New
Freedom Mental Health Commission. The consensus emerging from these
reports is that recovery and person-centered care are two tightly linked
concepts.

Recovery

Recovery, a term and concept frequently used in the alcohol and drug self-
help and treatment fields, does not have any single definition. Rather, it is

viewed as a process, a new way to live one's life beyond mere abstinence from alcohol and/or other drugs. Recovery defines how one lives life today, implying hope, healing, and restoration.

The mental health consumer/survivor movement, which began in the early 1970s, has truly championed the notion of mental health recovery with an emphasis on self-determination and empowerment. By the early 1990s, professionals began to take notice of the change in attitudes and expectations. In 1993, Anthony[1] endorsed the concept of recovery as a guiding vision for the mental health system after reading and listening to consumers' personal accounts of their struggles through and recoveries from mental illness. A recovery advisory group at a Virginia community mental health center describes recovery in the following way:

> *A process of re-emergence, awakening, or working towards the full life that you want and deserve to have, a life that includes the vision and dreams that you long for. A life in which each person is treated with complete respect at every moment. A life in which you have meaningful choices and you continuously move towards wholeness and healing from hurts, trauma, and/or darkness. A life in which you feel completely hopeful, completely empowered, and completely connected to the community.*

Another definition of a recovery-oriented system, and of recovery itself, in the mental health field, can be found in the National Technical Assistance Center for State Mental Health Planning's report *Mental Health Recovery: What Helps and What Hinders?*[2]:

> *Recovery can be construed as a paradigm, an organizing construct that can guide the planning and implementation of services and supports for people with severe mental illness. The outlines of a new paradigm recovery-enhancing system are emerging. Such a system is person-oriented, and respects people's lived experience and expertise. It promotes decision-making and self-responsibility. It addresses people's needs holistically and contends with more than their symptoms. Such a system meets basic needs and addresses problems in living. It empowers people to move toward self-management of their condition. The orientation is one of hope with an emphasis on positive mental health and wellness. A recovery-oriented system assists people to connect through mutual self-help. It focuses on positive functioning in a variety of roles, and building or rebuilding positive relationships.*
>
> *Recovery is an ongoing dynamic interactional process that occurs between a person's strengths, vulnerabilities, resources, and the environment. It involves a personal journey of actively self-managing psychiatric disorder while reclaiming, gaining, and maintaining a positive sense of self, roles, and life beyond the mental health system, in spite of the challenge of psychiatric disability. Recovery involves learning*

to approach each day's challenges, to overcome disabilities, to live independently, and to contribute to society. Recovery is supported by a foundation based on hope, belief, personal power, respect, connections, and self-determination.

On July 22, 2003, President Bush's New Freedom Commission on Mental Health released its final report, *Achieving the Promise: Transforming Mental Health Care in America.*[3] It stated the following:

A goal of a transformed system is recovery. Recovery refers to the process in which people are able to live, work, learn, and participate fully in their communities. For some individuals, recovery is the ability to live a fulfilling and productive life despite a disability. For others, recovery implies the reduction or complete remission of symptoms. Science has shown that having hope plays an integral role in an individual's recovery. Successfully transforming the mental health service delivery system rests on two principles:

1. Services and treatments must be consumer- and family-centered, set to provide consumers real and meaningful choices about treatment options and providers—not oriented to the requirements of bureaucracies.

2. Care must focus on increasing consumers' ability to successfully cope with life's challenges, on facilitating recovery, and on building resilience, not just on managing symptoms.

Out of the six goals put forth by the Commission to transform the mental health system of care, Goal Two is the one that addresses the issues related to individual planning for services. Simply stated, the report calls for mental health care that is consumer- and family-driven.

When a serious mental illness or a serious emotional disturbance is first diagnosed, the health care provider—in full partnership with consumers and families—will develop an individualized plan of care for managing the illness. This partnership of personalized care means basically choosing who, what, and how appropriate health care will be provided:

• choosing which mental health care professionals are on the team;
• sharing in decision-making; and
• having the option to agree or disagree with the treatment plan.

The Mental Health Commissioner of Ohio and chairman of the President's Mental Health Commission, Michael Hogan, PhD, fostered the development of his state's Department of Mental Health emphasis on a recovery-oriented approach to services. The Ohio model can be described by its emphasis on determining the recovery status of the individual and its process for developing a responsive individual recovery-management plan. The individual plan is clearly identified as central to a person-centered and recovery-oriented approach to services. "Nothing about me without me" has become a central theme and often-repeated refrain for many advocates of recovery-oriented person-centered systems change.

Person-Centered Care

The link between recovery and person-centered care is evident. The essential role of the individual plan in supporting both is explicit. The ideas of recovery, wellness, and resiliency embody a functional model of what it means to be person-centered; they simultaneously address both process and outcome. The concern is not only with the impact of services but also with the importance of the experience for the individual and family receiving services. The creation and implementation of an individual plan are the points at which these values should be most evident in practice. If service planning is not itself a person-centered process, then the entire service-delivery system cannot likely succeed. Planning is the foundation upon which the provision of person-centered services is built. Creating the plan is all about ensuring that our response to individuals is true to the vision and values of person-centeredness.

Re-Designing Health Care

Recently, the California Department of Mental Health's Statewide Quality Improvement Committee[4] adapted the IOM's six aims for health care quality in response to the concerns of mental health and addictive disorders systems stakeholders. Their translation of the aims is as follows.

Mental health and addiction services should be experienced as:

1. Equitable
   Access and quality of care do not vary because of client or family characteristics such as race ethnicity, age, gender, religion, sexual orientation, disability, diagnosis, geographic location, socioeconomic status, or legal status.
2. Safe
   Services are provided in an emotionally and physically safe, compassionate, trusting, and caring treatment/working environment for all clients, family members, and staff.

3. Timely

   Goal-directed services are promptly provided in order to restore and sustain the integration of clients and families into the community.

4. Effective

   Up-to-date evidence-based services are provided in response to and respectful of individual choice and preference.

5. Efficient

   Human and physical resources are managed in ways that minimize waste and optimize access to appropriate treatment.

6. Person-centered

   A highly individualized comprehensive approach to assessment and services is used to understand each individual's and family's history, strengths, needs, and vision of their own recovery including attention to the issues of culture, spirituality, trauma, and other factors. Service plans and outcomes are built upon respect for the unique preferences, strengths, and dignity of each person.

These six aims are inter-related and complimentary; it is difficult to achieve one without attending to the others. Together they articulate a vision of a system that is both recovery-oriented and person-centered.

The IOM also posited 10 new rules or guidelines for directing health care systems and service-delivery reform. Several of the rules suggest how person-centered care can be achieved. Table I includes 5 of the 10 rules that especially illustrate this point by comparing existing practices, values, and assumptions with a vision of a new and different approach. The concepts described within the "new paradigm" portion of the table are the guiding principles for this book.

These rules help breathe life into the notion of person-centered services and to make them less of an abstraction and more of a reality. Clearly, there is a need to involve individuals receiving services in decision-making and planning in a new and different way.

If these rules are followed, the provider should no longer solely determine outcomes for individuals and families. Treatment goals such as symptom reduction, decreased hospitalization, treatment compliance, or the elimination of behavior problems are for the most part generic and provider driven. Instead, the outcomes of services should be those changes identified and valued by the individual. Typically they will address personal and specific concerns about psychosocial functioning, improved clinical status, quality of life, and satisfaction with services. Outcomes should be person-centered and empowerment-oriented: all involve some degree of self-determination, self-esteem, and self-efficacy, and together lead to maximizing one's life and minimizing one's illness.[5]

TABLE 2.1   Changing Practice Guidelines

Current approach	New paradigm
Care is based primarily on visits	Services are provided in the context of continuous healing relationships
Professional autonomy drives care	Services are customized according to the needs and values of the individual
Decision making is based on training and experience	Decision making is based on evidence when possible
Information is a record	Knowledge is shared and information flows freely
Professionals control care	The individual is the source of control

Which Direction to Travel?

Donald Berwick, MD, was a member of the IOM's Committee on the Quality of Health Care in America and has subsequently attempted his own explanation of person-centeredness. In a groundbreaking article from Health Affairs,[6] Berwick describes four levels of organization in the health care system (Fig. 2.1). Beginning with the experience of "patients and communities," Berwick argues that health care should "honor the individual patient, respecting the patient's choices, culture, social context, and specific needs." Berwick goes on to describe this as *True North*: "like a compass guiding our journey, individuals and their experiences should be the 'defining force in health care delivery'. This is what orients the very basics of a service-delivery system."

Returning to the metaphor of individual planning as a journey, a compass is an invaluable tool for the traveler and explorer—without its guidance, it is easy to get lost. Without a fixed point of reference, setting and staying the course can be exceedingly difficult. In the same way that the magnetic pull of the North Pole has long helped direct human expeditions, the needs and experience of individuals and families seeking services should always be our point of reference and direction in organizing the resources required to address their needs.

Experience of Patients
and Communities

Microsystems of
Care
(*Where care occurs*)

Health Care
Organizations

External Environment of Care
Policy/Financing/Regulation

FIGURE 2.1

The other points of the compass are equally important. To the West are the "microsystems of care," providers and small clinical units that provide direct service. They in turn are supported by the East, which are "macrosystems of care" that include large provider organizations, HMOs, health care-delivery systems, and the like. The South points to the general, political, social, and economic environment in which health care systems function. In order for the experience of care for the individual to change to True North, it is often times necessary for change to occur at all points of the health care compass.

If we are to succeed in becoming person-centered, the entire system may need to re-examine its bearings. Those in the West, who have immediate responsibility for effecting change and the quality of care at True North, are also dependent upon support, influence, and factors that we cannot always control in the East and South. None of this, however, should minimize the importance of good practice at the level of microsystems where care is provided. Individual planning is all about ensuring that the needs of the individual and family at True North are identified, understood, and addressed.

Diversity

Nowhere is both the importance and the challenge of assuring a person-centered approach more evident than in considering the needs of an increasingly diverse American population and the disparities in access and quality of care for cultural, racial, and ethnic minorities in this country. The 2000 Surgeon General's report,[7] *Mental Health: Culture, Race, and Ethni-*

city—A Supplement to Mental Health: A Report of the Surgeon General established that in the U.S. today, many members of minority groups:

. have less access to, and availability of, mental health services
. are less likely to receive needed mental health services
. often receive a poorer quality of mental health care
. are under-represented in mental health research

There are many barriers—both real and perceived, both physical
and psychological—that contribute to these disparities. The chief
barriers are mistrust and fear of treatment, racism and discrimination, and
differences in culture, language, and communication. The ability of persons
receiving services to clearly and openly communicate with
providers carries special significance in the area of mental health and
addictive disorders service. These emotional and addictive problems impact
and affect thought, mood, cognition, and the highest integrative aspects
of behavior. The effective diagnosis and treatment of mental health
and addictive disorders greatly depends on the quality of verbal communication as well as trust and understanding between individuals, families, and
providers.

Attention to the role of culture in understanding the needs of each
individual in the process of assessment and individual planning must be
an essential part of the solution to these problems. The Diagnostic and
Statistical Manual of Mental Disorders IV-Text Revision (DSM IV-TR)[8]
includes often-overlooked guidelines for a cultural formulation in its
Appendix I. There has been considerable controversy and frustration with
the placement of this important component of diagnosis in an appendix,
which has, for many, called into question the field's real commitment to
cultural competence. Regardless, the outline specifically requires that the
following items and considerations be included as part of each assessment
and diagnosis:

. an inquiry about the individual's cultural identity (including issues of
  race, ethnicity, gender, sexual orientation, religion, spirituality, disability status, and other self-defining characteristics)
. the exploration of possible cultural explanations of problems
. consideration of cultural factors related to psychosocial environment
  and levels of functioning
. examination of cultural elements in the client-provider relationship
. an overall cultural assessment in establishing a diagnosis and development of an individual plan

In essence, both the Surgeon General's report and the Diagnostic and Statistical Manual of Mental Disorders—Fourth Edition—Text Revision (DSM-IV-TR) link a person-centered approach to understanding the unique needs of each individual and culturally competent service planning. Similar to the relationship between recovery- and person-centered approaches, the values and practice of culturally competent and person-centered mental health and addictive disorders service are also closely linked.

Self-Determination

The roots of a person-centered approach to care and planning can also be found in the mental retardation and developmental disabilities system of care. For over 20 years, clients and their family members in that system, along with practitioners and programs, have been actively involved in the process of developing individual plans. The focus has been on promoting the individual's right to self-determination and providing the necessary supports for the individual's highest level of participation in the community. In most cases, these practices would still be far from the norm in the mental health and addictive disorders service field.

Many of the ideas now spreading through the mental health and addictive disorders field about choice, self-determination, and self-directed care derive from the experience and knowledge developed in related human-service systems. The changes there have been accomplished not only by redefining the role of providers, but also most importantly by assuring the meaningful participation of the individual and their family in the individual planning process. This practice is in alignment with funding, licensing, and accrediting standards in the developmental disabilities field throughout the U.S. The behavioral health field has much to learn from developmental disabilities service systems where individual plans are rich, relevant, and meaningful tools for the consumers and their families as well as for the providers.

Professional Partnerships

One of the barriers to a person-centered approach in the fields of mental health and addiction services are the notions of transference and counter-transference, which remain a dominant framework. This strongly influences a provider's understanding of the dynamics and the relationship with the individual seeking services and shapes their interactions accordingly. While there may be some relatively tacit acknowledgment of the importance of a "therapeutic alliance," this is often given little attention in routine practice. Clearly it is a model based upon professional autonomy, professional control of services, and the presumed if not expected relative passivity of the individual receiving services. The idea of viewing the person as an active participant and partner—a member of the team—is relatively alien.

Many providers do not know how to establish a professional partnership with the individual receiving services. Nor are they especially comfortable with the idea and question its appropriateness. Many are threatened by the perceived loss of control and its multiple implications. Many providers voice the concern that empowering the individual and family-seeking services is tantamount to relinquishing their professional roles and responsibility. They have had difficulty in redefining their essential contribution in a realigned therapeutic relationship. It is easy to understand why for many providers the idea of being person-centered represents a difficult set of changes in practice that all too often are not achieved.

Somewhat in contrast to the prevailing practice in the mental health field, the idea of partnership has long been central to the addictive disorders field. Twelve-step programs are based upon peer-to-peer support and Alcoholics Anonymous is often described as a fellowship. This tradition, and recognition of the value and effectiveness of a helping alliance, should inform all of health care as we decide how to better help individuals articulate and achieve their own vision of wellness and recovery.

Historically, multidisciplinary team-based care was a distinguishing feature of psychosocial rehabilitation. Increasingly, multidisciplinary teams are now seen as an optimal service delivery model for health care services in general. The individual plan has always had an important function in multidisciplinary teams: the coordination of a range of services to address complex needs. But perhaps even more important has been the notion that the individual receiving services must be included as a vital member of the team if the desired goals and objectives are to be achieved. Whether or not it is a team of two—the individual and the provider—or a diverse team involving a range of mental health and addiction services providers, the idea of a team-based model can help to reinforce a person-centered approach.

Many providers have been trained in guild-based academic and clinical traditions. This approach has often focused on individual/provider dyads. As a result, many providers are not familiar or necessarily comfortable with multidisciplinary team-based approaches. Authority and secrecy have been the prevalent mode as compared to the need for cooperation, openness, and transparency among team members. The challenge now and into the future is to train the existing workforce, many of whom are experienced with a different model, in how to work effectively with the individual receiving services and family members in creating plans responsive to each individual's needs.

Clearly, there is compelling evidence that a person-centered approach to planning and services is the emerging new standard of care. Yet there is also substantial evidence that in daily mental health and addictive disorders practice, this is not what occurs. While we can see the future, we remain rooted in the past.

II. CREATING THE SOLUTION

Ultimately, the assurance of person-centered mental health and addictive disorders service lies in the process of individual planning. Based upon an individual and culturally competent assessment, the plan is in essence a contract between the provider and the individual, an agreement detailing who is to do what and when to help the individual and family realize their hopes and dreams. The individual plan belongs to the individual receiving services and is the written record of the agreed upon strategies and course. Individual planning is the essence of being person-centered.

Experience of Individuals and Families

Respect for the individual and family by the provider is an important component of a person-centered approach and an essential ingredient in planning. Although it is generally a well-understood concept, it can be difficult to explain. Responding precisely to the wants, needs, and preferences of each individual and family is the essence of respect. This implies that there are abundant opportunities for the provider to be informed about each person's unique attributes and perspectives. Another aspect of respect is the genuine inclusion of the individual and family in clinical decision-making consistent with his or her level of comfort, preference, and functional status.

While active participation is valued, it must be balanced with individual choice, preference, and comfort. This is often impacted by a whole host of factors ranging from age and gender to culture, ethnicity, and tradition. Past experience with seeking services—both positive and negative—may impact their ability to understand the process. Education and orientation, along with creating opportunity, can often go a long way towards facilitating meaningful participation and is in and of itself both healing and empowering.

Communication

Communication is another critical component of a person-centered approach to planning and providing services. Providers must assure the free flow of information, particularly about matters such as diagnosis, prognosis, services, and alternatives, as well as the attendant risks and benefits. It is essential that all information provided is accurate, perceived as trustworthy and credible, understandable, and tailored to the individual's preferences for involvement and participation. As much as possible, information must be communicated in a compassionate and empathic manner and should not compromise the comfort and safety of the individual.

Language is obviously core to communication. It is not enough to simply know the fluency and literacy of the individual and family; language preference may be even more important. It is not unusual to find that at times of distress, some people may find it easier and more comforting to communicate in their "mother tongue" rather than a second or third language.

Another key aspect of communication is sensitivity to the use of language. 'Person-first' language in and of itself goes a long way towards expressing respect and consideration. People are not diagnostic labels: a person may be diagnosed with schizophrenia but they are not "a schizophrenic." This awareness extends to providers and staff as well. Referring to those providing compassionate care as *direct-care staff* as compared to "front-line staff" who are "in the trenches" has its own connotations and implications. We are not at war with the individuals and families that we serve! Our use of language is an opportunity to focus on strengths and talents, identify successes, respect the individual's right to self-determination, and build an alliance between provider and individual.

Another component of language is the differences in terms between the traditional model of care and the person-centered approach. Table II provides a comparison of terms and preferred person-centered language.

The traditional approach keeps the focus on what is wrong, what is not working, and problems/abnormalities. In contrast, the person-centered approach is oriented to developing the resources of the individual, building solutions, and identifying possibilities.

TABLE 2.2   Comparison of Terms

Person–Centered	Traditional
• Person-centered	• Practitioner-based
• Strengths-based	• Problem-based
• Skill acquisition	• Deficit focus
• Collaboration	• Professional dominance
• Community integration	• Acute treatment
• Quality of life	• Cure/amelioration
• Community-based	• Facility-based
• Empowerment/choices	• Dependence
• Least restrictive	• Episodic
• Preventative	• Reactive

Family

The appropriate involvement of family and friends is yet another facet of a person-centered approach. Family is a vital source of information and knowledge about the individual, their history and needs, the role of culture in their lives, and other important details. At the same time, the physical and emotional support of family can be a critical component of each individual's recovery. If one component of successful rehabilitation and recovery is the individual's increasing reliance on natural supports and a decreasing dependence on professional services, the importance of family as a primary source of support cannot be underestimated. For most people, family includes the most important and significant relationships of our lives.

The role of family is often influenced by cultural factors, this makes an accurate understanding of the individual in the context of culture essential. Definitions of family should not be restricted to traditional notions; instead, the right of individuals (certainly each adult) to self-define their family and support system should be respected.

The Role of the Provider

Attention to the process of developing, documenting, and implementing an individual plan is part of a commitment to person-centered care. Actively involving the individual seeking services in the process of identifying goals, specifying objectives, and selecting services is the essence of being person-centered. For many providers this will be a shift in roles. The days of the provider as the source of expert knowledge and professional experience, knowing what is "best" for the individual, not sharing the assessment/ diagnosis results, not openly communicating, or not encouraging shared decisions are gone. Dismissing an individual's preferences and goals as being "unrealistic," or not soliciting them at all, ultimately fosters dependence rather than independence, and is the antithesis of recovery, wellness, and resiliency.

The concept of person-centered service does not suggest, however, that the provider no longer has any role to play in the recovery process. Simply put, the provider's role has changed from that of all-knowing, all-doing caretaker to that of coach, architect, cheerleader, facilitator, and/or shepherd. The provider builds a partnership with the individual, resulting in the individual plan that serves as the roadmap for service delivery and recovery. The provider uses the plan in four ways: to maintain focus on the individual's progress toward goal attainment, to track changes in needs or challenges, as a framework for identifying and organizing needed resources, and to measure growth and change.

The Plan

The individual plan should be a practical, understandable tool that the individual and the provider can utilize together to steer the course in the journey of recovery. It is *not* a document written by the provider in isolation without the participation of the individual. The plan is created by "meeting the person where they are" at any moment in time and not superimposing the provider's own goals and directions.

In order to be meaningful and effective, a plan must truly be the individual's road map. It is the focal point of each session with the individual. It needs to include personally defined goals along with realistic objectives that address relevant and immediate barriers and impediments. Plans need to be practical and reasonable in identifying specific services and interventions consistent with the individual's preferences and values. The plan should be sensitive to language choices and written in "plain English" or the individual's preferred language. The plan must be culturally relevant and outcome-oriented.

In contrast, it is worthwhile to be clear about what the plan is not. It is not written in jargon typically understood only by the professional provider. It is not disconnected from the assessment data and formulation, and does not stand alone with goals and objectives unrelated to assessment data. A plan is not merely a completed form that follows a computerized treatment-planning module with predetermined menus of goals and objectives that match diagnostic criteria. It is not solely based on the individual's deficits, disabilities, and problems. It is not written simply to satisfy funding and regulatory requirements, waved under the individual's nose for their signature, and then filed in their record never to be used again.

Ultimately, the plan is a communication tool for the provider, for the individual, for family and others involved in the individual's life, for payers, and for accreditation or regulatory reviewers. A written copy of the plan should be given to the individual and family to take with them and use. In this way the plan can help to evaluate the recovery progress of the individual and family.

III. MAKING IT HAPPEN

In a recovery-oriented, person-centered care system, the following conditions exist:

- individuals are encouraged and assisted in identifying their own goal(s)
- services are provided in the context of the individual's culture and community
- services facilitate an individual's and family's culturally appropriate interdependence with their community and are responsive to their expressed needs and desires
- the therapeutic alliance is directed by the expectation of the individual
- reaching goals for each person is facilitated by understanding their:
  - hopes and dreams
  - life roles
  - valued role functions
  - interest in work and other activities
  - spirituality and religious affiliation
  - culture and acculturation
  - educational needs
- individual differences across the lifespan are valued and considered
- there is a holistic approach in which assessment and intervention models are merged

- mutual reciprocity in a trusting hopeful relationship with providers is considered essential
- providers work from a strengths/assets model
- there is collaborative development of an individual service plan which identifies needed resources and supports
- the individual receiving services defines the family unit and their level of involvement

Much of this is realized through the process of developing, documenting, and implementing an individual plan.

Evaluation

Current practice should be evaluated against these criteria for person-centered care. There will no doubt be many examples of success and fidelity to the values and principles of this approach. It is equally likely that there will be opportunities for change and improvements that are identified at all levels within the service delivery system. The compass in Figure 2.1 is a useful framework not only for thinking about change for individuals and families but also for providers and care systems. Evaluating current performance at each of the four levels or points, and identifying strategies for change, is key to "making it happen."

Figure 2.2 reflects the interdependent relationship between the levels of system hierarchy and the elements of the IOM Quality Chasm framework. At the level of microsystems of care, providers are focused on assuring that the six core quality aims are satisfied; person-centered care is one of those core aims. This builds on the responsibilities of organized systems to employ and support the rules or guidelines for quality-oriented systems. Many of these rules are intended to assure person-centered approaches to providing services. Lastly is the importance of values, reflected and elaborated in policy, providing the basic structure and foundation of the service-delivery system. Each component of quality—values, rules, and aims—becomes an essential part of the individual's experience of a person-centered approach.

The four levels are inter-related, do not exist or function independently, and must be considered together. That is the essence of a system. Neither policymakers, health care organizations, direct-care providers, or individuals alone can assure that the systems and services they provide are person-centered. Success requires an alignment of values, policies and procedures, and principles and practice throughout the system in order to achieve this goal.

At the level of the individual and family, there are two important considerations. Knowing about the current (and future) experience of the care and service process is a key component of evaluating both provider and systems performance. There are several well-accepted surveys geared towards measuring the experience of care of the individual and family including the MHSIP (Mental Health Statistics Improvement Program) Consumer Oriented Survey[9] and the Experience of Care and Health Outcomes Survey (ECHO™) survey[10] which is part of the NCQA's (National Council on Quality Assurance's) HEDIS dataset as well as others. Other methods of understanding and evaluating the perspective of those seeking services include the use of individual interviews and focus groups. Every provider and organized system of care should have some mechanism in place to evaluate how service recipients experience the process and allow for suggestions for improvement and change. This is discussed further in Chapter 9.

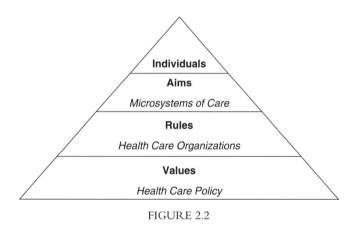

FIGURE 2.2

Alternatives

Another approach to changing and improving current practice at the level of the individual and family is to create "demand-side" change. It may well be that while individuals and families may be dissatisfied with a more provider-centered approach, they do not know what the alternative is or how it might be changed. In all too many settings, service recipients are not aware of the role of the individual plan—how it is created and how it directs services. In some cases, they may not even be aware of the goals and objectives that are supposedly determining the services they receive. By increasing awareness among individuals and families about the importance of the individual plan—and their essential role in its creation—a powerful ally in the process of systems change can be created.

Some of this can and should be part of the basic orientation to services that each individual and family should receive as they enter into the process of assessment and service planning. By making expectations and opportunities clear, the likelihood of meaningful participation and a truly person-centered plan is enhanced. This also provides an opportunity to understand the education or support an individual or family might need in order to meaningfully participate in his or her own plan and recovery.

Evaluating Providers

At the level of the provider and "microsystems of care," there should be multiple opportunities to evaluate and improve current practice. This can include self-assessment, peer-review, evaluation by a supervisor, or review by an external oversight authority. There are three key points of performance that can be considered:

1. Attitudes
   - How does the provider feel about the values and principles of person-centered care?
   - In what ways are they threatened or enthused by these ideas?
   - How does the provider regard the process and value of creating individual plans?
2. Knowledge
   - Does the provider understand the principles of a person-centered approach?
   - Has the provider received appropriate education and training in person-centered approaches to assessment, planning, and service delivery?
   - Can the provider identify the elements and phases of the planning process?
3. Skills and Abilities
   - Can the provider conduct a person-centered assessment that leads to a formulation?
   - Can the provider develop an effective alliance with the individual seeking services that supports their participation in planning and recovery?

- Can the provider work to develop, organize, document, and implement a plan that is responsive to the identified goals and objectives and is sensitive to the unique preferences and needs of the individual?
- Do individuals and families report feeling like they were treated with dignity and respect and supported in their own personal vision of recovery, wellness, and resilience?

Core competencies for providers need to be established and providers need to be evaluated as to their attitude, knowledge, and skills. The ability of a provider to develop person-centered individual plans should be one of those competencies. The IOM's *Crossing the Quality Chasm* report notes: "All health professionals should be educated to deliver patient-centered care as members of an interdisciplinary team, emphasizing evidence-based practice, quality improvement approaches, and informatics." If we are to achieve the reality of a consistent person-centered approach to providing mental health and addictive disorders service, this is an essential part of "Making It Happen."

In many cases this will necessitate additional education and training for the existing workforce as these represent a new set of expectations and skills from what has been the prevailing standard of care.[11] There is also a pressing need to evaluate and change the curriculum in current pre-degree professional programs as well as consideration of the post-degree pre-licensure training for those who are preparing to enter the mental health and addictive disorders service workforce. Lastly, we must recognize the important role in today's service-delivery system of para-professionals and peers—many of whom sorely lack adequate education and training to meet their substantial responsibilities. Hopefully this book can make a contribution to this education and training agenda.

Systems Change

Providing person-centered services requires endorsement and support at the level of organized systems of care. The expectations of quality care need to be aligned with the resources and supports required by providers in order to realize a person-centered approach. Structural barriers—including regulations, licensure standards, and payment requirements—are potential impediments to providing person-centered care and at this level need to be examined and removed. It is unfair to expect providers to change how they work without recognizing their dependence on these requirements and its impact on their meeting core quality aims. If person-centered approaches are to succeed, they must become part of the expectations and norms of organized systems and the resources necessary to meet this objective need to be available. This should be most clearly reflected in the requirements and expectations related to the development and use of individual plans in the service-delivery process.

Lastly, person-centered care must be clearly and unequivocally endorsed as a core value of our policy-making processes. The goals of the President's New Freedom Commission report begin to accomplish that clarification at a national level. It is quite significant that the need for proper service planning is identified as one of the six major goals and objectives of the report. There can be no clearer statement at the national policy level of the critical role of the individual plan in providing quality effective care. Only time will tell if the Commission's recommendations truly become an anchor point of policy and practice across the country. However, policy for mental health and addictive disorders services should not only be determined in Washington; it should also be elaborated on within states, counties, and commercial health plans. Our ability to provide a person-centered approach is inevitably dependent on the explicit endorsement and support at this level. Commitment to a person-centered approach must be made at the highest level of authority and influence in our care systems if organizations and providers together are to succeed in meeting the expectations of individuals and families.

In our endeavor to help individuals bring about positive changes in their lives, we need to recognize and accept the obligation to effect changes in values, policy, and practice within our own work and systems of care.

REFERENCES

1. National Technical Assistance Center for State Mental Health Planning. *Mental Health Recovery: What Helps and What Hinders?* Alexandria, VA: 2002, 9.
2. National Technical Assistance Center for State Mental Health Planning. *Mental Health Recovery: What Helps and What Hinders?* Alexandria, VA: 2002, 7.
3. New Freedom Commission on Mental Health. *Achieving the Promise: Transforming Mental Health Care in America.* 2003.
4. Committee on the Quality of Health Care in America. *Crossing the Quality Chasm.* Washington DC: Institute of Medicine, 2001.
5. Singh, Nirbay, PhD, Personal Communication, May 2004.
6. Berwick, D.M. A User's Manual for the IOM's 'Quality Chasm' Report. *Health Affairs,* 2002;21(3):80–90.
7. U.S. Department of Health and Human Services. *Mental Health: Culture, Race, and Ethnicity—A Supplement to Mental Health: A Report of the Surgeon General.* Rockville,

MD: U.S. Department of Health and Human Services, Substance Abuse and Mental Health Services Administration, Center for Mental Health Services, 2001.

8. U.S. Department of Health and Human Services. *Mental Health: Culture, Race, and Ethnicity—A Supplement to Mental Health: A Report of the Surgeon General.* Rockville, MD: U.S. Department of Health and Human Services, Substance Abuse and Mental Health Services Administration, Center for Mental Health Services, 2001.

9. www.mhsip.org.

10. http://www.hcp.med.harvard.edu/echo.

11. Daniels, A., et al. Current issues in continuing education for contemporary behavioral health practice, *Administration and Policy in Mental Health,* 2002;29(4–5):359–376.

## CHAPTER 3

The Value of Individual Planning

*"If you really want something, you CAN figure out
how to make it happen."*

Cher

I. STATING THE CASE

Chapter 2 focused on the subject of person-centered services and the important role of the individual plan in achieving this quality aim. However, there are several other important parts of the service-delivery process that touch upon the plan, ranging from ensuring outcomes and quality improvement to documentation of the medical necessity of services for utilization review. This chapter explores these other important functions of the individual plan. Figure 1 provides a graphic summary of these functions and emphasizes the integrative role of the plan. The individual plan becomes central to the entire process of mental health and addictions service delivery.

Some of the more specific functions of the individual plan include:

- building an alliance with the individual and family seeking services
- assuring that assessment and services are culturally competent
- describing the strengths, needs, preferences, and role of the individual
- identifying and establishing criteria for expected outcomes and transitions or discharge
- documenting medical necessity and anticipation of frequency, intensity, and duration of services
- supporting service documentation and billing

- considering and including alternatives, natural supports, and community resources
- identifying responsibilities of team members—including the individual and the family seeking services
- increasing coordination, collaboration, and multidisciplinary interventions within the team
- promoting the use of evidence-based practices
- decreasing fragmentation and duplication
- prompting analysis of available time and resources
- establishing the role of the individual and family in their own recovery/rehabilitation

Development and documentation of individual plans is often considered by many to be both an acquired skill as well as a clinical art that provides an opportunity for creative thinking: the plan helps to integrate information about the individual and family receiving services, facilitates prioritization, and provides a strategy for managing complexity.

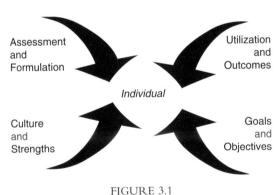

FIGURE 3.1

Outcomes of Planning

It is not unreasonable to ask what differences in services or outcomes should be expected if providers more consistently utilized a person-centered approach to mental health and addictive disorders service planning. The benefits might include:

- improved *access* to treatment when people are treated as individuals and respected for their heritages and cultures, and when families (as defined by the individual) are included in the process

- better *retention* in treatment as a result of improved engagement, collaboration, and partnership between the provider and the individual
- demonstrated *outcomes* that are goal-oriented, practical, clear, and meaningful to the individual and family
- a *strength-based* and *recovery-oriented* approach to service delivery

Additional benefits for providers who properly attend to the task of individual planning include the consistent satisfaction of regulatory requirements (e.g., state licensing, code, Medicaid regulations, and so on) and accreditation standards. Mental health and addictive disorders service providers throughout the U.S. and Canada are seeing an increased demand— and, in some cases, mandate—for achieving accreditation as well as satisfying other requirements for quality and accountability. CARF...The Rehabilitation Accreditation Commission's 2003 to 2004 Behavioral Health Standards Manual[1] includes specific requirements for service planning. These include the expectations that:

- goals be expressed in the words of the person served
- goals be reflective of the informed choice of the person served or parent/guardian
- individual plans be developed with the active participation of the person served

The Joint Commission on Accreditation of Healthcare Organizations' (JCAHO's)[2] standards on treatment planning require that:

- individuals be encouraged to participate in developing their treatment, care, or service plans, and such involvement is documented
- the treatment, care, or service plan include advocacy services when indicated to enhance the natural support system, facilitate environmental modifications, or create new supports

In addition to accreditation standards, there are government regulations and insurance requirements for payment that include the proper completion and documentation of an individual plan. From traditional insurance plans to managed care organizations in the private sector to the Centers for Medicare and Medicaid Services (CMS), all require service plans and quality documentation as a condition of payment. And expectations are moving beyond the satisfaction of minimal requirements. The old adage "If it isn't documented, it didn't happen" has now been replaced by "Just because it is documented does not mean you will receive payment." In Virginia, for example, state Medicaid regulations closely resemble the national accreditation standards by emphasizing the need for a person-centered approach to planning and documentation. In other words, simply having complete service planning forms in the record is not sufficient—it must be a properly developed and documented plan.

At the federal level,[3] CMS standards and attestation statements for psychiatric hospitals state: "The patient and the treatment team collaboratively develop the patient's treatment plan." Medicaid standards concerning documentation, and the subsequent audits of programs based on these regulations, reveal that provider organizations continue to struggle with meeting standards of care and documentation. For instance, APS Healthcare Inc.,[4] a Georgia external review organization for Medicaid funding in that state, found that in 2001, the top 10 areas of non-compliance included four issues specific to the service plan:

1) goals, objectives, and interventions were not specific, measurable, attainable, realistic, and time limited
2) goals, objectives, and interventions did not address symptoms, skills and resources
3) each service provided was not linked to a goal, objective, or intervention
4) the diagnostic assessment was not necessarily linked to a goal, objective, or intervention on the individual services recovery plan

Medical Necessity

Another component of administrative requirements attached to the development and documentation of the individual plan is the need to clearly demonstrate the "medical necessity" of services. Medical necessity has been a concept in both public and private insurance programs since the initial introduction of the Medicare and Medicaid programs in the 1960s—if not before. Simply stated, the documentation of medical necessity is the clear demonstration that there is a legitimate clinical need and that services provided are an appropriate response. While there is often some confusion about how to best document and demonstrate medical necessity, the clearest and most effective approach is through the proper development of a clinically relevant individual plan.

Medical necessity is not only about *what* services are provided but also includes some consideration of *where* services are provided (i.e., at what level of care). For example, motivational counseling for addictive disorders can occur in an outpatient program or in a residential program—the most appropriate and necessary setting is determined by a host of specific issues and needs for a given individual and all are components of medical necessity.

Medical necessity is also about billing and revenue. Today, most organized systems of care have some form of utilization review or quality management function. Increasingly, health care providers are concerned about how scarce resources are applied and want to minimize waste and unnecessary services while at the same time assuring that individuals and families receive indicated and needed services. The plan helps to organize decisions about services and the documentation of medical necessity.

The concept of medical necessity can be divided into five components. Most payers will only pay for services that satisfy these five criteria. Services must be:

- indicated
- appropriate
- efficacious
- effective
- efficient

While these components can be considered individually, they are also very inter-related.

Services are *indicated* when there is a diagnosis. The latest version of the International Classification of Disease Manual (ICDM) or the Diagnostic and Statistical Manual of Mental Disorders (DSM) is typically the reference used. While psychosocial factors may complicate an individual's needs, there must be a recognized and diagnosable "medical" condition identified in order to demonstrate the need for services and to justify billings. In most cases, "V" codes are not considered to be an acceptable diagnosis and will not support medical necessity or billing. In some settings, eligibility for services is closely tied to the concept of indication and plays a part in determining program enrollment and service availability.

Appropriateness refers to the match between a service and the individual's or family's needs and is closely linked with the idea of efficacy. Often, cultural factors as well as other individual attributes will play a part in determining appropriateness. For example, it is not appropriate to treat an individual at imminent risk of self-harm in an outpatient setting; nor is it appropriate to automatically place an individual in residential treatment when they have an adequate support system and have never before attempted or failed seeking help for their problems. In past years, depth-oriented psychoanalytic psychotherapy was considered to be an appropriate treatment for schizophrenia. Today, while there is an important role for some psychotherapy and counseling for individuals with this disorder, antipsychotic medications and psychosocial rehabilitation are seen as the most appropriate primary intervention.

Efficacy is about the likelihood that a particular intervention or service will be effective, and is tightly linked to the principles of evidence-based practice. Efficacy is often determined in research and controlled settings. While predictive of outcome and helpful in deciding which course of action to pursue, efficacy alone does not guarantee the desired results or outcome. In initiating any service or intervention, the challenge is to identify those activities that are most likely to have a positive impact for that individual and family. At the same time, individual choice and preference must be a factor in determining efficacy, and should be balanced with expert opinion and research data in determining what will most likely work for a given individual. Unacceptable interventions, no matter how powerful the evidence base to support them, will in all likelihood ultimately fail.

Effectiveness refers to determining the actual impact and value of the services and interventions provided. Did they work? Did they have the intended impact? Were there unanticipated negative consequences? Was a partial result obtained? These are all essential questions in the process of reviewing and updating a plan. It is surprising, if not shocking, how often ineffective services are provided on an ongoing basis. How can services be "necessary" if they do not in fact make a difference and support desired change?

Efficiency is closely tied to the concepts of appropriateness, efficacy, and effectiveness. It is not efficient to provide inappropriate, inefficacious, or ineffective services that are inherently wasteful of resources. For example, it is not efficient to provide services in a costly 24-hour setting when the individual can safely receive indicated treatment in an outpatient setting. Another element of efficiency is related to questions about the intensity, frequency, and duration of services. Intensity refers to how much of a service is provided: is case management for 30 minutes or for 90 minutes? Frequency refers to the pattern of service: is counseling provided twice a week or only once every other week? Duration describes the length of the intervention: will residential treatment be for 2 weeks or for 6 months? It can be difficult at times to determine the most efficient way to provide services, but understanding common practice and evaluating individual response to services can help. Regardless, it is essential to consider the question of efficiency in determining and demonstrating the medical necessity of services.

Medical necessity can be a useful and helpful concept in developing a plan of action in response to the needs of individuals and families. At the same time, there is no question that the principles of medical necessity have been inappropriately applied in some settings and systems, in effect, to deny individuals and families access to needed services. However, the concept itself is sound, useful, and central to developing meaningful and effective individual plans. The service plan should provide the clearest and most cogent documentation of medical necessity. When asked to demonstrate the medical necessity of a service for prior authorization or billing review, the capable provider should be able to present an organized and coherent plan clearly documenting the five core components.

The Role of the Team

Perhaps one of the most vital functions of the individual plan and the planning process is the way in which it supports the work of a treatment team. The team should be viewed as the basic unit of clinical performance and accountability. The composition of a team may vary based upon a number of factors, but the complexity of the needs of the individual and family should remain the most important consideration. In traditional psychotherapy or addictive disorders counseling, the dyad of provider and individual can be considered a team. As the complexity of the needs of the individual and family increases, the need for multidisciplinary inputs and responses escalates at least proportionately and should be reflected in the composition of the team. The essential role of the individual and family seeking services, as key members of the team, should never be overlooked.

A team is the proverbial example of the whole being greater than the sum of its parts. It is more than a group of people assigned to the same work unit or the same caseload. At its simplest level, a team can be defined as a group of people working together for a common goal: a group of people joining together to share a common task or challenge with the recognition that the group can succeed where no one individual can; success is a result of the integration of inter-dependent activity. Coordination of that input and contribution is essential if the potential of the team is to be realized. Developing an individual plan can provide the glue that holds the team together and supports its success.

The challenge in responding to the needs and preferences of the individual and family seeking services is created and solved anew for each person and group. There is no standard road map or route—a personal map must be drawn in response to the unique needs and desires of each individual and family. The process of developing a plan brings the team together to plan the journey to recovery for each person. There is no substitute for the focus on individual planning as a team process—involving all the members of the team—if the goals of the individual and family are to be met. The individual plan provides an opportunity to specify goals, identify the barriers and objectives, and design the action steps needed to provide the necessary help and support. Sometimes the best way to proceed is not at all clear, and the problem-solving requires benefits from the multiple inputs and perspectives in creation of a plan that only a team can provide.

Managing Complexity

Ideally we want to match a person's needs with what we know to be the most efficacious interventions. Drawing upon an evidence base is ideal but not always possible. Some of the emerging evidence-based (or best) practices in the mental health and addictive disorders field require complex, multi-system, and multi-service inputs. This in turn requires the coordination that can only come from a team-based approach to developing the individual plan.

As stated earlier, one of the important shared functions of a team and the individual plan is its ability to provide an approach or tool that assists in managing complexity and organizing and prioritizing responses to the individual's and family's needs. Both the team itself and the plan will change in response to the scope of needs. Figure 3.2 provides a graph that describes the relationship between the intricacy of the individual's and family's needs and the complexity of response or level of care.

The first or lowest level of care, natural supports, and self-management, often precedes professional help-seeking. As needs become more complex, the response increases directly and proportionately; the configuration of the team moves from an individual provider to a multidisciplinary group and to multi-system response. In parallel, the importance and complexity of the individual plan increases accordingly. If all interventions are provided under the guidance of one service organization, the planning process, documentation, and elaboration of the plan will be different than if the individual and family require services from multiple providers and organizations.

It should be abundantly clear that creation of a plan is an essential step towards generating an effective response to the needs of each individual and

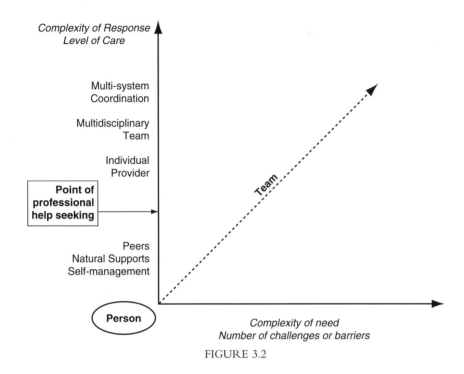

FIGURE 3.2

family. It is hard to imagine proceeding without a plan in place. If done well and with appropriate investment of time and thought, an individual plan can quickly move from being a seemingly useless administrative burden to an essential clinical tool at the center of the response to each individual and family.

II. CREATING THE SOLUTION

In the mid-1990s, Michigan implemented a state code which required person-centered planning for publicly funded services (mental illness, addiction disorders, and development disabilities). The law further required that individuals must have the ability to choose among available services and providers, including in-home and peer-delivered services. Pennsylvania, Maine, and Connecticut have also mandated an individualized, person-centered approach to planning that acknowledges the value and utility of this approach.

In an effort to make such mandates real and practical, Connecticut has developed clinical best practices for developing a culturally competent service plan. The state specified that all persons should be:

> . . . *assured a clinically appropriate treatment plan that incorporates the mutually agreed upon choice of relevant, attainable goals, culturally compatible treatment/rehabilitation services, and alternative treatment/rehabilitation strategies when so determined. Strategies may include use of family, community supports, spiritual leaders and non-traditional healers. Plans will be individualized, client-centered, based on individual strengths, and developed within the context of family and/or social networks in a treatment rehabilitation partnership. Plans will be formulated and reviewed during multicultural competent supervision of clinicians.*"[5]

Mandates and requirements such as those previously mentioned may be necessary but not sufficient to effect a systems change. There are serious questions about the skill and ability of the existing workforce to change prevailing practice and fulfill the vision embedded within these initiatives. But what are the skills required? How would training need to change in order for providers to be able to fulfill this vision?

Workforce Competencies

In a 2001 report commissioned by the United Kingdom's National Service Framework Workforce Action Team entitled *The Capable Practitioner*,[6] the Sainsbury Centre for Mental Health specified the mental health workforce competencies required to meet the demands of an increasingly complex service-delivery system as well as the increasingly complex needs of individuals and families seeking services.

> *It is a challenge not only for practitioners in the field, but also for service managers to create an optimal environment for best practice and for educators to equip trainees with the requisite values, skills, and knowledge. Earlier models of core competencies did not adequately address the comprehensive array of the needs of practitioners when working in these new service environments. Practitioners require more than a prescribed set of competencies. They need to be capable of providing the benefits of both effective and reflective practice. This requires an underpinning framework of values, attitudes, and knowledge in addition to competencies along with an ability to apply these in practice, across a range of clinical contexts from acute inpatient care to community-based crisis resolution and assertive outreach teams.*

This is a clear acknowledgment of the important role of provider competency in systems change and the ability of the current workforce to meet the changing and evolving expectations of advocates, consumers, and policymakers.

Experience demonstrates that there is a serious and significant incongruity between the importance of individual planning and the attention paid to developing the necessary skills in both pre-degree course work and post-graduate clinical/rehabilitation training. This becomes an even greater concern in light of the increasingly important role of non-degree para-professionals in today's mental health and addictive disorders service-delivery systems. Given the lack of training and skills, it should not be a surprise that providers devalue individual planning and so frequently fall short of meeting service recipients' needs.

Although planning is both a requirement and integral part of the clinical process, little attention is paid to assuring that providers have the skills necessary to complete the task. Creating the solution to the current state of practice involves, in part, a clear articulation of the knowledge and skills required of providers. This is essential if they are to have the necessary abilities to properly plan and appropriately involve individuals, families, and other natural support systems in the process. However, these competencies have not been well articulated in the past. This may well explain why individual planning is missing from curricula and training, and why attitudes and skill levels are poor.

A clear articulation of the competencies necessary to be effective in developing individual plans is an important step towards improving current practice. The work of the Sainsbury Centre is useful in its clear specification of a core set of competencies to improve current practice. These include the capacity of the provider for

- effective communication
- effective partnership with individuals and families
- effective partnership in teams

In order to achieve effective communication, some of the skills listed below are essential. Providers must be able to

- exchange information with individuals, families, and other members of the team
- listen to individuals and families and at the same time maximize opportunities for them to be heard

- educate individuals and families about the role, function, and limitations of mental health and addictive disorders services

The development and maintenance of effective partnerships—with both individuals and families as well as with other members of the team—involves a set of complimentary skills that build on the communication skills previously described. These include the ability of providers to do the following things:

- develop functional working relationships with individuals and families
- understand the fundamental importance of relationships to social and psychological well-being
- facilitate a cooperative alliance and partnership through the use of flexible responses and strategies
- establish safe and consistent mechanisms for continuing communication with individuals and families when they transition to other services
- maintain a respectful, non-judgmental, and empathic approach at all times
- support the development of opportunities for individuals and families to participate in all aspects of care
- facilitate the participation of individuals and families in the development, delivery, and evaluation of individual plans
- encourage and support individual, peer, and citizen advocacy
- lead or participate effectively in multi-disciplinary, multi-agency team
- articulate the roles and functions of the team, the services that it will provide, and the outcomes that it will seek
- identify the roles, tasks, systems, structures, and processes essential for multidisciplinary, multi-agency team collaboration
- identify the issues and key tasks involved in the implementation of effective teamwork into routine care
- appropriately and flexibly negotiate professional boundaries to meet the needs of individuals and families

In addition, there is knowledge and skills specific to the development of an individual plan, coordination of services, and review that can also be elaborated. Providers' competencies should include the ability to do the following things:

- participate in the development and documentation of written care plans
- identify, describe, and document the aspirations of individuals and families for improved quality of life

- identify problems, needs, and required interventions
- actively involve individuals and families where appropriate
- conduct a comprehensive assessment of health and social care needs of the individual and family
- access and coordinate the health, mental health, addictive disorders, and social services required to meet identified needs
- develop positive risk management strategies and a crisis action plan
- regularly and systematically monitor, review, and evaluate outcomes

The Center for Addictive Disorders Treatment Technical Assistance Publication (TAP) Series #21[7] also identifies addiction counseling competencies for service planning, such as having knowledge of the following:

- the stages of change and readiness for treatment in addiction recovery
- motivation and motivating factors
- the role and importance of client resources and barriers to treatment
- the impact of client and family systems on treatment decisions and outcomes
- sources of assessment information

Additionally, service providers should have demonstrable skills in the following areas:

- establishing treatment priorities
- working with people of different ages, developmental levels, and gender, racial, and ethical cultures
- interpreting data

Lastly, provider attitudes should reflect the following qualities:

- appreciation of the strengths and limitations of the client and significant others
- recognition of the value of thoroughness and completeness

The clear articulation of these competencies is an important first step in any effort to change current practice. How to transfer these abilities and skills into the provider's everyday routines remains a question.

III. MAKING IT HAPPEN

There is the old story about the young music student lost in the streets of New York. He approaches an old man playing violin on the corner with an open case in front of him for donations. The student asks, "How do you get to

Carnegie Hall?" The old man replies, "Practice, my son, practice, practice." The same holds true for learning to develop and record proper individual plans for providers, organizations, and systems. Providers can make it happen through education, training, and practice to master the requisite new skills.

Possible Solutions

Establishing changes in practice that appropriately value and utilize individual planning will ultimately require solution-focused changes in policy, leadership, education and training, and practice. A real commitment to individual planning as a central process and as an essential tool is a necessary element of change. As long as a lower standard of performance is tolerated and accepted, change will be difficult to achieve.

The use of law, mandate, and regulation is one strategy for effecting change, but without also attending to the issues of workforce competencies, it alone will not likely succeed. Connecticut, and the other states previously referenced, have not only mandated the use of a culturally competent, person-centered, recovery-oriented approach to service planning and delivery, they are also providing system-wide training and tools to assist with the implementation of such a model. Change in practice requires attention to the training needs of the workforce—it is not reasonable to ask providers to do something they have never really been educated or trained to do. This will require changing curricula as well as post-degree internships along with new efforts at continuing education for the existing workforce.

Education and Training

There are two primary components to this kind of education and training: 1) didactic and 2) practical. Training must be ongoing, and give providers constructive feedback on their performance. A "one-shot" approach to training will usually not accomplish the goal of increasing provider competencies. Competency-based training for staff, as already required by accreditation organizations, should be offered on an ongoing basis.

The didactic portion of the training should include presentation of both the theoretical and conceptual basis of person-centered planning for mental health and addictive disorders service. Understanding the principles, the concepts, and the terms, as well as having examples of good practice, are all useful in the learning process as students move towards mastery and current providers work to change existing practice. However, there is ample evidence in the literature that lectures, seminars, and even books do not necessarily change clinical practice. A more practical hands-on approach, building upon didactic knowledge, is required. This is especially true for the skills required in individual planning.

Teaching the practical skills for individual planning can be frustrating for both instructor and student alike. The leap from conceptual understanding to responding to the very real and sometimes overwhelming complexities of the individual's and family's needs could confound the learning process. It is one thing to understand the principles, its yet another to translate them into practice.

A useful approach to learning individual planning skills is to work with clinical case vignettes—relatively refined and limited bits of clinical information built upon assessments. This presents the student with a more manageable amount of data and complexity so that the learning focus can be on skill development rather than on responding to real human need.

In one training model, students or providers are asked to work in small team-like groups, with one member role-playing the part of an individual seeking services. The "team" is then asked to develop an individual plan based upon a formulation or integrated summary derived from the assessment data. The plans are usually limited to one goal and one or two objectives.

The participants are then asked to record their work on transparency sheets and to present their plans to the trainer and other trainees. In doing so, everyone gets to participate in a process of critical review; this works to reinforce the learning process. Trainees have the benefit of learning from both their own success and errors as well as those of others. This also helps to develop critical review skills that are valuable for ongoing learning and skill development. It is not unusual to find that as several vignettes are completed, skill levels and abilities increase dramatically as students benefit from the experience and feedback received.

Having developed some mastery in the isolation of the training room, students and providers should then be ready for the next step in developing mastery—applying the skills to everyday practice. This is an important and often challenging step in the learning and training process because of the very real time and caseload demands of most work settings. Yet finding the time and support necessary for providers and teams to consolidate their skills and proficiency is essential. With practice, most providers and teams can follow the learning curve and quickly become facile with a new approach. At that time, providers and the individuals seeking services can reap the benefits that result from a well-done plan.

Financial Incentives

While education and training are essential to enabling genuine change in systems and practice, skill development alone will not necessarily produce the desired changes. Changes in the care paradigm as well as systems operations are also required. In some instances, solutions may arise from negative consequences; the threat of disallowances and recoupments can be a powerful motivator for change. Paybacks, sometimes resulting in millions of dollars, can result from poor planning and documentation (e.g., not soliciting the individual's satisfaction with services, not matching the assessment conclusions to the written plan, having objectives on the plan that are not measurable and time-limited, and so on).

Systems, organizations, and individuals all tend to resist change, and often only endure change because of perceived self-interest. The first three chapters clearly indicate that current systems of care need to change if a commitment to person-centered mental health and addictive disorders service is to be realized. The changes need to occur in several ways and at multiple levels. Valuing the process of individual planning, and investing the resources necessary to ensure that providers have the knowledge, skills, abilities, and time to do it correctly, is an essential part of the overall process of change. With commitment, study, and practice, these skills can be learned and mastered, to the benefit of individuals and families in need of services.

REFERENCES

1. CARF Behavioral Health Standards Manual, 2003 to 2004. www.carf.org.
2. Joint Commission on Accreditation of Healthcare Organization. www.jcaho.org.
3. §(482.61© CARF Behavioral Health Standards Manual, 2003 to 2004
4. APS Healthcare Inc. *Top TRIGRS Issues*. 8/14/01.
5. The Connecticut Department of Mental Health and Addiction Services. *Assessment Guidelines for Developing a Culturally Competent Service System for an Organization or Program*. January 2000.
6. Training and Practice Development Section of the Sainsbury Centre for Mental Health, *The Capable Practitioner: A Framework and List of the Practitioner Capabilities to Implement the National Service Framework for Mental Health*. 2001.
7. *Addiction Counseling Competencies: The Knowledge, Skills, and Attitudes of Professional Practice*. Technical Assistance Publication Series, # 21. Center for Addictive disorders Treatment, 1998.

SECTION II

Getting Started

We are now prepared to launch into the journey of individual planning and recovery. Section I, Planning the Trip, outlined the preliminaries. This section will deal with the specifics of actually getting under way. Chapter 4 on Assessment and Chapter 5 on Understanding of Needs are essential to the effort—together they begin to set the individual's course, to define the purpose of the journey, and to set in motion the destination as well as the route.

Chapter 4 will focus on finding a balance between gathering information and building a relationship. Information about the particulars of the journey is essential as well as the bonhomie and partnership of the fellow travelers. Chapter 5 will discuss the transition from data to information and knowledge. This will become the fuel that sustains the trip. We may know where we want to go, but without understanding, we do not have a good idea about how to get there.

## CHAPTER 4

Assessment

Knowing is half the battle.

G.I. Joe

I. STATING THE CASE

Ostensibly, the purpose of an assessment is to gather information; this is the essential first step in creating a person-centered plan. It has been said that any plan is only as good as the assessment. There are many books and references that consider the challenges and issues in the assessment for mental health and addiction recovery services at a level of detail that is beyond the scope of this book—it is a rich and complex topic worthy of its own book and exploration. However, taking the time to understand the process of assessment is a worthwhile investment for the success in providing person-centered services. Understanding the unique attributes and needs of individuals and families is the essence of being person-centered.

The Process of Assessment

Providers have a responsibility to fully understand the individual and family, their strengths, abilities, and past successes, along with their hopes, dreams, needs, and problems in seeking help. Only this knowledge prepares the provider to help create a responsive, efficacious plan, which is consistent with the expressed values, culture, and wishes of those receiving services.

But assessment is more than the mere gathering of information; it is the initiation of building a trusting, helping, healing relationship, the forging of an alliance upon which to build a plan responsive to the individual's and family's needs. In terms of the road trip metaphor, this is the point of "getting started" on the road, and gathering the needed provisions in order to begin the trip. While there is no question that the accuracy and quality of information that we gather is important, *how* the information is gathered is perhaps even more critical. In many instances, it is easy to confuse the process of assessment with the requirements of paperwork and forms, but ultimately assessment is primarily about building a relationship. While forms and documentation need to be completed, it may be better to pursue a natural conversation rather than following a linear approach to completing these forms.

This is akin to the allegory of the road map. Following a decision to travel and the choice of destination, preparations begin, the route is laid out, and the intermediate stops are selected. Simply beginning a journey without a destination should be avoided, to prevent heading in the wrong direction and having to double back. Without following these basic steps, reaching the destination is unlikely. Assessment is the "getting started phase," identifying what we need to bring with us, choosing the provisions, gathering the essentials, and packing for the trip. In the journey of creating an individual plan, information is the fuel that propels us.

Before continuing with the discussion on assessment, it may be helpful to clarify the terminology. The words "triage," "screening," and "assessment" are often used interchangeably, resulting in some degree of confusion. While they are related processes, they also represent distinct clinical functions.

Triage	A process of assigning priorities for access to treatment based on urgency and risk, typically but not necessarily used in emergency or crisis situations.
Screening	A cursory of preliminary assessment process for determining the need and appropriateness of services, often times used in initial determination of eligibility, level of care, and so on.
Assessment	An in-depth gathering of data and information, typically conducted at the initiation of treatment, needed to understand an individual's or family's needs as a pre-requisite for developing a plan of care.

This chapter will focus on assessment.

Establishing a Relationship

Too often, initiating an assessment begins by asking and focusing on what is wrong. In a recovery-oriented, person-centered approach, the challenge is to think about more positive, inviting, and affirming ways of responding to and engaging individuals and families seeking help. The need to accept and "meet the person on their own terms" is an often recited phrase, but its real meaning needs to be examined in response to an individual's or family's request for assistance. Sometimes simply asking the neutral and inviting question "How can I be of help?" begins to realign some of the inherent and at times undermining power differentials in the relationship between the provider and the person seeking services. This helps to set the stage for a more positive and productive course. There are times when this process is framed as one of alliance-building or engagement. While this may at one level be accurate, the importance of the tone, quality, and experience of the relationship cannot be overestimated. Treating people with dignity and respect should always be our standard of practice and guiding rule, regardless of the circumstance.

The importance of a strengths-based approach to assessment cannot be overstated. A focus on problems and deficits often leads to feelings of shame, blame, and failure. This does not promote or support engagement and does not set the stage for recovery. A deficit-based approach emphasizes a negative perspective and often leaves the individual and family feeling that they are the problem. Instead, there is an opportunity to be empowering even in the process of gathering assessment information. In a strengths-based and person-centered approach, the focus is on action rather than the revealing of all of the problem areas.[1] This helps to build trust, cooperation, and meaningful involvement by the individual and family.

Another approach is to actually begin with some form of an orientation rather than immediately engage in data gathering and assessment. There are multiple levels of orientation to consider: orientation to the larger concept of mental health and addiction, orientation to the planning process, orientation to the service organization and available services, and/or orientation to a particular program. Depending on the needs, experience, knowledge, and sophistication of the individual and family, all four levels of orientation might be indicated. Although providers are generally very familiar with the mental health and addiction services process, many of the individuals and families seeking help are not. For many people, each new experience in seeking services promotes anxiety and uncertainty. Both children and adults will frequently carry fears and misconceptions, not knowing what to expect. Beginning with an explanation or overview of the whole process can help in reducing anxieties, beginning to build the alliance, and supporting the assessment.

Organizing the Steps

Figure 4.1 begins to show a hierarchy for the process of creating a plan. Each step in the pyramid builds upon the preceding one. Like the metaphor of building a house, creating the foundation is the essential first task. Each successive step must not only be completed in order, but must be done properly if the final result is to succeed. Skipping a step or jumping ahead will typically not work well. Perhaps not surprisingly, assessment is the first level of the pyramid. It is metaphorically as well as practically the start of the process in response to a request for help. The important underpinnings of culture and identity cannot be underestimated and, although often in the background, they influence the entire structure.

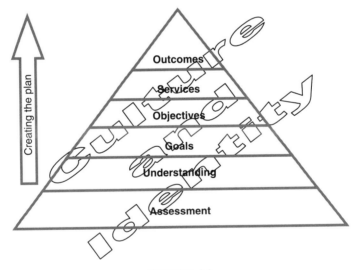

FIGURE 4.1

The pyramid itself can be a useful orientation tool that provides a simple graphic explanation of the various steps or phases in the process. Actually reviewing this diagram provides an opportunity to reassure individuals that the focus is on understanding their unique and individual needs. Being person-centered in not only *what* is done, but also about *how* it is done. In this way, individuals and families seeking help can be assisted in developing a plan for change that is reflective of their own expectations and goals. This is often in and of itself empowering and helps set the stage for successful outcomes.

Developing a plan begins with an assessment interview involving the individual and his or her self-defined family, and is an opportunity for the provider to engage the person in treatment and begin building a successful alliance. From the data gathered in assessment, a formulation or understanding is created. Next, long-term global recovery and outcome-oriented goals are identified; ideally, these are captured in the words and language of the individual receiving services and represent a potential endpoint or transition in the service delivery process. The objectives or the action steps the individual will need to take to lead to their goal should follow. In a person-centered plan, these time-framed and attainable near-term changes build upon the individual's needs, preferences, abilities, and strengths. Services or interventions (also referred to as strategies and methods), which are culturally sensitive and appropriate, are then provided in support of the objectives and consistent with individual preference. Ideally these services help build the skills and capacities of the individual and whenever possible, interventions should include services utilizing and building on the natural supports in the community. Ongoing reassessment and evaluation of timely progress and change are essential to keeping the entire process on track. This may also suggest the need for additional objectives or services to help the individual along the way in the journey towards reaching his or her goals and transitions.

In this hierarchical process, assessment is the base upon which the creation of the plan is built. In responding to a request for assistance, either self-referral or involuntary commitment, the first step is to engage the individual as a partner in telling the story and gathering information.

There are always circumstances in which an individual or family will have only one visit—typically an assessment. Sometimes this is appropriate, but many times the lack of follow-up reflects a failure in our ability to adequately initiate or establish a relationship and engage people seeking help in the process. And there is increasing evidence that under some circumstances, individuals and families may experience contact with the mental health and addictive disorders delivery system as not merely unhelpful but rather as traumatic. This is a particularly critical issue in serving diverse multicultural multi-ethnic communities where the issues of stigma, avoidance, and the ability to trust mental health professionals may be even greater. This makes the task of conducting a good assessment even more challenging. However, with careful attention to each person and sensitivity to his or her unique cultural and ethnic background, success in building a relationship and learning about their needs can be achieved.

The Cycle of Assessment

Assessment is often described as being both "initial and ongoing." Assessment should definitely not be considered a one-time event. Every step along the way we should be conducting an assessment or reassessment, evaluating the impacts of services and the changes that occur over time. Achieving a personal vision of recovery and wellness is inevitably a dynamic process in which we must attend to the new and different information that is generated in each individual's journey. Responses to services and interventions shed new light and have the potential to set new directions and priorities. People's lives and their environments are not static and changes are occurring apart from the provider's efforts to assist. Figure 4.2 describes how the planning and service processes have both linear and circular elements. Beginning with an effort at outreach, or a self-initiated request for assistance, all the way to the desired change, it can be viewed as linear. At the same time, assessment is a focal point in the overall process and part of a loop which is circular and repeated until the intended outcome is achieved. The cycle from assessment to plan to services and back to assessment revolves around a central theme: understanding of the individual and family in the context of their culture.

A common problem in many service-delivery systems and settings is the lack of documentation of formal, regular, and periodic reassessment. Providers will frequently claim that they have in fact been conducting an ongoing process of assessment and reassessment consistent with good practice. Both here and throughout the service-delivery process, the old adage applies: "If it's not written down, it didn't happen." While many providers often feel that they are crushed by the burden of paperwork and documentation, creating an accurate record is inevitably as much a part of the helping process as any other activity. Above and beyond the requirements of regulatory authorities, payers, and the like, our ability to assure continuity, consistency, and coordination is greatly enhanced by recording thoughts and observations as the service process unfolds; often, the information gathered proves to be useful for the individual and other providers in the future. Properly recording our assessment data helps to assure continuity of care over time.

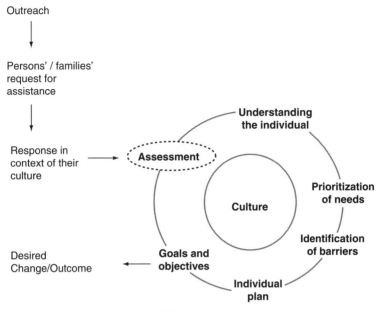

FIGURE 4.2

Although there are no standard rules or instructions for the proper period of review and update of an assessment, it should be timely and relevant to the provision of services. Oftentimes, regulatory agencies and funding sources will establish criteria for reassessment. In evaluating actual practice in a wide range of settings, it is not unusual to find current service plans based upon assessments that are quite old. As a guiding principle, a formal and comprehensive reassessment should be considered in the provision of long-term services at minimum every year; in all likelihood, briefer and focused reassessments will occur more frequently. In more short-term or acute service settings, the period of reassessment should correspond to the time frames in each individual's and family's plan and be related to the anticipated or average length of services. Midpoints are often convenient times for some formal reassessment. Individuals who continue beyond the customary duration of services are also good candidates for reassessment.

What To Collect

If assessment pertains to gathering information, then it is reasonable to ask a few quesions: How much information is enough? What is the right volume of data? What is the right level of detail? Ultimately the answer is this: an amount of information sufficient to adequately understand the individual and family. In practice, the service setting often shapes this amount. Long-term services responding to long-standing needs and problems will likely require more detailed assessments, while more short-term programs and plans will require less. External demands from accreditation organizations, licensing bodies, and funding sources may require certain types of information to be included, domains to be addressed, or even standardized assessment instruments, such as the Addiction Severity Index (ASI), to be utilized. A person-centered assessment does not have to exclude these requirements, nor is it necessarily in conflict with such requirements; a person-centered assessment is more a matter of focus and approach than specific data elements.

As we consider the scope of our assessment and the range of topics to address, perhaps one domain is more important or essential than all of the rest: identifying the individual's and family's strengths. Not only is this information important in and of itself, but the message communicated in efforts at recognizing and validating the individual is also engaging and healing as well as supportive of the larger process of assessment. Knowing about a person's hopes, dreams, accomplishments, and self-esteem helps us to better understand that person's challenges and needs. This becomes the essence of the experience of dignity and respect for the person seeking services, and ultimately it is these attributes upon which we will build a successful plan to address the individual's challenges and needs.

Conducting a comprehensive assessment is often aided by organizing the data gathering into domains or broader topic areas to minimize the risk of overlooking critical information. People's lives are unique and complex. An individual is far greater than his or her presenting symptoms and whatever challenges they may cause. For many people, it is not easy to be immediately forthcoming about every detail of their lives—particularly at a time of distress. Assuring that an assessment is comprehensive means that no important facet is overlooked and the individual seeking services is given ample opportunity to identify his or her needs and strengths. Sometimes this approach requires more than one assessment appointment and challenges the flexibility and creativity of providers as well as organizations and systems.

What does it mean to be comprehensive? How is an assessment tailored to the needs of each individual and family? Individual characteristics such as age, gender, ethnicity, and disability may provide some initial guidance. For example, it is typically appropriate to inquire about educational issues for a child and work issues for an adult. Health concerns are an issue across the lifespan but may be more critical in understanding the needs and circumstances of an older adult.

Detail and depth should not be confused with breadth. While being broad or comprehensive is a general criterion, the depth or detail of an assessment may vary depending on the immediacy and severity of an individual's circumstances and the treatment setting. Although it is important to touch on and consider a broad range of life areas, not all require the same depth of inquiry or detail. Many accrediting organizations, licensing bodies, and other standard setting groups will generate long and exhaustive list of items to be included in a comprehensive assessment—but clearly not all of the items are always relevant or appropriate to an individual or family.

Tailoring an assessment to each individual is part of being person-centered. There may be times when this impacts the depth of exploration in any one particular area more than the breadth of the assessment overall—particularly when there are licensing or accreditation standards proscribing domains or topics that must be addressed. However, the recognition of the need to be flexible and less proscriptive or absolute is reflected in recent changes in the 2005 JCAHO Behavioral Health standards. This new approach requires that "the organization defines in writing the data and information gathered during the psychosocial assessment,"[2] without the previous emphasis on specific or required domains.

From What to Why

It cannot be repeated too often that collecting information is but a first step. Weaving that data into understanding is a separate but closely linked, critical, and often-overlooked task. Chapter 5 on Understanding Needs will discuss this in greater detail. For now, it is important not to confuse *what* and *why*. In general, assessment describes *what* and hopefully with sufficient detail we can begin to understand *why*. The why of an individual's or family's needs is often the critical factor in developing a successful plan of response. Without this there is a risk of not truly addressing the issues and problems. Ultimately, the measure of an adequate assessment is its ability to support a meaningful level of understanding.

For example, knowing that an individual does not take their medicines as prescribed is a simple bit of information—and a not uncommon issue in mental health services. That fact alone may suggest the need for all kinds of support and supervision to assure adherence to the prescribed regimen, even to the point at times of suggesting the use of long-acting injections. However, there may be many reasons an individual does not take prescribed medicines. A list of possible reasons might include the following items:

- unwanted side effects
- lack of apparent benefit
- forgetfulness and disorganization
- a belief that they are cured
- lack of financial resources
- religious beliefs
- lack of understanding the purpose of the medication
- family opposition
- preference for alternatives, such as vitamins and homeopathy
- auditory hallucinations with negative commentary about treatment
- lack of trust in the physician
- trauma associated with past treatment

Research studies have found that not taking medications as prescribed is often a conscious decision by individuals based on adverse effects, price, or personal choice. According to a Boston Consulting Group study, *The Hidden Epidemic: Finding a Cure for Unfilled Prescriptions and Missed Doses,*[3] 20% of patients who forgo medications do so because they perceive a drug's side effects to be undesirable or debilitating, 17% because they find the medicines too costly, and 14% because they do not think they need the drug. Patients in this last group view themselves, not their doctors, as the best ultimate judge of what medications they should take and when they should take them. Among those actively not adhering are the 10% of patients who said they find it difficult to get the written prescription to the pharmacy or to get the filled prescription home.

Depending upon the reason, i.e., the understanding of the "why" lying behind the simple fact of non-adherence, a provider's response is likely to be quite different. For example, the response to unwanted side effects should be quite different than the supports and assistance provided to address financial burden, and different yet again from the psychoeducation initiatives needed to address family opposition. It is easy to see how the data alone, without an accurate understanding that goes beyond the mere facts, are not sufficient for preparing an effective helping response.

Dual Diagnosis of Co-Occurring Disorders

In their many articles and training sessions, Minkoff and Cline[4] have posited that "dual diagnosis is the expectation, not an exception." Research has proven them correct: 55% of individuals in treatment for schizophrenia report a history of substance use disorders, and 60% of individuals with substance use disorders have an identifiable psychiatric diagnosis. The message should be clear—when assessing individuals who present at either a mental health or an addictive disorders program, providers need to be prepared to view them as whole persons, with multiple needs and issues not necessarily fitting into one diagnostic category! Using an integrated assessment instrument to conduct a single biopsychosocial assessment (not having the individual be separately assessed by the mental health "experts" and the addiction "experts") is recommended. There should be "no wrong door" and individuals and families should be able to receive a complete assessment regardless of where they seek services. Minkoff[5] has recently developed practice guidelines that can be useful and relevant for providers in developing integrated approaches to assessment.

Cultural Issues in Assessment

With the changing demographics of American society and the increasing diversity of our communities, attending to the issues of culture in the process of assessment is also critically important. The lack of equity in access and health status of ethnic and racial minorities in the U.S. and other countries is a serious concern that has been well documented. Removing barriers—linguistic, cultural, physical, psychological, and others—has increasingly become a mandate for health and human services delivery systems. If assessment initiates the process of responding to need, then assuring the cultural competence of our assessment is essential. In many respects, a person-centered approach that focuses on the unique needs of each individual and family is the essence of a culturally competent approach.

The importance of cultural awareness, sensitivity, and competence, not just in assessment but also in the entirety of mental health and addictive disorders services, cannot be overstated. In this context, it is important to remember that culture does not refer only to matters of race and ethnicity but to the myriad ways in which people self-identify and affiliate. Understanding this is central to any notion of being person and family-centered. Individuals and families must be understood in the context of their culture and experience with full awareness of the ways in which culture can create barriers to an appropriate response.

The March 2003 Santa Fe Summit convened by the American College of Mental Health Administration (ACMHA) gathered together a diverse group of stakeholders including payers, providers, policymakers, recipients of services, government, professional associations, and others to examine the marked disparity in access and quality of mental health and addictive disorders service for many Americans. This leadership group concluded that services must be more culturally relevant and appropriate for individuals and families. There was a clear consensus that the process of assessment is a critical component of cultural competence. The group established that assessment must include recognition and appreciation of the person's culture as a crucial part of developing a formulation and should include cultural considerations that can influence diagnosis and care. These are essential elements in creating a service plan that includes culturally appropriate interventions and can lead to better outcomes for individuals.

It is useful to have a working definition of the concept of culture. A simple but effective approach is to recognize culture as a shared set of beliefs, norms, and values in which language is a key factor. Other factors that play an important role include ethnicity, race, sexual orientation, disability, and other self-defined characteristics. Equally important is to remember that culture is not fixed or frozen in time but rather exists in a constant state of change that is learned, taught, and reproduced. A framework for considering human diversity can be thought of using the ADDRESSING pneumonic and includes the following factors:

- **A**ge and generational influences
- **D**evelopmental and acquired **D**isabilities
- **R**eligion and spiritual orientation
- **E**thnicity
- **S**ocioeconomic status
- **S**exual orientation
- **I**ndigenous heritage
- **N**ational origin
- **G**ender

While this list is not exhaustive, it provides a handy tool to help assure that providers remember to consider those qualities that make every individual unique.

Issues of culture, ethnicity, race, and other attributes which individuals use to self-identify impact the quality of interactions with providers and thus the assessment. Cultural tradition, experience, and bias—by both the individual as well as the provider—are all part of an unstated but powerful dynamic in the helping relationship that impacts how information is provided and received. Providing an emotionally safe environment for disclosure and to allay the fears, anxieties, and preconceptions of those seeking help is critical to success in assessment. Understanding and being sensitive to the roles of status and power should also be a part of our approach. Knowledge about other cultures, awareness of one's own limits, and a willingness to seek help and consultation when necessary are also key ingredients for success.

Assessment must also consider how culture and social contexts shape an individual's symptoms, presentation, and meaning, as well as coping styles. In addition, family influences, attitudes towards help-seeking, stigma, and the willingness to trust helping professionals are all influenced by culture. The relationships between the provider and the individual and family are also potentially shaped by differences in culture and social status. Our efforts at assessment are impacted by factors including styles of communication, capacity for rapport, comfort with disclosure, the perception of safety and privacy, and the experience of power, dignity, and respect, all of which are to a degree culturally determined. The impact of a number of other factors including acculturation and immigration stress, identity, racism, marginalization, or discrimination, all affect help-seeking and successful engagement, and must also be considered. Issues of assimilation, alienation, and cultural trauma can also affect the experience of seeking and receiving services.

Ultimately, efforts at assessment should result in providing the information necessary to develop a cultural formulation as specified in the Diagnostic and Statistical Manual of Mental Disorders-Fourth Edition-Text Revision (DSM-IV-TR). The five key elements of such a formulation include consideration of:

- cultural identity
- possible cultural explanations of illness
- cultural factors related to psychosocial environment and levels of functioning
- cultural elements in the client/provider relationship
- the role of cultural assessment in diagnosis and service planning

Efforts at understanding the individual and family will inevitably be limited without the completion of a cultural formulation.

Standardized Assessment Instruments

Commonly used, scientifically reliable, and valid assessment tools for mental health and/or addiction treatment include any number of standardized instruments. A partial list, including some examples of commonly used instruments and tools, is as follows:

- Addiction Severity Index (ASI)
- Adolescent Drinking Index (ADI), for adolescents using alcohol, ages 13 to 17 years
- Beck Depression Inventory-Second Edition (BDI-II), for adults and adolescents with life functioning and behavior problems
- Behavioral and Symptom Identification Scale (BASIS-32), for adults with risk factors/symptoms/life functioning issues
- Brief Psychiatric Rating Scale (BPRS), for adults with major psychiatric disorders
- Child and Adolescent Functional Assessment Scale (CAFAS), for children and adolescents experiencing life functioning, family, behavior, and/or risk factors
- SF-36 Health Survey, for adolescents and adults with severity and/or risk factors and life functioning problems
- Minnesota Multiphasic Personality Inventory (MMPI)
- Michigan Alcoholism Screening Test (MAST), for identifying adults who potentially abuse alcohol or are alcoholic
- Substance Abuse Subtle Screening Inventory (SASSI), for adults who may be abusing substances
- Stages of Change Readiness and Treatment Eagerness Scale (SOCRA-TES), for adults presenting with alcohol and other drug issues
- University of Rhode Island Change Assessment (URICA), for drug-using adults
- biological methods, including breath tests, urinanalysis, and blood tests, to determine substance use

These standardized data-gathering tools may be helpful in terms of assessing the individual's severity of symptoms, life functioning abilities, problem behaviors, domains of impairment, degree of alcohol-related problems and alcoholism, and so on. However, standardized assessment tools may not be culturally sensitive or competent, and they are often too proscriptive and not sufficiently flexible to be useful in a person-centered approach. While there is some value in standardization, this must be balanced with a need for appropriate modification—through supplementation or editing—to ensure that each assessment is truly responsive to the individual's and family's unique attributes and circumstances. In comparison, standardization in terms of breadth or comprehensiveness is less of a problem than the use of structured assessment tools that limit our ability to individually explore the important topic areas in detail.

In summary, assessment is the first and, therefore, most important step in initiating a person-centered plan. It is the gathering of the provisions needed (the data), packing them into a suitcase (the formatted documents of the clinical record), selecting the destination (as described in the narrative summary) that will lead to understanding (the narrative summary) and, ultimately creating the map (the written individual plan).

There are many barriers within existing practice that make gathering information, developing understanding, and creating a person-centered plan difficult. Yet changing current practice to be more person-centered and creating the information and understanding needed to better serve individuals and families is quite doable within existing systems and resources: it is about changing the *how* of assessment as much as it is a matter of changing the *what*.

II. CREATING THE SOLUTION

Ironically, thinking about how to be more person-centered in assessment seems perhaps more difficult than in other phases of developing individual plans. This may be the case because assessment should be far more about process than about product—so much so that it is difficult to think about how to evaluate the "person-centeredness" of an assessment. What is the written demonstration of a person-centered assessment? How is it different from other assessment styles or approaches?

Gathering Data

The objective of assessment is to gather information about the individual and family—something that on the surface would appear to be the essence of being person-centered. However, there is a real need to shift the focus away from an emphasis on the quantity of information. Instead, greater importance ought to be placed on the quality and type of information gathered and the experience of the individual and family in the course of the process. With a greater concern about the process employed in gathering information, there is some assurance that assessment will be person-centered.

This is not meant to suggest a radical transformation of many providers' current practice. Rather, it is about a shift in emphasis, focus, approach, or style that has the potential to have a powerful effect on how providers as well as individuals and families, experience the process of seeking and receiving help. However, it is not entirely unusual that in the effort to meet a whole host of regulatory, accreditation, payment, and other standards—not to mention the demands of a full schedule and much-too-large caseload—the preferences, needs, and values of the individual and family are overlooked. At that point, assessment is not about the individual and family. Rather, it is driven by the obligation to gather all of the necessary information in a specified (and oftentimes too brief) period of time. The following pages contain some tips and tools that can assist providers in their efforts at being more person-centered in assessment and data gathering as a first step in the journey towards creating a meaningful and relevant individual plan.

Provider Attitude

It has been suggested that the attitude of the provider, expressed in terms of empathy, respect, warmth, genuineness, and concreteness, is the key to the practice of person-centered assessment. This approach provides the individual and family an atmosphere in which they can explore, understand, and benefit from the assessment process. Two essential elements of the provider's attitude have been identified. It can be said that assessment is person-centered when

- each person is viewed as a person of worth and is respected as such, and
- each individual has the right to self direction, i.e., to choose their own values and goals and to make their own decisions[6]

In this framework, the assessment provides the individual and family with an opportunity to learn about potentially desirable changes in their lives and to better participate in the planning process. It is not for the benefit of the provider.

Steps to Collecting Data

Re-ordering the process of collecting information in the assessment can help a provider to be person-centered. There are often a host of administrative requirements that determine the elements of a comprehensive assessment and often unreasonably shape the assessment process. This domain-based and structured approach can unwittingly lead to a deficit and problem-based approach. This can leave the individual and family seeking help feeling exposed and criticized. Instead, a person-centered approach places emphasis and focus on understanding the goals, hopes, wishes, and strengths of the individual and family in terms of their own self-defined identity and related cultural concerns.

A recent text on treatment planning suggests that "A semi-structured [interview] format is recommended as the best means of gathering information from the patient [sic] . . . this ensures that all interview information that is generally helpful or needed in formulating a clinical picture of the patient is obtained."[7] Instead, a "conversational and less formal" approach, which fosters a relationship with the individual and family rather than merely collecting information or promoting a particular service, is more likely to succeed in being person-centered.[8] Experience shows that one of the best ways to engage individuals is to focus on their goals, hopes, wishes, and dreams. This is primarily and closely tied to a strengths-oriented approach that is at the heart of recovery, wellness, and resiliency.

Domains

While every individual and family is unique and different, there are unifying concepts or concerns that can help to organize an assessment. These are frequently called domains. These broad categories are a useful framework by which to organize the collection of data. The following list is offered as an illustration of commonly considered domains:

1. Identity
   - may include issues of culture, race, ethnicity, sexual orientation, spiritual beliefs, etc.
2. Health and medical status
   - including diet and nutrition, efficacy of current or previously used medications, medication allergies or adverse reactions, risk-taking behaviors (e.g., intravenous drug use, sexual transmission of diseases, and so on), dental, hearing and eye care needs
3. Psychiatric and psychological status and history
   - may include mental status exam, identification of urgent needs, issues of personal safety, history of abuse and concerns (either as a victim or the perpetrator), co-occurring disorders identified
4. Alcohol and other drug use (present and past)
   - including alcohol and misuse of prescribed medications, as well as illegal drugs, caffeine, and tobacco
5. Treatment history
   - may include past hospitalizations, outpatient encounters for both mental health and addictive disorders

6. Family life
   . including history, present status, family members with mental illness/addiction issues
7. Community participation
   . may include all types of relationships, including use of natural supports, need for and availability of social supports, recreational pursuits, use of transportation
8. Housing status
   . including independent living, homelessness, incarceration, shelter living, group homes, and so on
9. Education and employment
   . including level of education attained as well as level of functioning
   . may include present and previous employment, vocational aptitude
   . financial status and ability to manage funds
10. Legal status
    . may include current legal situation, conviction history, incarceration
11. Developmental history (particularly for children)
    . including developmental age factors, motor development and functioning, speech, visual and hearing functioning, learning ability and intellectual functioning, prenatal exposure to alcohol, tobacco or drugs, and so on
12. Levels of functioning
    . cognitive, emotional, behavioral functioning, including living skills

This list is only a starting point. In particular settings and in response to specific individual and family needs, other assessment information may be indicated or even required. For instance, additional assessments for individuals in criminal and juvenile justice programs will likely require additional information and consideration. Regardless, content must always be balanced with process.

Strengths

The notion of strengths-based approaches is often invoked, but it is not necessarily well understood, in part because there are many definitions or interpretations. Moreover, many providers are not well trained in identifying strengths given the traditional focus in clinical training programs on diagnosis, problems, and deficits. One approach to understanding individuals lies in the concept of recognizing each person's "core gifts" or strengths. This language is important in its implicit valuing of these individual attributes. By not emphasizing deficits and problems, providers create an opportunity to see possibilities, options, and opportunities for change and improvement.

A basic inventory of strengths should at minimum include consideration of:

- abilities, talents, competencies, and accomplishments in any range of settings from home to school and work or other social settings
- values and traditions
- interests, hopes, dreams, aspirations, and motivation
- resources and assets, both monetary/economic, social, and interpersonal
- unique individual attributes (physical, psychological, performance capabilities, sense of humor, and so on)
- circumstances at home, school, work or in the community that have worked well in the past
- family members, relatives, friends, and other "natural supports" (both formal and informal relationships) within the community

Stages of Recovery

The idea of stages or phases in the recovery process can often be useful in understanding an individual's or family's responses and ability to participate in a person-centered assessment. Townsend et al.[9] have proposed a model in which individuals are placed in one of four stages of recovery, as detailed in Table 4.1. Often providers will report feeling overwhelmed by the number and severity of an individual's needs and their reluctance to engage. Recognizing that the individual may be at Stage I, dependent and still unaware of their own potential for recovery, can help guide the assessment and work towards assisting the individual, and enhance their ability to articulate a vision for their own recovery.

Boston University's Center for Psychiatric Rehabilitation has proposed another schema for staging, which describes individuals as being in one of the following states with regard to their challenges, disabilities, or illness:

1. overwhelmed by
2. struggling with
3. living with
4. living beyond

This model is useful in understanding that a hopeful progression and course exists for individuals and families to follow.

Osher and Kofoed[10] have proposed a "stages of treatment" model for integrated mental health and addictive disorders service. This is an adaptation of Prochaska's stages of change model, which was developed for the addiction-treatment field. The stages of treatment parallel the recovery process:

1. engagement
2. persuasion
3. active treatment
4. relapse prevention

In the engagement stage, the alliance between the provider and the individual is established. The goal of the persuasion stage is to develop the person's awareness of substance use as a problem and motivate the individual to change. The active treatment stage has its focus on reducing substance abuse, with an ultimate goal of abstinence, and the relapse prevention stage has stability, further recovery, and the prevention of relapse as its goals. Understanding the individual's stage at initiation of services (either voluntarily or under duress) is helpful in assisting the individual to succeed in plan development and ultimate outcomes.

TABLE 4.1   Stages of Recovery: Ohio Model

Stage I • dependent and unaware	The individual is dependent on the mental health and disabilities system and unaware of the potential for their own recovery.
Stage II • dependent and aware	The individual is dependent on the mental health and disabilities system but is aware of the possibilities and potential for their recovery.
Stage III • independent and aware	The individual is not dependent on the mental health and disability system, and is able to make choices about his/her life and aware of additional opportunities.
Stage IV • independent and aware	The individual is interdependent, involved in the life of the community, and aware of the possibilities for themselves and others.

Level of Care

Another component of assessment is helping to determine the breadth and intensity of services or level of care the individual and family will likely require to address their needs and concerns. This is a component of medical necessity and utilization management as well as an element in quality of care. Assessment data are the critical starting point in determining the appropriate level of care.

In the mental health arena, the Level Of Care and Utilization Scale (LOCUS)[11] developed by the American Association of Community Psychiatrists (AACP) for adults as well as children and adolescents (CALOCUS) has gained wide acceptance as a tool to support medical necessity determinations. The six domains of assessment for the adult LOCUS include:

- risk of harm
- functional status
- medical and psychiatric comorbidity
- recovery environment
- treatment and recovery history
- engagement

The CALOCUS for children and adolescents effectively uses the same domains with age-appropriate modifications and an emphasis on resiliency rather than recovery.

In the addictive disorders field, the American Society of Addiction Medicine's (ASAM) level of care tool, the Patient Placement Criteria (PPC-2R),[12] has become a virtual standard for level of care assignments. The ASAM criteria are based upon an assessment of multiple biopsycho-social factors to help support consistent and objective, clinically based placement decisions and to determine the appropriate level of care for adults and adolescents (e.g., outpatient, residential, inpatient, and so on) requiring addictive disorders treatment. Six domains or dimensions are considered in the ASAM schema:

- intoxication and withdrawal
- biomedical conditions
- emotional/behavioral conditions
- treatment acceptance/resistance
- relapse/continued use potential
- recovery environment

Based upon the findings in each of the six domains, guidelines are provided to suggest an appropriate level of care, for example, intensive outpatient or medically monitored residential treatment. There are striking similarities between the LOCUS and PPC-2R in their design and logic. Both of these systems use a matrix of criteria or domains and the individual's status or symptoms in each domain to guide decision-making. However, each of these tools or instruments includes its own specific decision rules to help determine the most appropriate level and location of services. While much of the required data can be routinely included in the assessment process, it is useful to be aware of some of the specific elements and how they are integrated into these decision support tools.

Culture

How can providers be culturally sensitive and competent? The answer lies in learning to understand how culture and social contexts shape an individual's and family's mental health symptoms, presentation, meaning, and coping styles along with attitudes towards help-seeking, stigma, and the willingness to trust helping professionals—all of which are factors in assessment influenced by culture.

As a first step, it is important for providers to be aware of their own cultural experience and orientation as well as limitations and biases. Stereotyping and making assumptions based upon culture is an unacceptable, dangerous practice that is the essence of discrimination. Within any ethnic or cultural group there is a tremendous amount of heterogeneity. Thus, a person-centered approach that focuses on understanding and appreciating the role that culture and ethnicity plays in the life of each individual and family is so important. In this way we can build an effective trusting relationship that helps to ensure an accurate assessment. Sadly, service providers are not immune to racism, either overt or covert. Systems may have institutional barriers to full access by all individuals. Honesty, self-awareness, and a willingness to confront these issues by providers as well as supervisors and administrators are important first steps towards assuring cultural competence in person-centered services and reducing disparities.

Language is a key factor in removing cultural and ethnic barriers to access and services. Understanding the fluency of the individual and family is necessary but not sufficient. For example, if English is a second language, it may not be the preferred language. Conducting an assessment in the language that provides the greatest comfort and ability in expression and communication for the individual becomes the prerequisite of conducting an effective assessment.

Competencies

We can perhaps begin to identify a minimal set of competencies required for providers to succeed in assessment, particularly in their work with diverse multicultural communities. Providers need to have awareness, knowledge, and skills. Table 4.2 provides a brief summary of some key competencies.

While this list is by no means intended to be comprehensive, we have identified some key elements or considerations in understanding the roles of culture and identity for both individuals and families:

1. Conducting a culturally competent assessment begins by clarifying the identity of the individual and family. Oftentimes the simple question *How do you see yourself?* helps to provide vital information about race, ethnicity, sexual orientation, religion, color, disability reference group, and other factors important to the individual's and family's sense of self and place in society.

2. Language is another set of important concerns that shape the entire assessment process. Inquiring about language fluency, literacy, and, perhaps most importantly, preference is essential. Conducting an assessment in the individual's and family's preferred language is always ideal; the use of an interpreter is second best. Family members should be used as interpreters only as a last resort when it is clear that no other resources are available.

3. Understanding the individual's and family's experience and history of immigration, the country of origin, and possible trauma is important. Did they leave voluntarily or were they victims of persecution or even torture? Were they refugees? Did they seek political asylum? Similarly, understanding attitudes and perceptions of acculturation, assimilation, discrimination, and alienation are equally important.

4. Evaluation of family composition, relational roles, and dynamics should be considered.

5. Considering the impact of culture and language on the description of distress and symptom expression is important. There are times when somatic concerns may represent emotional distress. Awareness of possible culture bound syndromes is essential along with idioms of distress. Inquiry about the experience of symptoms in relation to cultural group norms may help to explain the cause of the problem.

Preferences for and experiences with professional and "popular" or traditional providers should also be explored. It may be advantageous to involve racially/ethnically/culturally specific providers, when possible and appropriate, to assist in gathering and understanding data either directly or through consultation.

6. If formal assessment tools and forms are used, they must be normed and validated for the specific cultural group as well as be linguistically appropriate.

7. Providers should consider the individual's and family's preference for linkages with their identified racial, ethnic, or cultural community.

8. Evaluation of the psychosocial environment, the interaction and multiplicity of stressors, and availability of supports along with levels of functioning and disability is often revealing of important data.

9. Understanding the individual's and family's beliefs and practices with regards to mental health and substance abuse, including attitudes about stigma and shame, is essential. Also important is an appreciation of any gender bias in help-seeking behavior that may be culturally determined or influenced.

10. Consideration of the possible impacts of poverty, discrimination based upon race ethnicity and/or sexual orientation, and spirituality and religious affiliation should also be included as part of the assessment.

This set of information provides the database necessary to ensure that the overall planning process is culturally sensitive and informed, by supporting a DSM-IV-TR cultural formulation as part of the overall process of assessment.

TABLE 4.2   Cultural Competencies

Awareness *of* . . .	• their own culture and social status
	• power differentials in relationship
Knowledge *about* . . .	• how theory and practice are culturally embedded
	• history and manifestations of racism
	• sociopolitical influences on lives of persons served
	• culture specific diagnoses
	• differences in family structures and roles across cultures
Skills *to* . . .	• understand the person's conceptualization of their illness
	• self-assess their own cultural competence/bias
	• modify assessment techniques/tools so that they are culturally sensitive and appropriate
	• design and implement non-biased effective service plans

III. MAKING IT HAPPEN

Three specific techniques and tools are presented in the following pages of this chapter. They include **a**) understanding the individual's stage of change, **b**) using motivational interviewing, and **c**) some sample interview tools that can help draw out the individual's recovery goals and concerns. These represent but a few of the many strategies available to ensure a person-centered approach to assessment. Without a doubt there are others, but these three build on existing provider skills and can be easily mastered as possible ways to enhance skills and current practice. This section concludes with four examples of person-centered assessments.

Stages of Change

In an attempt to better understand the process of recovery, rehabilitation, and wellness, Prochaska, DiClemente, and Norcross[13] described four stages of change. Most if not all people pursuing recovery seem to move through these stages, but the process is not always linear or direct. These stages are not unlike those described earlier in *Creating the Solution*, but here the focus is largely on the issue of motivation for change.

Understanding the stage of motivation of an individual and family is not only a product of the assessment; it is important information that guides and structures the assessment and the entire planning and service process. The four stages are as follows:

- precontemplation
- contemplation
- preparation (determination)
- action and maintenance

This approach derives in large part from the experience and tradition of practice in the addictive disorders field but has much broader applicability in helping to support a person-centered approach. It provides insight into people's fears, anxieties, and ambivalence, as well as their drive for change. Identifying an individual's current stage and the provider's role in helping them, is empowering for everyone involved.

In the *precontemplation* stage, the individual has not yet considered the possibility of change and seldom presents voluntarily for treatment. In this circumstance, the provider's job is to increase the person's perception of risks and problems with his or her current behavior. In the *contemplation* stage, the individual is ambivalent, vacillating between motivations to change and justifications for not changing. At this stage, the provider should strengthen the person's ability to change his or her current behavior by heightening awareness of the risks of not changing. *Determination or preparation* occurs when the individual experiences the motivation to change and the provider helps the person determine the best course of action to pursue. The *action* stage is the point at which the individual seeks services and the provider helps the person take the necessary steps toward services. *Maintenance* is when the individual attempts to sustain the change and the provider helps to identify strategies to prevent relapse and promote ongoing recovery.

The stages-of-change framework also helps to explain the individual's or family's current view or outlook on their situation. The entire construct offers a positive perspective and allows for re-framing problems and circumstances in a way that leads to alliance, hope, and success. For example, instead of using language with a negative connotation, such as saying the person is "in denial," the provider can help the person to understand that they are in a precontemplation stage and are in the earliest phases of the change process. This also supports the idea of mapping out what lies ahead. This perspective brings up the question, what will it take for the individual to get to the next stage? The answer, once learned or discovered, can play an important role in shaping and directing the individual plan. Using the stages of change framework, along with motivational interviewing, embodies respect for the individual, a true person-centered approach to assessment, the development of a trusting and helping relationship, and a style of orientation that will hopefully produce better information and outcomes.

Motivational Interventions

A complement to this model is the practice of motivational interviewing largely developed and refined by Miller and others at the University of New Mexico.[14] This approach follows the stages-of-change model and is useful for improving efforts at person-centered assessment. In this approach, providers use their skills and understanding to encourage individuals to analyze their own behavior and derive their own conclusions. Responsibility for change remains with the individual, while the provider is nonjudgmental and does not assume the role of the "expert." The individual, with the provider directing the assessment interview, identifies any reasons to change and the goals of the treatment episode. Through a discussion about the findings of the assessment, the authors contend that this dialog helps the individual to explore his or her decisions and, therefore, the process of decision-making is the foundation for change. Assessment then is the understanding of the individual and the meeting of his or her needs as well as recognition of his or her strengths and abilities.

The acceptance and recognition of the value of motivational approaches has expanded and is continuing to grow beyond its popularity in the addictive disorders field because it offers an alternative to traditional techniques and is consistent with the values of a person-centered approach. This is particularly valuable in working with individuals who require services via the civil or criminal justice systems and are resistant or not ready to make life changes. However, even highly motivated individuals enter into mental health and addictive disorders service with some ambivalence and resistance to change.

Tools

There are other techniques that can be used to promote a person-centered assessment. Some providers and programs utilize self-report questionnaires that the individual and family complete independently in order to describe their needs, desires, preferences, and/goals. Others may use a worksheet that is completed in conjunction with a more traditional interview. A very simple approach to eliciting the individual's own sense of recovery is demonstrated in the following example. For some individuals, expressing these thoughts and feelings in writing provides another opportunity and alternative to verbal communication that allows them to feel more in control. These are a few semi-structured questions that can serve as their self-assessment of strengths and resources:

Recovery Planning Worksheet

- What are your greatest stressors?
- Are there any signs/triggers of wanting to use substances or feeling like you are not doing well?
- What has helped your recovery in the past?
- What are your goals for yourself?
- What can the staff do to help?
- What can you do to help?
- Who else can help?

A culturally competent assessment process[15] might include more open-ended questions as opposed to structured questions on the form, such as:

- How do you define your problem?
- Who is your family? Who do you trust?
- Have you ever been a member of a faith community?
- Are you now going or have you ever gone to an indigenous healer for help with your problem?
- With whom do you have intimate relations?
- How do you identify culturally/racially/ethnically?
- Have you ever experienced racism, police brutality, discrimination and/or oppression?
- What do you know about your culture?
- Has your family always lived in this area?
- What were the messages about your culture that you received while growing up?

These questions will often elicit a richer and more meaningful response then merely asking about the individual's "spirituality" or "sexual orientation" (oftentimes difficult topics for providers).

In the beginning of this chapter, it was suggested that a simple question such as "How can I be of help?" could provide a powerful alternative to the usual approach of "Tell me what's wrong." Process and approach in data gathering can make a big difference in assuring that assessment is person-centered. Below are nine suggested action steps and fresh approaches that providers can use to facilitate a person-centered assessment:

- *Ask* the person
  - what they are seeking
  - what services they want
  - what they hope to accomplish from this treatment episode/this particular service experience
  - what his/her hopes and dreams for the future are
  - if he/she has any preferences in receiving services or assistance
- *Listen* to the individual's concerns before interrupting with an opinion
- *Assist* the person to understand reasonable alternatives
- *Use* the assessment interview to begin to engage the person in services, even if they are a reluctant participant or coerced into treatment
- *Help* the person identify his/her strengths and resources

- *Include* the family member and other members of the person's support network in the interview process and elicit their feedback
- *Respect* the individual's preferences, needs, and values
- *Determine together* the individual's current stage of recovery
- *Share* the findings from the assessment with the individual

In implementing these steps, the provider can become an effective partner with the individual and family, use the assessment process as an opportunity to clarify the individual's expectations of the provider, and collaborate with their decisions and choices.

Examples

Ultimately, *Making It Happen* is about translating theory into practice. Examples are always useful for demonstrating the transition. In this chapter, and each to follow, concepts and principles will be translated into the practicalities of providing services.

Four examples of individuals and families with various needs and challenges have been collected from practice around the country, and the documentation for each is included in his or her respective appendix. A presentation and commentary on each, to highlight certain issues, begins in this chapter and follows throughout the book. These sample scenarios address a variety of settings, populations, diagnoses, lengths of stay, voluntary versus mandated services, and situations that require different goals, objectives, and interventions.

These examples are drawn from real people and circumstances, but each story may well include elements from several different instances and individuals. These examples are by no means all encompassing. However, they will hopefully serve to illustrate the principles presented in the chapters about data gathering, formulation, and planning services. They are not intended to be clinically correct; the examples do not reflect the one and only diagnosis, proper mental status exams, perfect conclusions via the narrative summary, or the only way to "fill in the blanks." This book was never designed to be a "how to" on providing treatment or matching diagnosis to treatment interventions. Rather, the intent is to use real-life stories to illustrate how to develop a person-centered individual plan.

The scenarios presented are those of the following four people:

1. Aaron, a child in foster care who has mental health needs
2. Sally, an adult who is court-referred for addiction services
3. Sam, an adult with mental health and addiction challenges
4. Carmen, an adolescent struggling with suicidal thoughts

The presentation of these examples is not intended to suggest the perfect or ideal comprehensive biopsychosocial assessment document. A variety of forms are included as examples of the work of some leading providers, including forms based on the Ohio public sector model and Genesee County Community Mental Health in Flint, Michigan. These two in particular are built on a sincere commitment to the principles of recovery, resilience, and person-centered care. However, they have been modified by the authors to reflect language and principles consistent with this text.

The inclusion of these examples is not intended as an endorsement of either form or approach. There are many styles and formats of forms that document a comprehensive assessment and are suitable for particular settings or programs and are responsive to local regulatory, accreditation, reimbursement, or policy requirements. Signature pages or additional items that provider organizations may wish to have on assessment and plan documents are not included. Instead, the focus is on presenting a person-centered approach independent of format and setting that can easily be inserted into existing documentation systems and standards and adapted to meet local needs and requirements.

Aaron

Each scenario presented tries to demonstrate not only different histories and conclusions, but also different approaches to conducting an assessment. For instance, the comprehensiveness of the assessment information of Aaron Howard may not be suitable for all treatment settings. On the other hand, children currently in programs across the U.S., particularly in community mental health centers and child guidance clinics, are often challenged by complex needs, family concerns, and involvement in multiple systems and agencies in the community, making a highly comprehensive and integrated assessment essential. The data addressed includes barriers to achieving goals, developmental issues, an in-depth description of the family environment, family relationships and custody issues, and school functioning—all of the information that is needed for assessing a child. In addition, the assessment is organized around an inventory of strengths and needs with pre-identified domains. This assessment also demonstrates how a cultural formulation can be included, how a narrative summary can be structured using the "Six P's" referenced earlier, and how the CALOCUS worksheet is completed and utilized.

With Aaron, there are many issues that arise; they may or may not be ultimately addressed in the individual plan. For example, the diagnosis will need to be finalized at some point. The challenge for the provider will be to synthesize the information in the narrative summary and clearly identify priorities.

Sally

In the example of Sally Hamilton, there is less detail in the data since she enters services with some reticence; she is in the pre-contemplation stage of change (as assessed by the provider). Her initial assessment may be enriched with more information as she progresses through stages of change and more is revealed. This example demonstrates how the ASAM PPC-2R criteria can be embedded in and used in an assessment form. An alcohol and drug treatment history is also included in the assessment. Sally's diagnosis is not complete since there is an acknowledgment that she clearly has patterns of abuse, but it is not clear if she is alcohol-dependent. She enters treatment reluctantly (under court order), and with little motivation other than to resolve her legal difficulties. The challenge for the provider in this assessment is to make the plan truly person-centered even when there is lack of motivation for services and a defined curriculum or program to adhere to.

Sam

The assessment of Sam Hewlett provides an example of a more narrative style and approach to both conducting and recording the assessment. The focus is not as much on completing specific data fields as on assuring that a comprehensive overview of the important facets of Sam's life and history are well considered in creating the clinical database to support the remainder of the planning process. This approach has an implicitly warm and friendly tone that many providers will find comfortable and individuals will find comforting. This is intended as an example of how the information-gathering process can be used to build a collaborative relationship between the individual, family, and provider.

Prominent in the assessment is a description of Sam, his current circumstances, and his stated needs. In terms of format, this is consistent with a person-centered approach in that it avoids the traditional language of "chief complaint" and "presenting problem." Even the identifying information moves quickly beyond the more descriptive facts of Sam's life and helps to understand him in the context of his request for help. It is important that his stated goals and intentions are included early on—this suggests that the focus of the process was on this level of understanding and engagement and this data should precede an exploration of all the explanatory and complicating details. It is the essence of a strengths-based approach.

The narrative structure and format give the provider significant latitude in collecting and organizing the assessment data. For less experienced providers, this may be difficult and they may find that it is easy to get lost in the process. But for those providers who can "go with the flow," this approach helps to provide a rich and contextual assessment that can readily be tailored to the unique needs of each individual and family.

It is also important to note that this is a form of re-assessment; Sam has a long history of seeking services and much of his life history and past efforts are well documented in the records. The flexibility of this approach allows the provider to focus on and bring forward that information which is most immediately relevant to the individual's circumstance and current needs while at the same time recognizing that there is a long and elaborate history of past success and failures. The challenge in such an assessment is to sift through very lengthy documents and records in order to extract the information and history that is meaningful and relevant to Sam's immediate needs and goals.

The sample assessment is fairly comprehensive and reasonably detailed—without question, one could do more. This could be considered an example of a "good enough" assessment and not intended to be the very best. At the same time, if such assessments were the standard of practice in the field today, the challenge of creating individual person-centered care plans would be much advanced. The ultimate test of an assessment is how well it prepares and supports the subsequent steps of creating a plan.

Carmen

The assessment of Carmen Suarez at the Pine Grove Mental Health Center is an example of yet another approach that could be considered a semi-structured format in comparison to the other samples. There is a reasonable balance between a focus on data fields and a more narrative approach. This example was adapted from the forms and format used at Genesee County Community Mental Health of Flint, Michigan.

The use of the parent/child questionnaire is noteworthy. This provides the family and individual an opportunity to present their concerns and needs in their own hand and word. This is usually completed prior to an interview and helps to give the provider(s) important background information before proceeding with the remainder of the assessment.

As with the assessment for Aaron, this evaluation of an adolescent places an emphasis on developmental history, both prenatal and perinatal, as well as during early childhood. In some respects the psychosocial history may not be as complete in this assessment as that seen in others—but it is reasonably adapted and targeted to issues especially germane to understanding the needs of children and adolescents.

This tool also includes a checklist approach to recording the mental status exam—this too has its advantages and disadvantages. It helps to assure that a standard and comprehensive mental status exam is completed, but it potentially lacks for more subtle descriptive elements. The narrative portion that follows helps to make sure that all of the important components of the exam are recorded.

The other important element of this assessment is the inclusion of a cultural formulation closely likened to the diagnostic conclusions. For Carmen and her family, issues of ethnicity and culture factor prominently into understanding her needs as well as organizing a response. The proper cultural formulation, following the outline included in Appendix I of the DSM-IV-TR, helps to highlight and give meaning and relevance to these issues. The assessment of this individual and family would be sorely inadequate and lacking without this essential component. Issues of culture and identity and their importance are not unique or limited to ethnic minorities and persons of color; they should be a component of every assessment.

The question remains: How do these forms shape provider behavior and interaction with the individual and family seeking services? There is always room for improvement, and the future will bring new challenges and opportunities. With the increasing use of electronic record systems, it becomes important to assure that form follows function; information systems should not dictate provider behavior. The examples provided here are only sample written products of the information-gathering process. Recording that information in a usable format is certainly important, but a focus on documentation should not distract from the primary aim—a person-centered approach to assessment and planning.

REFERENCES

1. Wagner, R., Clark, H.B. *Strength Discovery Assessment Process for Transition Aged Youths and Young Adults*. University of South Florida. http://tip.fmhi.usf.edu/files/StrengthDiscoverModule.pdf.
2. www.jcaho.org.
3. *The Annals of Internal Medicine*. www.annals.org.
4. Regier, D.A., Farmer, M.E., et al. Comorbidity of Mental Disorders With Alcohol and Other Drug Abuse. *JAMA* 1990;264:2511–2518.
5. Minkoff, K. *State of Arizona Service Planning Guidelines: Co-occurring Psychiatric and Substance Disorders*. 2000. Draft.
6. Patterson, C.H., Watkins, C.E. Some essentials of a client centered approach to assessment. *Measurement and Evaluation in Guidance* 1982;15:103–106.
7. Maruish, M.E. *Essentials of Treatment Planning*. New York: John Wiley and Sons, 2002.
8. Hodge, M.S., et al. *Practical Application of Recovery Principles in Clinical Practice—The Ohio Experience*. Unpublished manuscript, 2003.
9. Townsend, et al. *Emerging Best Practices in Recovery*. 2003.
10. Addiction Exchange, Vol. 3, No. 15: *Substance Abuse Disorders and Serious Mental Illness*, September 17, 2001, http://wwww.mid-attc.org.
11. http://www.comm.psych.pitt.edu/finds/locus.html and http://www.comm.psych.pitt.edu/finds/calocus.html.
12. www.asam.org.
13. Prochaska, J.O., DiClemente, C.C., Norcross, J.C. In search of how people change: applications to addictive behaviors. *Am Psychol* 1992;47:1102-1114.
14. Miller, W., et al. *Motivational Interviewing, Second Edition: Preparing People for Change*. 2nd edition. New York: Guilford Press; New York, 2002.
15. Ali, O.S. ATTC-NE Course. *Developing Culturally Competent Recovery Plans—Person-centered Planning Within Recovery Oriented Systems of Care*. 2004.

## CHAPTER 5

Understanding Needs: The Narrative Summary

We all face problems and challenges; the way we frame them is the first clue to our ability to deal with them.

C. Tollett

I. STATING THE CASE

The gathering of information in the assessment is only the beginning. Integration and summary of data and clinical formulation are essential but often-overlooked steps in the process of developing an individual plan. The assessment data is about *what*, and the narrative summary and formulation is about *how* and *why*. Understanding the problem from the perspective of the individual and family, as well as understanding their needs, strengths and resources, is the foundation for identifying barriers and developing personal goals.

Following the data-collection efforts of the assessment, preparing a narrative summary is the next step in moving towards creating an individual plan. The narrative summary, alternatively referred to as the formulation, interpretive summary, diagnostic summary, clinical impression, and so on, is more than a mere compilation and re-telling of the assessment data. Rather, it involves integration of the data and it draws upon the provider's insights and interpretation. It is similar to weaving a whole cloth from a collection of threads; out of the bits and pieces of the assessment data, we can create an understanding of the individual and family that extends beyond the mere facts.

Provider Role

Creating a narrative summary draws upon the skill, intellect, training, experience, intuition, and creativity of the provider. This step in the overall planning process is where the provider has a unique if not essential contribution to make. If the individual and family understood their problems and needs, then they might not require assistance to address them. It is often because they do not understand the issues or cannot envision a solution that they seek help. The value of the provider's contribution is very apparent.

The ability of the provider to integrate data into understanding, and the sharing of this insight and perspective with the individual and family, is often in and of itself a powerful intervention. It is the essence of empathy, a key ingredient of successful helping relationships. The provider is not merely a sponge absorbing facts and detail but rather a skilled partner working in collaboration with the individual and family. Sharing the understanding and formulation that emerges provides an opportunity to further that alliance. How is their request for assistance understood? What does all of the information gathered mean for this individual and family? What has been learned about them to help prepare an effective response? In a person-centered approach, this understanding brings forward the unique abilities, talents, skills, and strengths that serve as the cornerstone in development and implementation of the plan.

The written narrative summary documents the rationalization and justification for the provider's recommendations and suggestions. It creates the platform from which the individual and the team launch into creating the individual plan and charting the course for recovery and resilience. The summary explains the goals, identifies the barriers, orders the priority of tasks and objectives, substantiates the level of care, clarifies the diagnosis, explains the role of culture, and ultimately justifies the interventions or services provided for each individual and family.

The special contribution of the skilled and seasoned provider is their capacity to interpret the data. While other less-trained and less-experienced members of the staff might be able to help collect the data, it is the experienced provider's clinical leadership that vests them with the ability and responsibility to develop formulations. At the same time, that responsibility is not solely theirs—the person-centered collaboration with the individual and family is only truly realized when the summary is shared. In this way, the individual and family are fully informed partners and are given an opportunity to contribute their own perspectives, to add to the provider's understanding, and to make sure that their personal vision of recovery and resiliency is truly understood and appreciated. Sharing the narrative summary with the individual and family may also be a way of engaging and motivating them. This creates yet another opportunity for dialog and discussion about their goals, hopes, and dreams.

Returning to the journey metaphor, we are reminded of the famous question posed to mountain climbers about why they pursue their passion and seek ever-greater challenges. The classic reply is: because it is there. The journey of individual planning is perhaps less philosophical and more practical. We need a reason, an explanation, and a justification for this trip. We need clarification about not only where we are going, but also why we are going there and what we hope to find. This informs many subsequent decisions about what to take, how to choose the route, the modes of travel, and how to structure the trip. Not unlike mountain climbing, this must be done as a team, with all members working towards the same destination. It would not work if one climber on the team took on Everest while the others pursued K-2. In the recovery journey, the provider cannot be working towards one set of goals based upon an understanding that is not shared by the individual, the family, and any other members of the team. The narrative summary helps to assure that common understanding and purpose.

Requirements and Standards

For many years, CARF... The Rehabilitation Accreditation Commission's standards for behavioral health have emphasized the importance of the narrative summary. The standards state that the summary should "integrate and interpret all history and assessment information collected."[1] The CARF guidelines for conformance to standards further detail how the intent of the standards can be met and identify some key components or elements. The guidelines suggest that the summary should include:

- a central theme about the individual
- the findings from history and any assessments conducted, including medical, psychological, vocational, and so on
- the perception of the individual of his or her needs, strengths, and abilities
- the provider's perspective about what might affect the course of treatment

- recommended treatments and the level of care
- anticipated duration of services
- goals of the treatment encounter

Other elements to add might include the following:

- the provider's insights into the underpinnings of the problem in terms of psychodynamics, family systems, cognitive behavioral styles, personality traits, or any other relevant perspective/framework
- a hypothesis for an effective response plan
- speculation or understanding about the success and failure of past treatment efforts
- identification of barriers to the individual's goals
- anticipated outcomes and transition or discharge options

This summary is derived from all of the data gathered about the individual and family, not just the results of the face-to-face interview and the completion of a bio-psychosocial assessment instrument. If the individual has had any standardized testing, or there is medical information, discharge summaries from previous treatment experiences, referral source information, and so on, these documents should be reviewed in order to gain a broader perspective to help in the interpretation of the data. The narrative summary also provides an opportunity to integrate the data from several components of a multidisciplinary assessment source into a coherent and comprehensive assessment.

Current Practice

Despite the importance and value of the narrative summary in individual planning, experience demonstrates that it is the most often overlooked or neglected part of the process. Some examples of the problems encountered in completion of this important step include:

1. The narrative summary is only written from the perspective of the provider who actually conducts the psychosocial assessment or intake interview. Other data that is rich in information and meaning is ignored simply because that particular provider has not personally collected the additional information, such as the medical history and physical, psychological testing, or vocational evaluation. If the provider does not utilize all of the information available, it is not possible to formulate conclusions and write a complete narrative summary.

2. The provider lacks the skill and sophistication necessary to prepare a narrative summary. In some settings, particularly community-based multi-program organizations, the narrative summary is one more form that is left to the case manager or intake worker to complete. Yet these are often entry-level positions and this person may have limited education, training, or experience, or/and lack the skills to create a meaningful summary. The question of who is actually able to interpret all the data raises an important issue of competency.

3. Sufficient time and resources are not provided to prepare a proper narrative summary. A specific team meeting in which all of the data and information resources are brought together and a shared hypothesis is generated is a particularly effective way of benefiting from the rich talent and perspectives of a multidisciplinary team. This requires a commitment to the value of formulation and the expectation that it is part of the planning process.

In one way or another, all of these examples involve the issue of time and human resources necessary to complete a narrative summary. There is no question that this task requires an effort and investment of resources in systems that often seem to be already limited and stretched. However, the alternative is really unacceptable. To proceed without understanding carries the risk of doing the right things for the wrong reasons or vice versa. That is a waste of resources that no one can afford.

It is not uncommon to hear providers express discomfort in making an interpretation of the data. They question their qualifications, fear drawing the wrong conclusions based on limited assessment data, and worry about the impact of incorrect interpretations. Providers are often concerned that they might be held liable in some way for the impact of their determinations, and at the same time report that they are uncomfortable sharing their findings with the individual and family. Providers need to be reminded that assessment and formulation are not one-time events, but rather part of an ongoing process of successive approximations and refinements leading to goal attainment. In the process of helping the individual and family, there should be ample opportunities to clarify information and make corrections if necessary. The emphasis should be on involvement, exchange, and empowerment, not on precision.

At times it seems that formulation and preparation of a narrative summary has become a lost clinical art. Historically, the critical thinking involved in formulation has been at the heart of clinical training. Regardless of the theoretical framework, providers were taught analytic skills and trained to look beyond the mere facts for understanding to shape their helping responses. Perhaps it is the pressure on time and resources over the past 10 to 20 years, or an unbalanced emphasis on behavior and outcomes that have seemingly relegated this kind of understanding to history. It is time to revive and renew the practice and once again make formulation a central part of what providers do in response to a request for help. This can be revitalized with a person-centered approach and the involvement of the individual and family in refining the formulation.

Prioritization

The narrative summary also supports the important early task of prioritization. Even the best at multi-tasking can only manage so much at one time, and deciding what comes first is often a challenge. This is true for both the provider as well the individual and family. Ordering and organizing the problem-solving skill inherent in the individual plan is a valuable contribution that helps promote success. Maslow's[2] hierarchy of needs is a useful schema for helping to establish priorities. For example, Maslow pointed out the primacy of health and safety concerns. There should be little argument that if an individual is homeless, ill, unemployed, and lacking money, the immediate objective, even if the individual is currently abusing alcohol and other drugs, is probably not lifelong recovery and abstinence from drugs. The first priority for the individual is probably to obtain shelter and medical care. All too often, however, the goal on that individual's plan is merely abstinence, usually because it is a program requirement.

As previously noted, there are times when agreement on priorities is not as obvious or easy. A provider may have an understanding of the goals based on professional experiences and perspectives only to find that the individual or family may have other self-identified priorities and needs. Sometimes people simply feel unprepared or reluctant to address particular problem areas. This often occurs when drug and/or alcohol use is a part of the individual's and family's problems, but for a variety of reasons they are not yet able or willing to acknowledge the impact of their drug use. Our efforts at formulation should help us to understand and continue to work with the individual and family. Instead, providers often experience these differences as a virtual roadblock to further progress and a crisis in the treatment process that precludes development of an individual plan.

A recovery-oriented person-centered approach offers an alternative. Building on the philosophy and skills of motivational enhancement therapy, as well as the work of Patricia Deegan, PhD, in her Intentional Care[3] framework for promoting recovery and resilience, the provider can find a ready solution: recognition that decisions ultimately lie with the individual and family. This is not to suggest that such differences should lead the provider to abandon the individual and family to "the natural consequences of their choices." Nor does it suggest that the provider violate their own sense of professional duties, ethics, or, in some circumstances, legal obligations. Utilizing motivational interviewing, providers can encourage individuals to analyze their own behavior and derive their own conclusions. Providers remain non-judgmental, while supplying a combination of information and encouragement intended to help the person move to the next stage of recovery. These techniques are particularly effective during the early, trust-building phases of treatment.

If there is not mutual understanding of the needs and problems or the priorities and goals to address them, how can an effective and meaningful plan be developed? Recognition of those differences and negotiation between the provider and the individual, and sometimes the family, can play an important role in clarifying the goals and priorities. Disagreements between the provider and the individual can be viewed as just another issue to discuss, a means to enhance understanding and opportunity to build a collaborative alliance based upon mutual respect. All too often providers shy away from this type of engagement and in a variety of ways reject the individual and family seeking help. There are times when the effort to create a narrative summary and achieve a shared understanding with the individual and family results in a mutual decision not to proceed further. Instead, hopefully, differences can lead to understandings which reflect an appropriate balance between the concerns of the individual, family, and provider.

If there is not a mutual understanding of the needs and problems or the priorities and goals to address them, how can an effective and meaningful plan be developed? Yet the need for a plan and the pressure to move on can result in a provider creating a plan that is not meaningful or relevant for the individual and family. Sadly, there are many times when services are provided on this basis with everyone simply going through the motions. It is no wonder there are high levels of frustration, dissatisfaction, and disappointment with outcomes. If the provider or service organization has admission criteria that the individual does not meet, if a provider does not have expertise in the identified areas of need, or if the program has treatment expectations that are not individualized to the person, then a referral to another program or provider may be necessary.

Barriers

The narrative summary also helps to identify the barriers that the individual and family may face in achieving their goals. Barriers may exist in many different forms and include personal needs, family issues, resource needs and other challenges. The identified barriers, whether a need for skills and supports, the resolution of interpersonal conflict, or the lack of access to transportation, should be articulated in the narrative summary. This is an essential step towards developing a responsive plan with appropriate goals and objectives. The impact of barriers on shaping the individual plan is so great that it warrants its own more detailed exploration and discussion. The issue of barriers is discussed in greater depth in Chapter 6.

Diagnosis

The assessment and formulation process should provide the clinician with the information necessary to determine and support at least a provisional working diagnosis. Much of this information is derived from the mental status exam and its inherent focus on symptoms but should also include other relevant data. The narrative summary offers an opportunity to integrate the report and observations of symptoms and behaviors with everything else that is known about the individual and family and their needs.

An emphasis on diagnosis may seem contrary to the principles of person-centered recovery—it evokes images of a person being "pigeon-holed" and classified rather than understood as a unique individual with strengths and resources in the context of his or her culture and community. However, the reality is that diagnosis is so ingrained in existing clinical practice, as well as systems of payment and accountability in both public and private care settings, that it is unavoidable. Although a person- and family-centered approach to the development of the plan is not necessarily driven by diagnosis, it is often necessary to establish a diagnosis for purposes of reimbursement, prescribing medication, and utilization management.

Current Diagnostic and Statistical Manual of Mental Disorders-Fourth Edition-Text Revision (DSM-IV-TR) and International Classification of Diseases (ICD)-9/10 diagnostic systems have their strengths and utility as well as their limitations. All too often a diagnosis is reached or recorded without much insight into the clinical thinking and reasoning to support that decision. The narrative summary provides an opportunity for the provider to record the rationale for a diagnosis. In sharing the summary with the individual and family, diagnosis can be a tool to help them to better understand the nature of their needs and challenges. This can often help build support for decisions about priorities, goals, objectives, and interventions. Historically there has been provider reluctance about sharing the diagnosis with individuals and families. Withholding such information, however, would be contrary to the principles of a person-centered approach in which information is transparent and readily accessible to the individual seeking services. As stated earlier, this sharing of understanding tends to build and strengthen the collaborative partnership with the individual, family, and provider. At the same time, it should be evident that an individual's preference not to receive such information should always be respected.

Diagnosis should inform but not drive the development of the individual plan. There is substantial literature on treatment planning[4] that proceeds from the notion that a somewhat standardized plan with prescribed goals, objectives, and interventions can be generated primarily from the diagnosis or type of service. Many treatment planning models in electronic clinical record systems are based on the same approach and philosophy with a menu of selected goals and objectives for each diagnosis. While there may be some utility and efficiency in such an approach, it does not embody the spirit of person- and family-centered planning and is generally not helpful in creating the plan.

Ashra Misha, MD, a psychiatrist and associate professor at Virginia Commonwealth University, emphasizes the importance of a "person-first" style. The person is not the illness; rather, "the illness is a part, but not the whole part, of the person." Regarding diagnosis, she says, "the burden should be on the professional . . . not to go in with preconceived notions about a diagnosis. Labels stick . . . I stay away from labels in general."[5] Therefore, a diagnosis may be needed to meet administrative and regulatory requirements, but the narrative summary should truly reflect the provider's thoughtful understanding of the individual and family as a step towards creation of the plan.

Co-Occurring Mental Health and Addictive Diagnosis

It has been said by Cline and others that the co-occurrence of mental health and addictive disorders problems should be the expectation, not the exception.[6] It seems to matter little whether individuals and families identify their needs in one area or another—assessment frequently reveals that issues and needs exist in both. There is strong epidemiological evidence from recent studies and surveys to substantiate this claim.[7] The problem is not necessarily limited to immediate circumstances. Given the cross-over between the two, the individual with current addictive disorders needs is significantly at risk of future mental health problems and vice versa. A "no wrong door" approach has been advocated at a systems level with a focus on organizing funding and services to better integrate services. Regardless of larger systems issues, it is important that both areas be addressed in a narrative summary to include consideration of not only past and present needs but also potential future concerns and risks.

Experts in the field[8] have proposed a two-by-two matrix for considering the co-occurrence of mental health and addictive disorders needs in a dynamic model (Figure 5.1). This diagram illustrates how co-occurring mental health needs (MH in the figure) and addictive disorders needs (SA in the figure) can be sorted into four categories based on the severity of each of the disorders. This matrix and its interpretation in the narrative summary can be used as a guide for service planning. This helps to inform decisions about the location as well as the intensity of services.

Service needs can be divided and recognized as ranging from low to high severity for each disorder. Individuals with high mental health needs usually have severe and disabling mental disorders and require continuing integrated care in a multidisciplinary mental health treatment setting. It is appropriate to treat individuals with high addictive disorders service needs with episodes of addiction therapy in an addictive disorders specialty services setting with varying degrees of integration of mental health capability. The greatest challenge is often in responding to the needs of those individuals in quadrant IV who have high needs in both areas and require services with a high level of integration and coordination.

The integrated summary should consider the possibility of co-occurring disorders and evaluate the interrelationship between the two. Assignment to a quadrant on the matrix can help inform the level of care as well as establish service priorities.

Cultural Formulation

Although the DSM-IV includes specific recommendations for the inclusion of a cultural formulation as part of diagnosis, they are buried in the appendices of the manual and many providers are not even aware of their presence. If the narrative summary is about assuring that we understand the individual, then accounting for the role of culture and ethnicity is critical to a true appreciation of the individual. If the outline for a DSM cultural formulation were actually included in the narrative summary and consideration of diagnosis, the commitment to being person-centered would be in many respects honored and fulfilled. Given the emphasis on sharing the narrative summary with the individual and family, the inclusion of cultural factors in the diagnosis and formulation opens additional opportunities for dialog, understanding, and partnership. Cultural sensitivity is a key component of cultural competence.

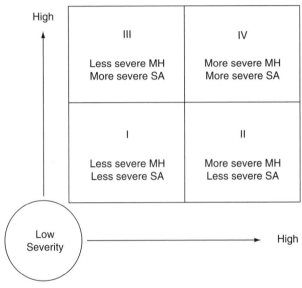

FIGURE 5.1

Transition and Discharge Planning

Last, but not least, the narrative summary should also include consideration of the level of care, the anticipated length and intensity of services, and ideally some notion of when the individual may be able to transition to another level of care or be discharged. Accrediting and other standard setting organizations commonly call for early transition/discharge planning. Preparation of the narrative summary creates an opportunity for providers to identify the criteria for transition/discharge, even if the individual is likely to require long-term services. Understanding the individual's needs determines the anticipated length of stay. Instead of expecting everyone to "complete the program"—the antithesis of individualized services—the type and duration of services must be organized and tailored to meet the unique needs of each individual.

In practice, the anticipated discharge or transition shapes the individual plan's objectives and helps to identify the barriers. Specifying the criteria for discharge or transition is crucial. In doing so, the idea of a journey becomes more than a metaphor. By integrating all of the information gathered and creating a narrative understanding, the trip is launched and the resources are set in motion. The individual plan becomes the map and the narrative summary becomes the tour book.

II. CREATING THE SOLUTION

If many providers are uncomfortable with formulation, and the creation of a narrative summary has become a lost art, it is reasonable to ask: What knowledge, skills, abilities, and competencies do person-centered, recovery-oriented providers need to develop a formulation? Below are several suggestions for provider activities and competencies that can help support a person-centered approach to assessment, formulation, and the documentation of a narrative summary. They include the ability to:

- be empathic and non-judgmental in reviewing assessment data, and developing summaries with an inclusive approach that promotes an open and frank dialogue about the conclusions
- work collaboratively with the individual and family to create and sustain a helping partnership and not assume an all-knowing, authoritarian role implying that "I'm the expert and I'm going to tell you what you need to do"
- use respectful person-first language that avoids the use of jargon or labels; examples of person-first language include speaking of a "person with a diagnosis of bipolar disorder," not "a bipolar," or someone with a "history of depression," not "suffering from depression"
- engage the individual and family through motivational interviewing
- encourage the individual to determine who is present during the assessment and planning meetings and take into consideration information and perspectives from all of the participants
- be culturally competent and sensitive to the influence of cultural factors in understanding the needs of individuals and families

- implement a team approach that includes the individual, family members, and providers in reaching agreement about a formulation
- actively support the individual's and family's choices even with the realization that some choices will likely be unattainable
- seek feedback on his or her performance through focus groups and surveys completed by individuals receiving services
- participate in regular peer/supervisory review of the records to: 1) receive feedback about the narrative summary, and 2) evaluate whether goals established on the plan are in reasonable alignment with the conclusions of the narrative summary

A narrative summary that appropriately describes the individual's and family's needs, strengths, abilities, and challenges helps to prepare an individual plan that is relevant and helpful in achieving their desired outcomes. The outcomes that are identified in the plan—self-management, improved quality of life, symptom reduction, overall recovery goals, meaningful activity/work, and so on—comprise what is in essence a treatment contract between the individual and the provider. These outcomes are impossible to accurately identify if the understanding of the individual, reflected in the narrative summary, does not occur. The competencies previously described include important skills for the provider's success.

Coordinating the Team

How is a narrative summary actually created? What is the analytic process? How is the data integrated? How does the team collaborate? Below are three models or approaches to creating a narrative summary. Each of these models gives the provider prompts and helps structure the task. Not every item is appropriate in all cases, and each area of response may be only a few sentences, but length and verbosity are not what is important. Rather, it is all in the interpretation of the data! These models need not be rigidly applied; embedded within each approach are tools that can be mixed and matched to help providers improve their skills in formulation and preparing narrative summaries.

Regardless of the model, thinking about how to actually coordinate and integrate the multiple inputs from the perspectives of the various members of a team is time well spent. For the team that is simply a dyad of provider and individual, this is a relatively easy task, but it does require the commitment of time by the provider, individual, or family to develop and review.

However, for a six- or eight-member multidisciplinary team, finding the time, integrating and coordinating the various assessments, and developing a consensus process can be a real challenge. One approach is as follows:

- Each provider conducts a discipline-specific assessment, prepares summary conclusions and forwards a copy of the assessment to the team leader prior to the team meeting
- The team leader integrates the assessment data from each of the disciplines and prepares a draft narrative summary including a proposed formulation
- At the team meeting, each team member presents a brief (2- to 3-minute) summary of their key assessment findings
- The team leader presents the draft narrative and formulation for consideration and discussion by the team and helps the team to reach consensus on a final summary and formulation
- The team leader or another team member shares the summary and formulation and key findings with the individual and family as part of the individual planning process

Clearly this workflow will not apply or be useful in every setting. It is, however, an example of the kind of organization, task assignment, and coordination that can help to make creating a narrative summary a manageable, meaningful, and relevant task.

Model I: The Six Ps

This approach identifies six components to consider and include in creating a narrative summary. Conveniently, each focus begins with the letter "P." In each category there are a number of factors to bear in mind. However, the suggestions below are by no means intended to be exhaustive. The list includes consideration of the following items:

Pertinent History
Some of the details included in this section may include age, marital status, children, educational history, work history, cultural affiliation, languages spoken, history and duration of mental illness, first hospitalization, number of hospitalizations, reasons for hospitalizations, longest hospitalization, medication history, therapy history, suicide, violence, arrests, addictive disorders, and so on.

Presenting Symptoms
A succinct description of major or significant symptoms that help to support the diagnosis and may explain in part why the individual and

family are seeking help at this time. This may include the experience of hallucinations, delusions, depression, anxiety, trauma, personality disorders, and/or other behaviors, and should include information about the onset, duration, and course of these symptoms.

Precipitating Factors

This helps to answer the important question, why now, and typically includes consideration of psychosocial life events and stressors, e.g., losses (death of a loved one, job, home, pet, and so on), poverty, immigration, trauma, and lack of support from family or significant others, community, and friends. Possibly relevant biological concerns such as substance use, medical conditions or physical trauma, non-compliance with medication, and so on, should also be included. The list is only suggestive and by no means complete.

Predisposing Factors

Biological factors predisposing an individual to challenges and the need for assistance might include genetics (i.e., family history), medical needs (trauma, seizures, general health conditions), alcoholism and other addictive disorders, and medications along with other medical concerns. Psychosocial factors could include early family dynamics, abandonment, loss, neglect, abuse, traumatic experiences, and exposure to violence.

Perpetuating Factors

A number of issues play a role in perpetuating an individual's or family's needs. This might include the nature of mental illness or addictive disorders problem, a persistent medical problem, a history of not following through with medications, difficulty with engaging in psychosocial treatment and services, a lack of outside support or poor support structure, or the lack of a relapse prevention plan, as well as many other factors.

Previous Treatment and Response

This section should include a description of what services and interventions the individual has previously received, their effectiveness, and any problems associated with the services. This may include consideration of acceptability, preference, tolerance, culture, risk and benefit or outcome.

This organization of the assessment data helps set the stage for completing the formulation. The *Six P's* is a useful framework to help bring forward the most relevant and compelling information collected and supports the process of understanding. These six factors and the specific details in each should be the basis upon which the formulation is built.

This approach anticipates the phrase: "And in conclusion . . ." which should then lead to some interpretation or finding of significance and meaning embedded within the facts. For example, if perpetuating factors seem to be the most compelling part of the individual's story, then the circumstances that sustain the individual's needs or challenges should inevitably become a focus of the individual plan. On the other hand, recognition that the individual's needs are situational will direct the focus and the plan to the precipitating factors. Often an understanding of the impact and benefit from previous treatment and services is essential. Knowing what has or has not worked in the past can inform current plans. There is no need to recreate the process, nor is there in general any justification for repeating things that have not worked in the past. This does not mean to imply that only one factor must be the identified focus—several may inform our understanding and plan development. The ability to extract that kind of knowledge from the assessment is the real value of the narrative summary.

Model II: Narrative Outline

In this approach, the narrative summary is a less structured document that integrates all of the assessment data and abstracts several appropriate, dominant, and explanatory central themes. It should also begin to suggest strategies for response and issues to consider in the creation of a plan. Typically, the narrative begins with a brief description of the individual or family and typically includes consideration of:

- the reason(s) the individual and family is seeking services
- the individual's and family's acceptance or understanding of the problems/needs
- strategies for relapse prevention
- the individual's apparent strengths as well as challenges and limitations
- potential barriers to community inclusion/integration
- successful attainment of goals and movement toward recovery
- complicating co-occurring conditions/disorders including substance use and serious medical conditions
- the choice of goals
- the balance between appropriate risks and choice

This model is an outline with prompts for including and considering several important topics. Although organized somewhat differently, it is not entirely unlike the Six P's and leads to a similar outcome. Perhaps the first item is the most significant: the reason for seeking services. The word *reason* could simply imply the individual's and family's accurate explanation of their needs. However, there are times when it is important to go beyond the individual's description and develop a deeper explanation of how the problems came to be and why the individual and family need help in addressing them. This is the essence of understanding and the platform from which to build an effective plan.

Model III: Eclectic

This approach is called eclectic because it builds from and includes the successful experience of a number of different providers and settings. It is a blending of several approaches that is a complement to the models previously described. In this approach the narrative summary should include the following steps:

1. A summary of the individual's mental health needs and substance use problems, along with a clear statement of their goals (with appropriate consideration of other life concerns and issues) using the full scope of assessment data.

2. An evaluation of the stage of recovery based upon a summary of the individual's and family's perception of their behavioral health needs, including consideration of other life problems as well as a description of motivation and commitment to resolve these problems.

3. An explanation of the source of the problem or needs and an understanding or hypothesis about the barriers that prevent the individual and family from attaining their goal(s).

4. A summary of both the positive and negative factors likely to affect the course of treatment and outcomes after discharge that includes but is not limited to consideration of identified strengths, assets and abilities, skills and supports needed, previous successes, relapse issues, and cultural factors.

5. A realistic description of mental health and addictive disorders service goals that will be the focus of the individual plan including anticipated transition or discharge criteria and needs, the type and range of services (or level of care) required, and the estimated length or intensity of services.

6. Identification of additional services and/or referrals that the individual and family will likely need to improve their quality of life, promote community inclusion, and facilitate recovery.

In this approach, perhaps item 3, the explanation of the source of the problems, is the most important.

Removing Barriers

If we reconsider the schematic in Figure 5.2, identifying the barriers at points B, C, and D that keep the individual from moving from A to E informs and structures the successful individual plan and is an important part of the narrative summary. Developing a plan and specifying objectives relies heavily on understanding the factors that cause and perpetuate a particular need. A narrative summary and formulation should provide the insight and understanding required to create a map like this simple but effective diagram.

A novel alternative approach to reaching this kind of understanding is to borrow from the problem-solving techniques of quality improvement and the use of a tool alternately referred to as an Ishikawa diagram, cause-and-effect diagram, fishbone diagram, or root cause analysis. Figure 5.3 provides an example of such a diagram.

The basic concept in the diagram is that the goal or need is entered on the left side of the diagram at the end of the main "bone." The factors leading to the need and the barriers to its resolution are then drawn as bones off of the main backbone. Brainstorming among members of the team, including the individual and the family, can help to identify possible causes and barriers to the main "bones." This subdivision in terms of increasing specificity continues as long as the challenge areas can be further subdivided. The practical maximum depth of this tree is usually about two, or at most three, levels.

When the fishbone is complete, a rather comprehensive picture and understanding of the possible factors leading to and sustaining the need emerges. The Ishikawa diagram provides a powerful visualization and knowledge organizational tool. Placing the ideas and insights of the team in this systematic way facilitates the understanding of the issues. This in turn can support the planning process by focusing attention on causes and removing the barriers towards reaching the goal. Ultimately, the objectives of the plan will help to resolve the identified problems and the description

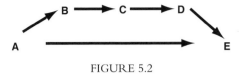

FIGURE 5.2

of the underlying issues and causes will help inform the selection of services and interventions necessary to remove the barriers.

This exercise can empower the whole team—it is the essence of creating the roadmap. The real value of the narrative summary is its ability to identify and explain the underpinnings of the needs of the individual and family. By understanding the barriers that have made the issue irresolvable for the individual and family, the provider is able to be strategic and effective in planning and providing services. Actually creating a fishbone diagram and including it in a narrative summary—with a bit of explanation—is a practical way of satisfying many of the planning process requirements and giving the treatment team the tools and directions needed to plan for the individual's recovery journey.

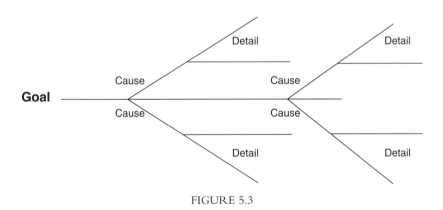

FIGURE 5.3

III. MAKING IT HAPPEN

A written narrative summary must be part of every assessment or periodic reassessment. It may be documented in the individual plan itself, be attached to the assessment documents, or be included in the general notes section of the record. It does not need to be lengthy, but it must be complete. It should include some of the following elements:

- diagnosis, cultural formulation, and justification of the diagnostic con-clusions based upon key elements of the assessment and mental status exam
- an understanding or explanation of the individual's and family's needs and goals in the context of their culture (including the role of religion and spirituality as appropriate) with insights into precipitating, per-petuating, and other complicating factors
- recognition of the strengths, abilities, and resources of the individual and family
- identification of the barriers that inhibit goal attainment
- anticipation of the level of care and possible length of services
- consideration of the priorities in helping the individual and family to reach their stated goals
- description of the individual's and family's preferences for participation in planning, language, services, and other components of the helping process

There is no substitute for experience in learning to prepare a narrative summary. A relatively small number of essential criteria to use in creating and evaluating a narrative summary can be articulated. A checklist to use in reviewing and evaluating a narrative summary will be discussed in the following text. This is designed to give providers, peer reviewers, and supervisors a tool by which to evaluate a narrative summary and identify areas for improvement. Not every box will or should for that matter be checked off—there are many times when a particular issue is not relevant or appropriate.

There is no such thing as a perfect narrative—even a narrative that meets all the criteria stated could have room for improvement. But an adequate narrative summary can be described and modeled. The very fact that the summary is narrative and not a matter of check-box forms and simple data fields creates significant anxiety and discomfort with some providers. Hopefully the models in the *Creating The Solution* section, along with the following examples, can make a difference. They are intended to give providers the tools and confidence they need to be more person-centered and effective in their work with individuals and families.

Figure 5.4 is a useful checklist tool that providers and supervisors can use to review and evaluate narrative summaries. Providers unfamiliar with the task of writing narrative summaries may need to simply dive in, while seasoned practitioners may find some of the tools and prompts included helpful in refining and improving their skills. Providers are encouraged to

---

NARRATIVE SUMMARY CHECKLIST

☐ Moves from what (data) to why (understanding) with
    ☐ clear formulation or explanation of meaning
    ☐ description of a central theme for the individual and family
    ☐ identification of stressors/precipitants
☐ Integrates and summarizes the data collected to include
    ☐ results from standardized tests
    ☐ previous treatment experiences
    ☐ discharge summaries
    ☐ school evaluations and reports
    ☐ face-to-face psychosocial interviews
    ☐ psychiatric and psychological
    ☐ mental status evaluations
    ☐ at least a tentative or initial diagnosis
☐ Summarizes the perceptions of the individual
    ☐ describes choices and prioritization
    ☐ explains what's most important and what comes first
      consistent with the individual's and family's
      concerns/perspective
☐ Identifies
    ☐ the individual's strengths
    ☐ personal/family values
    ☐ cultural nuances
    ☐ abilities and past accomplishments
    ☐ interests and aspirations
    ☐ resources and assets
    ☐ unique individual attributes
☐ Provides
    ☐ the foundation for developing treatment plan goals and
      objectives by setting the stage for prioritizing needs and
      goals
    ☐ behavioral descriptions of the needs and problems
☐ Identifies the barriers to achieving desired goals
☐ Reflects a balance between the understanding of the individual and the
  provider
☐ Identifies co-occurring disabilities /disorders
☐ Recommends a course of treatment and determines the levels of care
    ☐ specifies the stage/phase of recovery
    ☐ anticipates transition/discharge (length of services)
    ☐ recommends referrals, tests, special assessments, as indicated
    ☐ documents the recommended intensity of services

FIGURE 5.4

self-evaluate their narrative summaries against the checklist. While the principal source of feedback should be the individuals and families seeking help, supervisors and peers can also offer valuable input. Providers should not be afraid to share their work (with appropriate protections of privacy and confidentiality) with colleagues for review and comment. Although it is not commonly done, it is a very useful, if not powerful, tool for changing and improving practice. Reading texts alone will not likely change practice, but taking risks and being open to constructive criticism, as well as praise, can greatly help to develop new clinical skills and habits.

Examples

Four examples of narrative summaries based on the individuals previously introduced are provided, with an important caveat. They are not necessarily clinically perfect—they are intended as samples of at least one reasonable interpretation of how data can be integrated to support individual planning. Readers may well come to different conclusions from their review of the assessment data. Each case is illustrative and instructive in its own way; accordingly, important aspects of the narrative summary are highlighted in conjunction with each example.

Far more important than the specific formulations, however, are the organization and thought processes reflected in these examples. No doubt there are many different possible interpretations of the data presented in the sample biopsychosocial assessments. Without knowing the individual or having their direct input into the process, the preparation of a narrative summary example requires a bit of conjecture. Examples removed from the real world of practice are inherently limited. However, they can serve to illustrate how a meaningful transition from data to understanding can be accomplished without a mere repetition of the assessment. The real test of their adequacy will be clearer as the subsequent elements of an individual plan, built upon these summaries, are introduced and the process is examined in the chapters to follow.

Aaron

The documentation for Aaron Howard includes a separate cultural formulation as well as a narrative that utilizes the "Six Ps," a framework to organize and present the narrative and formulation. In this analysis, key factors that help to explain Aaron's past difficulties and current challenges are identified—precipitating and especially perpetuating factors seem to be most significant. The formulation is rich with insights and a hypothesis to help understand the underpinnings of Aaron's challenges and needs, and provides a basis for organizing an effective set of interventions that are responsive to these factors.

The summary also incorporates the results of the CALOCUS level of care instrument that provides suggestions and guidance about the intensity and setting of services for Aaron, and is consistent with the current referral while acknowledging the risk of placement at a higher level of care if he is unable to succeed in the current setting. While Aaron himself is not likely to be able to understand all of the ideas presented in the summary, nor perhaps the foster family either, it will be important for the other members of the team entrusted with Aaron's care to have a thorough understanding of his needs, his strengths, and his abilities. The provider can then share a synopsis of the summary with Aaron and his foster family which should help Aaron to understand that although his desire to reunite with his mother is understood and supported by the team, there is real concern that achieving this may go beyond the scope and influence of the services being planned.

While Aaron's summary identifies multiple emotional, physical, and behavioral problems, it also notes his strengths, which can be built upon in developing the plan. Although his overall dream is to be reunited with his biological mother, the narrative summary identifies immediate barriers that Aaron and his foster family face and the priorities that must be attended to first.

Sally

The summary of Sally Hamilton demonstrates the simple narrative approach. It is relatively straightforward and to the point—Sally's presentation and needs do not appear to be highly complex, and the length and detail of the summary seem to be appropriate. Along with a brief review of the relevant history, the summary incorporates the ASAM dimensions and the Addiction Severity Instrument. The narrative clearly states that Sally is not initiating treatment willingly and that the provider sees more problem areas than Sally does. At the same time, the narrative summary demonstrates an openness, honesty, and thoughtfulness that hopefully create an opportunity to engage in further dialogue with Sally about her use of alcohol and its impact on her life.

Sally's stage of change is identified as "pre-contemplation;" therefore, appropriate interventions are suggested, such as motivational counseling, in addition to her court-ordered educational classes. Although it may be clear to the provider that Sally has a long history of alcohol abuse/dependence and needs additional, longer-term services, the provider is respectful of Sally's current thinking. The anticipation of the exit interview sets the stage for re-evaluation and reconsideration of Sally's needs following an initial set of interventions.

Sam

The narrative summary for Sam Hewlett flows from the assessment data and is well integrated into the entire assessment. The narrative is far more than a recitation of the facts; rather, it gathers the salient details and important innuendos that help explain Sam and his current needs. The narrative starts by highlighting what is important, significant, and different at this time in contrast to Sam's past experiences in seeking help—the fact that Sam has come voluntarily as compared to fulfilling an external mandate is extremely important. The narrative focuses on Sam's strengths and past accomplishments with a balanced acknowledgment of his past problems and failures.

This narrative helps to provide guidance and justification for the medical necessity of services and the appropriate level of care. The use of a stage-wise model helps to clarify the impact and significance of Sam's current contemplative phase—especially as compared to his historical pre-contemplation and difficulty in sustaining active treatment. The use of the LOCUS helps to confirm that team-based outpatient services are the appropriate level and intensity of response to the various dimensions of Sam's needs.

The interpretative summary raises questions about Sam's diagnosis and the implications for treatment—it will be important to see how this is further addressed in the formal development of a plan. The summary also carefully considers an end point or discharge or transition criteria—this will be helpful in organizing the actual plan. The barriers section of the narrative is essential. This is an effective integration of history, insight, understanding, and present circumstances, and provides a realistic estimation of the challenges that Sam and his providers will face in helping Sam to achieve his stated goal. The barriers identified can easily be translated into objectives for the plan—as will become clearer in Chapter 7.

Lastly, the overall tone of the summary is hopeful, positive, and recovery oriented. It is intended to support Sam's goals for more independent and integrated participation in the community and builds on his capacity for resilience. There is a hopeful message embedded in the summary that leaves open the possibility of exploring additional future goals for Sam after his immediate needs are addressed.

Carmen

In the Carmen Suarez example, the narrative summary form is a document apart from the rest of the assessment. In some settings it is useful to have the narrative as a standalone document that can be shared with the team—including the individual and family for review, comment, and enhanced understanding of the needs, priorities, and goals, as well as a clear articulation of the strengths upon which to build a recovery plan.

The summary is fairly brief and to the point, and it effectively integrates the information from the parent/child questionnaire with the data from the provider interview and assessment. It nicely serves the function of being a conceptual and written transition between the assessment and the creation of the plan. In narrative fashion, the summary really begins to map out the journey for Carmen and her family—particularly in its clarification of the goal and its anticipation of treatments issues and modalities.

Perhaps most importantly, the summary provides a formulation and a hypothesis for understanding the issues and precipitants that lie behind Carmen's apparent depression. As objectives are identified, this will be critically important in framing the plan and selecting appropriate interventions. The linkage of her symptoms and diagnosis to cultural factors, and the speculation about the role of culture in her experience of the illness as well as her and her parents' understanding, are also key to successful engagement, treatment, and outcomes.

REFERENCES

1. CARF 2004 to 2005 Behavioral Health Standards Manual, p. 80.
2. Maslow, A. *Motivation and Personality,* 2nd ed., Harper & Row, 1970.
3. http://www.intentionalcare.org.
4. Jongsma, A.E. *The Complete Depression Treatment and Homework Planner.* New Jersey: Wiley Publishing, 2004.
5. *Changing the Face of Mental Illness in Virginia.* The Alliance for Increased Mental Health Awareness, p. 5.
6. http://www.zialogic.org/CCISC.htm.
7. Kessler, R.C. *The National Comorbidity Survey of the United States.* International Review of Psychiatry 1994;6:365–376.
8. *Indiana Task Force on Co-Occurring Mental Illness and Addictive Disorders.* Final Report, 1999.

On the Road

The three chapters of this section cover the core elements of any plan: goals, objectives, and interventions. We are about to begin our journey, the final destination is clearly specified, and at least some of the early signposts are identified. What we need to get there, what we need to overcome, and the tools and resources to assure our safe, successful passage are all part of being on the road.

The road movie is a favorite Hollywood genre, often filled with wonderful scenery and bits of humor and sometimes fraught with peril as the characters run or drive in pursuit of some dream. It focuses on the human spirit being quickened by the thrill of motion and change—new vistas, new challenges, and new opportunities. Ask people about hobbies, interests, and pastimes, and they often pick travel first. The opportunity to make a change and experience something different and new seems to be part of human nature.

Some trips can be aimless—the journey is the destination itself. However, the road to recovery seems to benefit from a bit of forethought and planning. The goals, objectives, and interventions are the implements of a complete expedition.

## CHAPTER 6

Setting Goals

If you don't know where you are going,
you will probably end up someplace else.
Lawrence J. Peter

Goals are dreams with deadlines.
Diana Hunt

I. STATING THE CASE

In setting the goal for the individual plan, the real creation of a map begins. The goal should reflect the individual's and family's clearest articulation of the destination—the optimal outcome from seeking help and receiving services.

A properly conceived and written planning goal should be a broad general statement that expresses the individual's and family's desires for change and improvement in their lives, ideally captured in their own words. A goal should be long term and written in positive terms. It is a simple statement of the individual's and family's anticipated changes and benefits that will result from receiving services—it is typically linked to their motivation in seeking help and reflects the resolution of their problems and needs. The goal statement should encompass the individual's and family's hopes and dreams, not only for resolution of their immediate problems and needs, but also to possibly address another major life area that needs attention.

Goals are not necessarily measurable. At the same time, however, their achievement or realization should be something easily recognized and readily apparent to all. Goal statements may be reflective of the individual's and provider's "meeting of the minds" about what can be reasonably achieved within the context of the helping relationship and service setting. The goal statement often reflects the implicit or explicit point of engagement with the individual and family and becomes the focus of further collaboration. If the plan is thought of as a contract between the individual and the provider, the goal is the "deliverable" specified in the contract.

For the most part, goals are not necessarily time framed, but may be if the time frame is meaningful and relevant to anchor their attainment to some point in the future. This is often influenced by a number of factors ranging from the service setting (e.g., inpatient or residential as compared to outpatient), the acuity of the individual and family's needs, externally imposed time factors, deadlines or requirements, and the specificity of the goal itself. When there are multiple goals, clarifying priorities and sequencing by setting time frames can help to provide clarity and organization to the development of the plan.

Types of Goals

Three different levels of goals can be identified: life goals, service or treatment goals, and quality of life enhancement goals; however, not every plan has to specify all three types. Often these three goals are closely related, if not one in the same, depending in part on the circumstances and service setting. Goals described as *life goals* may include aspects of the individual's life where they have hopes for overall improvement and may include aspirations such as "I want to be married" or "I want a job." Such goals may or may not appear to have an immediate relationship to service needs and are less likely to be time framed. Yet the difference in the power and momentum of the plan that occurs when "I want a job" becomes "I want to be working full-time within 9 months" cannot be ignored. Regardless, the recognition and acknowledgment of the individual in identifying and setting life goals can be a critical part of building and maintaining an effective collaboration.

Service or treatment goals address the resolution of the needs and concerns that are a barrier to discharge or transition from services. These goals are often closely linked to the issues and needs that prompted the individual and family to seek help and are responsive to the immediate circumstances. Treatment goals may be setting specific or address concerns for a particular episode of care or a particular level of service. In an inpatient or residential care setting, these goals are typically the positive reframing of the discharge criteria and the removal of the barriers for a transition to a lower level of care. These goals are often quite succinct and may be more specific or measurable. For example, an individual may have a life goal of a career as a teacher, but is currently living in a clean and sober housing program. The life goal might be: "I want to become a teacher" while the treatment goal in the current setting is "I want to return to living with my family."

In some settings or circumstances, as in the previous example, treatment goals may be a subset of larger and broader life goals. The more non-specific and larger the life goals, the greater the likelihood that there will be important, more specific, or immediate service goals to identify and achieve. Admittedly, this can be confusing and blur the distinction between objectives (short-term intermediate steps) and goals. At some level, the distinction between the two is qualitative and subjective and needs to be considered in the context of an individual plan. One could argue that returning home from a clean and sober housing program could be viewed as a short-term goal or objective—an intermediate step on the road to getting one's life back on track and pursuing the dream of becoming a teacher.

This is part of the art of individual planning—knowing how to organize a strategy that is most effective in helping the individual and family. A goal will typically have multiple barriers or steps that need to be resolved through a series of very specific objectives. In contrast, an objective is one of several efforts to focus on a measurable and targeted change in behavior or capacity within a specified time frame that helps the individual and family to attain their larger goals. There are typically few goals and many objectives. Goals are tied to discharge and transition; objectives are tied to the attainment of goals.

Enhancement goals include those other needs not expressly or immediately linked to seeking services or specific life changes, but typically reflect quality of life concerns for the individual and family. These goals may be fairly non-specific and may speak to human needs and concerns ranging from the mundane and material to a desire for some form of self-actualization. Often these goals will not be a succinct focus of the individual plan. Rather, the individual and family are able to build upon their success in attaining service goals or life goals and pursue these enhancement goals on their own. Examples of life enhancement goals might include such things as "I want to be able to travel more" or "I want to have more friends, a better job, live near the beach, and so on." Life enhancement goals are often of real importance to the individual and family but they are not as tightly linked to the needs, challenges, and barriers that result from the mental health and addictive disorders that are the focus of the plan.

The complexity of people's needs and challenges will often be reflected in the complexity of the plan and the number of goals that are identified. There are times when life goals and treatment goals may be one and the same. This is most likely to occur when needs are time limited and acute and the individual is not working to overcome a disability or other significant and long-standing challenge. In more long-term rehabilitation, a significant and meaningful life goal may provide an organizing principle for a series of more short-term, focused, and sequential goals leading to fulfillment of the individual's dreams.

Respecting Goals

There is perhaps no greater expression of respect, understanding, hope, and empathy by the provider than the ability to elicit, acknowledge, and accept the individual's and family's goals. In many respects, this is where individuals may feel most vulnerable—sharing their hopes, their fantasies, their desires. Individuals and families often seek help because they feel overwhelmed, frightened, and defeated by their needs and challenges. Rekindling a connection with their dreams and aspirations is an essential first step in creating a successful and effective plan. The standard should not be whether or not the goals are realistic. Rather, the criteria for success in this crucial planning step is whether or not the goals help to build the sense of trust, safety, and collaboration necessary for successful partnership and outcomes in a recovery process.

There are times when individuals and families will bring forward goals that seem utterly unattainable. The provider must resist any impulse, albeit it well intended, to dismiss or diminish them as unrealistic. This is not a time for "reality testing"—if necessary, that can come later. Inevitably, there is tremendous meaning and significance in the goals that are identified. The provider's task is to accept and understand. There was poetic insight in the lyrics of Crosby, Stills, Nash, and Young when they sang in their well known and prophetic song *Teach Your Children*:

> *You, who are on the road*
> *Must have a code that you can live by*
> *And so become yourself*
> *Because the past is just a goodbye.*
> *Teach your children well,*
> *Their father's hell did slowly go by,*
> *And feed them on your dreams*

The ones they pick, the one you'll know by.
Don't you ever ask them why, if they told you, you will cry,
So just look at them and sigh and know they love you.

And you, of tender years,
Can't know the fears that your elders grew by,
And so please help them with your youth,
They seek the truth before they can die.
Teach your parents well,
Their children's hell will slowly go by,
And feed them on your dreams
The ones they pick, the one you'll know by.
Don't you ever ask them why, if they told you, you will cry,
So just look at them and sigh and know they love you.

This acceptance can prove to be empowering for both the individual and the provider. It is the essence of being person-centered.

Clarification of treatment goals and quality of life concerns can follow from the individual's and family's identification of life goals. The provider's question then becomes: How can I be of help? What is in the way, what is keeping you from those dreams? What can I do to assist you in your journey? Plans can and should recognize life goals while at the same time creating a focus on more immediate service goals.

Common Errors

There are common problems and frequent errors encountered by providers in attempting to identify and include goals into the individual plan. These pitfalls include selecting goals that are not sufficiently:

- directed towards recovery
- responsive to need
- strengths-based
- broad or global

In addition, it is not unusual to see plans with too many goals. It is often if not almost always appropriate to have only one goal that captures the essence of the individual's and family's vision of their recovery and service needs. Having too many goals or goals that are too specific, can seriously undermine the rest of the planning process. This is perhaps the most frequently observed mistake in practice today.

A goal is broad and captures the big picture, while an objective is focused, specific, and incremental. A goal might be "I want a job," but a goal written as "I will be able to complete employment applications" is probably best treated as an objective. Not being able to complete a job application is likely a barrier to successful employment and, therefore, should be treated as an objective rather than a goal. If "job application" becomes the goal, then writing an objective for this goal can become tedious and the plan soon becomes a tangled web of unnecessary details that confounds rather than facilitates the individual's recovery. If there are too many goals, managing the plan (for both the individual and the provider) becomes overwhelming and renders it a fairly useless document. Providers are encouraged to carefully evaluate any plan that contains more than one goal and to question whether or not the plan is enhanced and strengthened by having multiple concurrent goals.

The other most common error is the inclusion of goals that reflect provider concerns and needs rather than those of the individual and family. Sometimes this is driven by the provider's sense of values and what is correct or most important. Other times this reflects a lack of meaningful involvement by the individual and family in the problem-solving and identification processes; it can be an early sign of trouble in the individual/provider partnership. The standard of good practice is that goals are expressed and documented in the individual's own words.

Goals developed by a provider should not be subsequently "translated" into the individual's words in an attempt to give them authenticity. Rather, as much as possible, goal statements should capture in a short phrase or sentence what individuals and families seeking services see as their needs and expected outcomes from the plan. It is perfectly acceptable for the provider to suggest language or ideas to facilitate the process. If an individual or family is unable to articulate goals, then the first task in the service process is to provide them the comfort, safety, tools, and supports necessary for them to be able to identify a goal. After all, it is their journey, their destination—the provider merely serves as guide, facilitator, and mapmaker along the way.

There are states and service-delivery systems that continue to have requirements—oftentimes tied to provider reimbursement for services—for goals to be elaborated for each domain of an assessment. Such requirements run the risk of creating detours on the road to successful planning; they create unnecessary complexity that confounds the service process and potentially dilutes the effectiveness of the plan. Yet, realistically, these expectations and regulations cannot be ignored. One practical solution is to identify some goals as active and inactive or primary and secondary, allowing the team to focus on a few more immediate and critical needs.

Developing Goals

Goals are developed from the information gained in the assessment and the understanding derived from the narrative summary. The assessment process helps to identify the unique attributes of each individual and family—including needs and problems, strengths, resources, barriers, and priorities in reaching the goals. In a person-centered approach, the provider's responsibilities are 1) to help the individual and family identify and express those issues and needs, and 2) to help to frame the resolution of those needs as goals to be included in the individual plan. Providers must guard against the temptation to step in and assert their experience, wisdom, and/or values in stating goals that reflect the provider's concerns or priorities rather than those of the individual and family. The provider's obligation is to respect the individual's and family's choices and preferences, and to assist them in achieving those goals.

The link between goals and anticipating transition or discharge from services is often neglected but essential. Goals should reflect the resolution of the problems or needs that initially led the individual and family to seek services. The treatment goals specified in the plan can be used as a yardstick to measure readiness for discharge or transition from services. If the individual achieves the goals, and there are no other goals that emerge, it is probably time for transition or new goals need to be identified.

However, clarity about discharge or transition criteria is often missing from mental health and addictive disorders service plans. In many instances it seems not even to be a consideration; the implication is that the relationship with the provider is forever and there is no exit for the individual and family. This implies fostering a codependency and a process with no end that lacks any accountability. An important function of the individual plan is to prevent this from happening through the identification of goals and the articulation of discharge or transition criteria linked to the goals.

The power of the goal statement is often in its simplicity. It is not necessary for goal statements themselves to reflect a sophisticated or highly developed understanding of the problem and needs—this typically occurs in the task of developing objectives or specifying interventions. Oftentimes the most effective statements of goals reflect the everyday basic concerns, wants, and needs of individuals and families. They might include such things as

- managing one's own life and being free of external control
- wanting a better quality of life with greater comfort or ease

- improved housing
- improved access to transportation and mobility
- the ability to work
- pursuing an education
- access to specific activity or accomplishments
- social opportunities and more satisfying relationships
- sexual satisfaction
- spiritual fulfillment
- better health and well being
- wanting to feel better and be happy
- the ability to have fun and enjoy things

While these are goals that may well be affected by mental health and addictive disorders services, they are not treatment or disorder-specific. Recovery and rehabilitation are concerned with helping people lead their lives to the fullest potential. These concerns and needs are at once mundane and profound. However, it is important not to lose sight of the need to understand and link these challenges to the barriers created by the mental health and addictive disorders that have led the individual and family to seek help.

Culture can also play a role in identifying goals and can affect both real and perceived priorities. The interplay of personal experience, culture, society, and the service delivery system is complex. Awareness of and sensitivity to this interaction is critical. Stigma and culture are often linked in intricate ways and may also play a role. The potential for an individual or family to self-limit their expectations for a better life, in the face of the challenges resulting from mental illness and addictive disorders, is real. Providing education about the potential for recovery, resilience, and wellness is part of supporting the process of goal identification and definition. The provider's task is to help people to see beyond what was to what can be by removing the blinders of fear, ignorance, and misunderstanding.

For example, individuals and their family members may have a limited vision about an individual's employment potential. They are resigned to a life of disability and unemployment based on old beliefs about benefits, treatment options, prognosis, and so on, or are unaware of the established success of supported employment programs for individuals with even the most severe mental health and addictive disorders challenges. Providers need to inform the individual of options, and share their professional judgment about what they believe would be most effective. Providers need to help the family and individual move beyond disability labels (e.g., "can't work," "low productivity," "won't stay on task"), and instead build on their hopeful vision for a different future.

Priorities

Priorities are an important consideration both for establishing goals as well as for setting objectives, but they differ in significance for each individual and each phase of the service process. Priority in goal-setting is really driven by the wishes and desires of the individual and family—with appropriate help from the provider as needed in clarifying those preferences and priorities. If multiple goals are identified, it is important that their priority, order, or sequence be identified.

Addressing the issue of priorities is perhaps one of the more difficult and potentially conflictual aspects of the planning process. There are times when the priorities of the individual and family are very different than those of the provider. Sometimes this is simply a matter of values and perspectives. At other times providers must give priority to protecting and preserving the basic health and safety of the individual, family, or community. Abraham Maslow[1] elaborated a hierarchy of needs that helps to shed some light on the perspective of many providers. Maslow identified five levels of human need as follows:

Physiological Needs: These biological needs are the strongest needs because if a person were deprived of all needs, the physiological ones would come first in the person's search for satisfaction.

Safety Needs: When all physiological needs are satisfied and are no longer controlling thoughts and behaviors, the needs for security can become active. Adults have little awareness of their security needs except in times of emergency, while children often display the signs of insecurity and the need to be safe.

Needs of Love, Affection, and Belongingness: When the needs for safety and for physiological well-being are satisfied, the next class of needs for love, affection, and belongingness can emerge as people seek to overcome feelings of loneliness and alienation. This involves both giving and receiving love, affection, and the sense of belonging.

Needs for Esteem: When the first three classes of needs are satisfied, the needs for esteem can become dominant. These include needs both for self-esteem and for the esteem a person gets from others. Humans have a need for a stable, firmly based, high level of self-respect and respect from others. When these needs are satisfied, the person feels self-confident and valuable as a person in the world. When these needs are neglected, the person feels inferior, weak, helpless, and worthless.

Needs for Self-Actualization: When all of the foregoing needs are satisfied, then and only then are the needs for self-actualization activated. Maslow describes self-actualization as a person's need to be and do that which the person was "born to do." "A musician must make music, an artist must paint, and a poet must write." These needs make themselves felt in signs of restlessness. The person feels on edge, tense, lacking something, in short, restless. If a person is hungry, unsafe, not loved or accepted, or lacking self-esteem, it is very easy to know what the person is restless about. It is not always clear what a person wants when there is a need for self-actualization.

Provider Perspectives

When the individual or family has significant physiological and/or safety needs, providers may have both moral as well as legal mandates and obligations that guide or direct their sense of priorities. In some instances, the provider may have requirements to file reports with various welfare or law enforcement agencies or seek the involuntary confinement and treatment of the individual. When the provider sees the individual and family as being at risk in a manner not recognized or acknowledged by them, an impasse that threatens the recovery alliance and plan can occur.

This circumstance of irresolvable differences seems to occur most frequently when there are differences between the provider, individuals, and families in the recognition of the impact of substance use and dependence on their needs. The challenge for the provider in such instances is to find a way to remain true to their professional, moral, and legal obligations and at the same time prevent a rupture or breach in the relationship. This often requires the most artful negotiation and ability to compromise, and some willingness to take risks. There is much in the literature to suggest that these are risks well worth taking.

For example, numerous past efforts to help people who are mentally ill and homeless, whose problems are complicated by substance use, have not succeeded because they have made shelter and housing a reward conditioned on good behavior, drug and alcohol abstinence, and compliance with medications. This is an instance of providers placing their own priorities above and beyond those of individuals. Recently, new initiatives and programs have demonstrated success with a different model. The alternative approach has been to offer and provide food, clothing, and shelter without the expectation of sobriety or treatment acceptance. This has not only helped to remove individuals from living on the streets, but it has often been a first step in building a trusting and safe relationship that over time has allowed the individuals to feel safe and able to consider their medical, psychiatric, and addictive disorders treatment needs. This is an excellent example of how critical the issue of priorities can be, and how success can be achieved when the individual's and family's priorities are allowed to direct the process.

Children and Adolescents

The process of identifying and agreeing upon goals raises some issues unique for working with children and adolescents and their families as compared to adults. Sometimes, the goals that are identified are more those of the family member(s) than the child or adolescent. Too often, the child's or adolescent's voice gets lost in the crowd of other interested parties: parents, social service personnel, guidance counselors, probation officers, and so on. If the goals of the plan do not reflect the child's or adolescent's views, input, and desires in a significant way, the plan is not likely to succeed.

Children and adolescents deserve care that is both family- and person-centered. Providers working with youths need to spend the time necessary to build a trusting relationship that allows children and adolescents to engage and express their own perspectives about the issues and concerns that have brought them to the service setting. For the child too young or otherwise unable to understand, it is often appropriate for the provider to play a more active role. Suggesting that the provider is there to help the child or adolescent improve their relationship with their parents, succeed at school, stay out of trouble with the law, or help them overcome a painful loss or trauma is quite appropriate. Offering and suggesting goals that the child can agree upon, acknowledge, and accept often helps to assure success in planning and services.

Even if the individual is a reluctant participant in the service program, as may be the case when schools, welfare agencies, and so on refer children and adolescents, the provider can use the principles of motivational interviewing to help build the youth's commitment to change. During the initial assessment phase, the child may not be able or willing to accept responsibility for the behaviors leading to the referral and will tend to blame others. Sometimes the provider's task is to help the child begin to simply acknowledge the consequences of their behavior without assigning responsibility. Even the smallest agreement upon a goal can be the start of meaningful engagement and the beginning of a positive change process.

II. CREATING THE SOLUTION

The solution to creating person-centered goals, the heart or focal point of the individual plan, lies in the provider's ability to put aside his or her own needs and desires to be helpful or the temptation to be judgmental. The task instead is to listen and understand the individual and family and to help them reveal their hopes and dreams. The successful plan is built upon the creation of a shared vision between the individual, family, and provider.

Reaching agreement on the goal is extremely critical—the entire process could be at risk. If the provider is unable to understand, appreciate, and capture the goals of individual and family, then the plan is inherently flawed. A team cannot succeed without a shared goal and common purpose—it is the essence of the power and success of a team. Every team member must ultimately embrace that goal or difficulty—if not, failure will inevitably ensue. In the words of John O'Brien,[2] an innovator in person-centered planning for individuals with developmental disabilities, "To put it simply, I do not see person-centered planning as the cause of change. I see it as a way to improve the odds that purposeful change will happen."

The provider's job is to help the family feel comfortable, safe, and sure enough about the process that they are able to share their goals. The goals that are established in the plan must have immediate meaning and relevance for the individual and family. They must speak to their concerns and motivation in seeking help. This may be contrary to what the provider thinks is the appropriate goal for the individual, but agreement in setting the goal is where the provider must be the most accepting and accommodating.

In addition, the provider must be aware of the distinction between life goals, treatment goals, and quality of life enhancements goals. It is perfectly acceptable to ask the individual and family about what they see as their goal in each category. Helping to clarify what goals the individual and family are hoping will be addressed through seeking services facilitates the process of agreeing upon goals to be recorded in the plan document. It can be useful to have a place on the forms or in the electronic record system to document all three types of goals.

Discharge and Transition Planning

It is commonly said that discharge or transition planning begins at admission, but common experience is that this adage is often forgotten or overlooked in mental health and addictive disorders service-delivery systems. However, given the link between goal-setting and discharge/transition planning, it is a step in the process that cannot be skipped. Discharge or transition criteria should be clearly stated in the plan and shared with the individual and family.

Setting discharge and transition criteria can be a straightforward task. The provider simply asks the individual and family to describe what would need to change so that they could manage on their own and not be in need of mental health and addictive disorders services. The answer to this question holds both the criteria for discharge or transition as well as the basic elements of a treatment goal. Life goals and quality of life enhancements may extend beyond the treatment goal. However, in creating the plan, the expectations of the individual and family and the role of the provider in attaining those goals should be made clear.

This question will inevitably make some providers uncomfortable; it often challenges deeply held beliefs about mental illness and addictive disorders, the provider's authority, and each individual's potential for recovery and wellness. Providers must learn to join with individuals and families, to envision a time when they might not be in need of or dependent on services in the same way. Embedded within this process is the essence of hope.

Re-Connecting with the Past

Another practical approach to helping individuals and families identify goals is to help them re-connect with their past. There are times when people are so overwhelmed or even defeated by their problems, challenges, and needs that it is impossible for them to imagine how things might be different. In such an instance, asking the individual and family to recall an earlier and easier time, before their difficulties began, can be helpful. Using suggestion, guided imagery, empathy, support, and other techniques, it is often possible for people to reconnect with an earlier sense of hopefulness and purpose in their life. When they were in high school, for example, what were their goals and how did they see their life unfolding? What happened that prevented attaining the goal? What would it take to resume, even with some modification, that original dream?

Within the answers to these questions may well lie the goals of the service plan. Revisiting this history can be painful, but it can also communicate a message of hope. Joining with the individual and family in acknowledging what was special, exciting, compelling, and satisfying about their earlier vision can be empowering and has the potential to carry with it a message of caring, hope, and possibility. In this way, creating a service plan is not just the completion of a form and satisfaction of an intrusive administrative requirement. Rather, it a powerful healing intervention that assures a person-centered approach to services and sets the stage for successful outcomes.

Addictive Disorders Goals

The challenge of prioritizing and agreeing upon goals is often greatest in working with individuals whose needs and concerns are complicated by ongoing substance abuse or dependence. In such circumstances, it has not been uncommon for providers to quickly identify abstinence as the goal. Sometimes sobriety becomes a condition of treatment instead of an outcome. This may occur especially when mental health and addictive disorders services are not provided in an integrated fashion. Regardless, this is not acceptable. Such actions unnecessarily force a set of priorities that often push the individual away rather then engaging them. Following Maslow's hierarchy, some form of harm reduction and assurance of safety should be a priority over demands for sobriety.

This is particularly a problem when individuals come seeking services in a less than voluntary fashion. It is not unusual for many people to initially seek addictive disorders services under a court order or other legal mandate. They often feel angry, resentful, and lack awareness of the impact of alcohol and/or other drugs on their lives. As a result, they have little real interest in being abstinent from these substances. A goal of abstinence, even in the face of a judicial mandate, will not likely succeed. It fails to recognize that recovery and effective addictive disorders treatment follows a stage-wise approach. If the individual is in the pre-contemplation stage, then the provider should focus on contemplation and engagement. Setting goals that have meaning and relevance to the individual and their stage of change, rather than imposing someone else's goals, are part of creating a successful person-centered plan.

Rarely are sobriety and abstinence clearly stated goals of the individual at the outset of seeking help. Many if not most individuals struggling with addictive disorders have tremendous ambivalence about relinquishing what has been at times a source of pleasure and enjoyment. Rather they want relief from the chaos and turmoil in their lives that is at least in part a result of the substance use. Engaging the individual and family by agreeing to help them resolve the problems and challenges in their life is an appropriate approach to setting goals—abstinence and sobriety will likely become objectives in the plan as the individual comes to better understand that their goals cannot be realized if their substance use continues.

Goal setting, especially for seeking help with a problem of substance use or dependence, should be informed by an understanding of their stage of recovery and their treatment readiness as well as their needs and preferences. Questions that help to assess the person's willingness to change and to participate in the planning process and treatment setting, include: What is your motivation for treatment? What is your definition of addiction? What experiences have you had with treatment programs (either for yourself or family members)? Do you see any connection between your use of alcohol and/or other drugs with this referral?

Every person with an addictive disorders problem is a unique individual with his or her own issues and needs. Yet in practice, it is not unusual to see sobriety become a one-size-fits-all goal with "the program" as the universal solution or service. Instead, each individual should have their own goal responsive to their life circumstances and needs. Sobriety, or even an initial reduction in use, may be an objective along with several others, and "the program" may be one of several services or interventions to help the individual attain the objective.

The Language of Goals

Whenever possible, goals should be expressed in the words of the individual and written in the person's primary language. Some criteria for evaluating the appropriateness of goals are included in Table 6.1.

Obviously not all criteria apply at all times, nor is the list in Table 6.1 intended to be complete. Rather these suggestions are offered to provide a handy reference to use in developing goals statements.

TABLE 6.1   The Language of Goals

Criteria	Possible Goals
Provide a focus of engagement/life changes as a result of treatment	• *I want to withdraw from drugs* • *I want to have a boyfriend/girlfriend*
Are consistent with a desire for recovery, self determination, and self-management	• *I want to learn how to . . .* • *I want to be able to drive a car* • *I want to open my own bank account*
Reflective of the person's values, lifestyles, and so on	• *I want to work as a . . .*
Culturally relevant, in consultation with individuals and their families Appropriate to the individual's age	• *I want to live with my family* • *I want my family to accept me* • *I want to stop getting in trouble with my parents* • *I want to be able to stay at home with my family* • *I want to get through the school year*
Based upon the individual's strengths, needs, preferences and abilities	• *I want to find out why I keep relapsing* • *I hope to live in my own apartment*
Written in positive terms, which embody hope, not negative in focus	• *I want to keep my job*
Appropriate to the stage of recovery	• *I want to get the judge off of my back (pre-contemplation)*
Alternative to current circumstances	• *I want to feel better by stopping grieving over my husband's/wife's death*

Parsimony

Simplifying goal setting, and resisting the temptation to elaborate too many goals, is one of the secrets to success in developing effective individual plans. It is possible that some plans will have three or more goals. The intent of the plan is to make change a manageable process, but identifying too many goals complicates and confounds the efforts of individuals, families, and providers. Having too many goals in the plan is simply overwhelming for everyone and undermines the entire process.

Encouraging parsimony in setting goals for individual plans is one of the important points of departure from common practice today. Providers are encouraged to have only one or perhaps two goals at a time. It is questionable whether having more than one or two goals adds to the value of the plan and the effectiveness of service. First, goals should be global and expansive—having too many is an inherent contradiction. Second, goals linked to discharge and transition criteria should be a stable element of the plan as the recovery process unfolds—having multiple goals that are short-term and narrow in focus means that this element of the plan will likely need frequent revision and render planning a burdensome chore. Instead, the focus for short-term change should be found in the objectives.

It follows that prioritization of goals is a necessity. The provider may have to help the individual brainstorm different approaches and options, or choose the areas that are most immediately important and educate the person about the possibilities. All of these activities are strategies for developing a partnership with the individual. Even the individual involuntarily referred for services will be hard pressed to deny or rebuff the team's interests in his or her strengths, preferences, interests, gifts, and competencies.

Some organizations have used the tool of having a "goal sheet" wherein the individual is asked to write down his or her goals (or dreams) in their own words (if they are capable of doing so). This worksheet is then utilized during the planning meeting as a mechanism to further define and priori-tize. A worksheet with topical headings such as, "What I want to do," "Where I want to work," "Friends I'd like to make," "These are my hobbies/favorite activities," and so on, may be useful for some people in helping them identify their goals.

Evaluation

How can one tell if the goals on an individual plan are truly person-centered? The following criteria are useful for evaluating individual plans. Upon review it should be clear that:

- the findings from the assessment and formulation have been shared with the individual and family
- a planning meeting has occurred with the individual (and perhaps others) to discuss and develop the plan

- goals are aligned with the information gathered in the assessment and described in the interpretive summary
- there is a connection between what are identified as strengths, needs, abilities, and preferences, and what are actually stated as goals
- the individual and family have been given useful information about services and treatment options to help them establish goals
- questions such as: "How do you want your life to be in the future?" "What is important to you?," and "What are your hopes and dreams?" have been asked to help elicit goals
- the goals on the plan are actually written in the words of the individual
- the individual and family member receiving services can articulate the goal(s) on their plan

III. MAKING IT HAPPEN

The solution to creating the proper plan does not lie in the "perfect" form. However, the forms used for the examples of individual plans included in the appendices prove to be useful at least in demonstrating and presenting the various elements of a plan. These forms, adapted from recently developed clinical tools at Metropolitan State Hospital in Norwalk, California, help to promote person-centered approaches to planning and make clear distinctions between goals, objectives, and interventions. This format facilitates the recording of each plan element and is used for all of the examples that follow. However, they have been simplified for their use as teaching tools and do not include various features such as signature blocks/ pages and other commonly required components. These samples are by no means the only choice for providers and organizations wishing to revise current forms to support person-centered planning, but hopefully are an example of acceptable simplicity and utility.

Examples

Please refer to the appendices for samples of goals for each of the following examples.

Aaron

In the example of Aaron Howard, there are three different goals identified:

- a treatment goal: *stabilize Aaron's current foster placement so that he can work toward reuniting with his biological family*
- an enhancement goal: *I want to have friends and improve relationships with others*
- a life goal: *I want to live with my mother*

These are all appropriate and credible goals that follow from the assessment and narrative summary. Together, they reflect the hopes, needs, and concerns of Aaron and provide a platform from which to build the rest of the plan.

The treatment goal, however, is not written in Aaron's words. This is an example of the provider's synthesis of the salient issues for Aaron—the goal that captures what needs to happen so that Aaron can move toward his life goal of reuniting with his biological mother.

Sally

For Sally Hamilton, only one goal is identified. This treatment goal—*to satisfy the legal requirements of the court order*—is consistent with and reflective of the information gathered in the assessment and formulation. Sally is in a pre-contemplative stage and has little investment in the treatment process beyond satisfying the court's demands. Resolving her legal difficulty is her only main treatment focus.

Sam

The individual plan of Sam Hewlett contains three inter-related goals. His life goal, *I want my own place to live,* which has motivated his seeking help at this time, is tightly linked with his service/treatment goal, *Sam demonstrates the necessary skills to be able to live independently with minimal ongoing support or supervision from the treatment team.* This goal is also tied to the discharge/transition criteria. For the time being at least, Sam is only interested in getting help with managing his symptoms so that he can get settled into his own housing using his Section 8 voucher.

The plan also identifies a life enhancement goal, *I want to have a better relationship with my parents,* and while this is not strongly identified as an issue in the summary, it was an issue that Sam brought forward when the plan was actually developed. His longing for acceptance and his concerns about his mother's recent diagnosis of cancer have weighed on him more than perhaps he has been able to acknowledge. Finding a way to improve his relationship with his family is something that Sam wants to focus on as he and his parents age. As such, is it not necessarily a key focus of services but something to attend to as his individual plan and recovery journey proceed.

Also tied to the setting of the goal and the identification of discharge/ transition criteria is the recognition of the barriers to attaining the goal and succeeding in transition. The barriers listed in Sam's plan are a succinct summary of issues and needs brought forward in the narrative summary. Their distillation here will help to frame the objectives that follow next in the plan—each objective and its interventions should build on the individual's strengths and resources to address, relieve, and remove barriers. This plan identifies four separate but related barriers to Sam's housing success that are immediately related to his mental and addictive disorders and are the appropriate focus of a service plan.

Carmen

Carmen Suarez also has three different goals: a life goal of *I want to graduate from high school*, a treatment goal of *resume regular classroom attendance, after-school employment, and social involvement*, and an enhancement goal of *I want to have my old relationship back with my father*. All three of these goals are readily identified in the assessment.

In the summary of her strengths, needs, and abilities section of the assessment document, the provider notes that Carmen's main interest is in graduating from high school and furthering her education. She also realizes that she may not be able to have the kind of relationship with her father that she would ideally like; the decision to focus on more immediate needs makes the relationship issue an enhancement goal. By working on her treatment goal of resuming her daily activities, Carmen should also make progress in achieving her life goal—although this may not actually occur during the treatment episode.

REFERENCES

1. Maslow, A. *Motivation and Personality,* 2nd Ed., Harper & Row, 1970.
2. O'Brien, J., Lyle O'Brien, C. Responsive Systems Associates. www.soeweb.syr.edu/thechp/rsapub.htm.

## CHAPTER 7

Focusing on Change: Specifying the Objectives

You don't just luck into things . . . you build step by step,
whether it's friendships or opportunities.

Barbara Bush

I. STATING THE CASE

Moving along the path to recovery and wellness, objectives can be thought of as the milestones and way-posts along the route toward reaching the goal or destination point. Sometimes objectives are called "short-term" goals. Building on the roadmap analogy, objectives are the directions and route plan to reach the destination, such as "drive 30 miles to the town of Success," "meet me at the Recovery Center Post Office," or "when you come to the circle, go halfway around and bear right and pull in to the Wellness Lodge." The individual moves closer to the final destination or goal each time one of these midpoints is reached or a change in his or her mental health and addictive disorders status and needs is achieved.

Objectives are the sequential or concurrent near-term changes necessary to help the individual and family meet their long-term goals. Objectives identify the immediate focus of treatment; they are the incremental changes and manageable tasks the individual and family will focus on, bit by bit, as they move towards reaching their goal. These are often seen as the real engine of the individual plan that drives overall progress. The focus of objectives is the removal of barriers; objectives should help the individual and family bring about changes in physical and psychological status, function, behavior, symptoms, potential, or capabilities that empower them to resolve the needs and concerns that led them to seek help. Objectives are typically described in action words and should not involve changes in thinking, understanding, insight, and so on. Rather, changes in behavior or function that result from such understanding or knowledge should be identified in the objective. Achieving objectives usually requires the individual and family to master new skills and abilities that support them in developing more effective responses to their needs and challenges.

Objectives are about action and change; they are not passive or abstract. Objectives are of the moment and practical; they are not distant or remote. A properly written objective should typically begin with the statement: "The individual and/or family will..." and describe a significant and meaningful change in behavior, status, or function as a step towards reaching the larger goal. An objective should include a measure of success as well as a time frame for its completion. Objectives should empower, engage, and motivate by making the larger goal attainable.

Attainment of an objective is supported by the activities, services, and interventions of the entire team, including the individual and family. These efforts may include a range of services from traditional professional treatments such as psychotherapy, and addictive disorders counseling, pharmacotherapy, case management, occupation or rehabilitation therapy, and so on, to psychoeducation classes, peer supports, and folk remedies. Overall, the emphasis should be on teaching skills, enhancing the ability of the individual to manage his/her own life, utilizing the natural resources of the community, and being less dependent on professional resources. Objectives should not be confused with services or interventions and *this is one of the most frequent errors made in developing individual plans*. While seemingly basic to the process, specifying objectives is often one of the most difficult tasks for providers in preparing individual plans.

Key Features

Objectives should be

- reasonable
- measurable
- appropriate to the treatment setting
- achievable
- understandable to the individual

- time-specific
- written in behaviorally specific language
- responsive to the individual's disability/disorder/challenges and stage of recovery
- appropriate to the individual's age, development, and culture

A popular mnemonic says that objectives should be SMART:

- **S**imple or **S**traightforward
- **M**easurable
- **A**ttainable
- **R**ealistic
- **T**ime-framed

Objectives are about success, realizing that things can be different, and experiencing the power of change. As individuals and families struggle to overcome challenges and address needs, nothing succeeds like success. Each objective should address or specify only one change at a time. Objectives should not be a description of what the provider or others will do to promote and facilitate the change—those activities are more accurately interventions and are examined in depth in the following chapter.

Role of the Team

The elaboration of objectives, and the development of a strategy that works to remove barriers and help individuals reach their goals, is one of the important contributions of the provider. Individuals and families seek help because they have reached a point where they are unable to address their needs and challenges on their own. They may be able to identify their destination or goals, but they cannot envision the route or overcome the barriers that lie in the way. Objectives work to help remove the barriers, and in the process, set the journey's course. The provider becomes the guide who can lead the way. The important role of the provider as counselor, advisor, recovery consultant, coach, and expert partner should not be underestimated or ignored. While the provider can and should offer experience and perspective to overcome barriers, it is important that the provider not unwittingly limit the individual's and family's choices or ability to take risks and try new things. The setting of objectives builds upon the strength of the individual and family as well as the collaboration and partnership between them and the other team members. The task

should reflect the mutual experience of dignity and respect for all participants.

The intermediate steps or objectives that an individual and family pursue
to achieve their goals should be substantial and significant, but at the same
time manageable. They should reflect valuable and meaningful change.
There is a tendency in current practice to trivialize objectives instead of
making them meaningful and relevant. For instance, if the problem is
"depression" and the goal is "I want to feel happier," merely stating "Susan
will keep a mood journal" does not explain how that action or activity will
help bring her happiness. In fact, this is a good example of how the difference between objectives and interventions can blur—keeping a mood journal is much more of an intervention than a significant change in behavior
or function. Individuals seek help and receive services because they have
reached an impasse and are unable to solve their own problems. The team
assists in helping to establish realistic, responsive objectives that individuals
can achieve as tangible steps towards meeting their goals.

Time Frames

Specifying a time frame for attainment of an objective is a critical component of the overall planning process. Goals are long-term; objectives are
near-term. The specific time frame established in an objective carries with
it a message for the provider as well as the individual and family: change is
expected. In many settings, the time to accomplish an objective is automatically tied to the minimum administrative requirement for review and
update of a plan. For example, if the plan needs to be reviewed every 6
months or every year, then all of the objectives have a 6- or 12-month time
frame for completion. This typically does not communicate a message of
hope or change.

A person-centered, recovery-oriented approach to planning and
services has time frames that are relevant to the scope of the objective,
the individual's and family's motivation, and the resources available to
support and facilitate the change. More importantly, setting extended
time frames subtly communicates a message of low expectations and hope-
lessness. While each objective must be individual and relevant to each
person's goals, as a general rule 90 days should be considered as an upper-
limit time frame in crafting objectives. If nothing else, 90 days is a reasonable period for review and reassessment, and in many settings it is a standard
of care.

Strengths-Based Approach

With much attention focused on the principles of a strengths-based approach, many providers struggle with how to actually employ strengths in an individual plan. Nowhere is the recognition and engagement of the individual's and family's abilities and resources more important than in specifying objectives. Objectives should not focus on deficits; rather, they should describe positive changes that build on past accomplishments and existing resources.

There are times when it can be difficult to recognize a person's strengths in the midst of their distress and need; their motivation is often overlooked. This alone can be a powerful strength upon which to build a plan and mobilize success. Imagine trying to create an effective plan without this resource to build upon. In fact, a lack of motivation is often a factor when individuals and families seek services only to satisfy the requirements of the courts, school, or other authorities. In these instances, providers could help individuals become motivated to change as a way of supporting and sustaining person-centered strengths. It could be appropriate to have a first objective statement which anticipates the individual's and family's ability to recognize and "own" the need for services and change. Such an objective might be: "Karen and her mother will be able to identify a self-defined goal and agree upon at least one objective that removes a barrier to that goal." In this circumstance, interventions would focus on the issues of awareness, motivation, and engagement.

As much as possible, objectives should reflect an increase in functioning and ability, along with the attainment of new skills, rather than merely a decrease of symptoms. In formulating an objective it is important to ask: What are the individual's strengths that can be utilized and enhanced to help bring about change? Objectives that build upon these existing resources and abilities are far more likely to succeed and sustain the journey. Objectives that merely ameliorate the current distress will inevitably lead to distractions and detours on the path to recovery and wellness.

Avoiding the "Dead-Man Standard" and Other Pitfalls

The creation of objectives that are simply the cessation of a particular behavior or symptom is another commonly observed error. For example, consider the objective "John will stop having temper tantrums." The problem with this objective is that if John were to die, he would meet the objective by no longer losing control of his anger. This is the "dead-man standard." It should be immediately obvious that objectives must describe active, positive change if they are to be meaningful midpoints, as well as measures of progress and success. A re-wording of this objective might be: "John will remain calm when faced with frustration" or "John will express his anger using a normal tone of voice at least 80% of the time over the next 3 months."

An objective is not the mere removal of the barrier—this runs the risk of reinforcing a deficit-focused approach. Rather, the objective should capture the positive alternative to the current needs and challenges. For example, if an individual is struggling with thoughts of suicide, the objective should not be that "Carla will report that she is free of suicidal thoughts within 30 days." Instead, the healthy alternative is that "Carla will report enjoying at least two activities that help her to feel life is worth living." While some might dismiss the difference as a trivial matter of semantics, experience is that this type of reframing is empowering and leads to better outcomes.

Another pitfall is the use of activities that merely indicate attendance or participation in service activities as an objective. Statements such as "Bill will attend medication groups weekly," "Gayle's mother will participate in family psychoeducation groups every other weekend," or "Juan will keep 70% of his cognitive-behavioral therapy appointments" are all examples of such objectives. These statements should be considered a description of interventions. They demonstrate how services and objectives can become commingled and confused. Attendance may be necessary to begin the process of change; however, it is not a meaningful change in function or behavior that helps move the individual and family closer to their goals. Mere participation in services in no way indicates that any learning, development, or change has occurred. Understanding, insight, or knowledge alone are not sufficient objectives. Instead, there must be some active and measurable demonstration that the input and benefit of services has been incorporated and helped to cause positive and desired change. The skill of developing an individual plan is to clearly articulate intermediate accomplishments in support of the larger goals and to understand how services such as medication groups, family psychoeducation, and case management, all contribute to meeting objectives and promoting change.

All too often, otherwise thoughtful and well developed plans are undermined by the efforts to do too much at once. There are no hard and fast rules about how many active objectives are required at any one time, except for the expectation that there is at least one objective for every goal. There are circumstances when it may be perfectly appropriate to have only one active objective; there may also be times when having two or three simultaneous and concurrent objectives is necessary and beneficial.

However, as with goals, there may be value in strategic parsimony (i.e., having fewer objectives that are more targeted and, therefore, make the overall plan more manageable). This alone may help to make a plan more effective. In general, plans with more than two or three current active objectives are too complex and should be carefully reconsidered. Objectives are the building blocks of successive learning and have an order and sequence. For instance, an individual may first need to be able to recognize and acknowledge his or her addictive behaviors before being able to demonstrate two alternatives to drug and alcohol use as a way to relieve uncomfortable emotions. Figure 1 is a reminder of the relationship between assessment (point *A*), goals (point *E*), objectives (points *B, C,* and *D*) and the services and interventions (*small arrows*). Although this diagram suggests that objectives are sequential, there are many times when two or more objectives are concurrent.

From Barriers to Success

The narrative summary should include at least some description of the identified barriers to attaining the stated goals. During the assessment process, some attention should be focused on understanding what stands between the individual and family today and their hopes, dreams, and goals for the future. For example, in Figure 7.1, what hinders pursuit of the direct course between *A* and *E*? The simple but powerful question "What keeps you from doing [blank] tomorrow?" is often an effective entrée into a discussion of barriers—those that are a result of a mental health or addictive disorder as well as those that are brought about by social, economic, and other challenges. Objectives in the individual service plan should reflect the removal, resolution, or mediation of those barriers. If the barriers are not

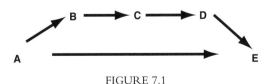

FIGURE 7.1

clearly identified or understood, then the creation of meaningful and effective objectives will be difficult if not impossible.

For example, a barrier to obtaining employment might be a lack of personal transportation (resource barrier) and a fear of using public transportation (personal barrier). In such a case, at least one of the plan's objectives toward the goal of obtaining employment might be: "Within 30 days, Taisha will be able to take the bus from her home to downtown and return by herself." If the narrative summary has identified social phobia anxiety, withdrawal, learning problems, and an overprotective mother as challenges for her to overcome in learning how to ride the bus, then the services provided should include a web of interventions and activities that address these challenges. With those supports and skill-building steps in place, Taisha should then be able to succeed in meeting her objectives and taking a first step towards employment.

A second objective might address the barriers and challenges she faces in either developing job skills or overcoming her fears and inexperience in submitting applications and enduring interviews. The sequential nature of the process becomes clear. It is the judgment of the individual and family as well as the provider as to whether or not objectives should be sequential or concurrent. A number of factors, including the complexity of the overall plan, the anticipated time frames, the ability of the individual to multi-task, and the viability of resources for both the individual as well as the service system all play a role in the selection and sequencing of objectives.

Review

Not all of the objectives need to be developed at the time the goal is established or the first objective is set. Sometimes it is possible to anticipate the entirety of the journey early on, while at other times it is only possible to see just a few feet ahead. The attainment or completion of objectives is a time for review of the individual plan as this success inevitably provides new information and may create new opportunities or possibly identify unanticipated needs and challenges. It is an opportunity to re-evaluate the goal, review barriers, and check on the overall course. New objectives that are accurate and responsive to the goal can then be established.

Such a review helps to inform priorities and the step-wise process of goal attainment. The individual and family must play active roles along with the provider in establishing objectives; they are often better able to participate as the entire process unfolds and they come closer to their goal. After all, the objectives and their successes should be empowering and should provide them with new skills and abilities to express their preferences as well as to meet their needs and challenges.

II. CREATING THE SOLUTION

A better understanding of the defining features of objectives often helps providers to write more appropriate objectives on the plan. This is not trivial—language and construction can make a tremendous difference. Properly worded objectives empower both the provider and the individual, while poorly written plans can create unanticipated roadblocks and impede progress. This section carefully examines the criteria and descriptions for a well-crafted statement of the objective.

A statement of the objective should generally satisfy all of these criteria. An objective should be the following things:

- *Measurable*
  The intended change should be obvious and readily observed by the individual and family as well as the provider. It is important, however, to agree about how that change will be measured or noted. This is often thought to imply the use of elaborate research-based scales and other measures, but that is not necessarily the case. It is perfectly reasonable and acceptable to measure the change specified in the objective by observation, self-report, completion of an assignment, statements made in group/individual/family therapy, reports from other agencies, and so on. This does not preclude the use of standardized tests and there may be instances when the use of laboratory studies, such as urine drug screens, may be useful and appropriate.

- *Appropriate to the treatment setting*
  Objectives need to be considered in the context of the level of care and discharge or transition criteria. In other words, if services are being provided in a 24-hour care facility or program, the objectives should focus on immediate treatment goals rather than more long-term life goals. There may also be restrictions in such a setting that make some objectives less appropriate or relevant. For instance, many residential detoxification programs do not allow contact or visitation in an effort to control the introduction of contraband. An objective that expects the individual to "strengthen their social network with friends" so that they can move toward their goal of "feeling included with peers," is

not appropriate to that setting. Instead, an objective focused on developing relapse prevention skills that prepares the individual to face the challenges of returning to the community is very appropriate to the setting.

- *Achievable*
  The individual should have the capacity to actually meet the objective—sometimes this is also about being reasonable. Expecting a child to *never* have any disciplinary problems at school is not reasonable. Instead, expecting that Jorge will reduce the frequency of aggressive outbursts at school from 3 to 1 per week may be attainable. *Achievable* should also include some consideration of the number of objectives. Having too many simultaneous active objectives for each goal is not realistic and probably not attainable!

- *Understandable*
  Writing objectives in a language and style that is understandable to the individual and family is essential. The objective should be practical, simple, and easy to recall—after all, it is the individual's plan! Writing in an excessively professional style does not meet the intent of a person-centered plan. An objective that seeks to "restore euthymia" for a depressed mother with a history of mood swings may not be particularly meaningful. Instead, an objective that states "Sheila and her husband will report 7 consecutive days of emotional stability and well-being within 2 months" meets the criteria for a well written objective.

- *Time-specific*
  Time frames are specific to the each objective and predict how long it will take the individual to achieve the change—be it 60 days, within the next year, or by a certain date. Time frames are not necessarily all the same, nor are they based on a program's established review dates for plans (i.e., quarterly, annually, and so on). Rather, they should be specific to the individual's and family's needs, strengths, and desires for change. Most people are responsive to deadlines and due dates; they often motivate our actions and organize our energies. While setting realistic expectations is important, it is possible to create hope and momentum by establishing relatively short-term expectations for success.

- *Written in action-oriented and behavioral language*
  Given the historic emphasis in the mental health field on process over outcomes, it is not uncommon to find objectives written anticipating

that the individual will "gain insight," "have understanding," or "be able to accept." These are not action-oriented changes that meet the criteria for an objective. Instead, the focus needs to be on what the individual and family will do differently with the insight, understanding, knowledge, and acceptance that transpire through services. Oftentimes these cognitive processes are components of behavioral change, but the focus of the objective is on the actual demonstration of new skills and abilities.

- *Responsive to the individual's unique needs, challenges, and recovery goals*
  The development of objectives needs to be informed by the assessment process. For example, if an individual is in the pre-contemplative stage about their use of alcohol and other drugs, then an objective that expects that "Jordan will meet with his narcotics anonymous sponsor weekly for the next 10 weeks" does not reflect an understanding of the individual's stage of recovery. However, if the individual has been in multiple treatment experiences, has had several relapses, has a sense of awareness of his or her addiction, and is motivated to maintain sobriety, then an objective which states: "Within 2 weeks Leroy will be able to identify three of his usual triggers (e.g., people, places, and things) to seeking heroin and develop a plan to avoid them" may be quite reasonable and meaningful.

- *Appropriate to the age, development, and culture of the individual and family*
  Objectives must be an individual match that not only builds on strengths and resources but also accounts for the unique qualities and attributes of each person and family. These characteristics are often determined by factors such as age, development, race, ethnicity, and culture. Expecting a young single woman from a family-centric culture to establish an independent residence may be an example of an inappropriate objective. Instead, an objective that focuses on resolution of cross-generational differences and expectations of autonomy and self-determination is consistent with a person-centered approach sensitive to issues of acculturation. Similarly, an objective seeking full-time employment for a 16-year-old boy may not be consistent with his age and development. An objective that focuses on his need to succeed in pre-vocational education is more likely to be acceptable to both he and his parents.

Risk and Choice

One of the more difficult challenges in setting objectives involves the questions of choice, preference, risk, and failure. Providers have an inclination to be risk aversive advocates for vulnerable individuals and families—they often try and steer individuals and families towards choices and options that the provider feels are safe. With the best of intentions, providers often act in a controlling and limiting fashion, offering a limited menu of "choices" for action that appear to be reasonable and protective. This can lead to conflict between the individual, family, and provider, especially when the individual has other preferences and priorities and feels constrained by the limited choices offered.

On the other hand, providers can become slavish adherents to the notion of choice and stand by passively while individuals make poor decisions that put them in harm's way. At some point leaving individuals and families to endure the "natural consequences" of their choices becomes a form of abandonment or neglect. What is a provider to do in the face of disagreement over individual preference and choice?

As mentioned in Chapter 4, Patricia Deegan[1] and her associates have developed Intentional Care Performance Standards to help bridge the gap between the principles of recovery and empowerment and the real-world application of these principles in the everyday work of direct service staff and their supervisors. These standards attempt to provide a framework to reconcile some of the differences and tensions that can occur. Some of the principles of Intentional Care include the ideas that:

. individuals and families deserve to have the dignity of risk and right of failure
. providers should always be advocates of individual choice over a wide range of options
. individuals should not be not abandoned to suffer "the natural consequences" of their choices
. neither providers or individuals and families are failures if a choice results in failure

Figure 7.2 depicts some of these ideas in a simple graphic. The suggestion is that providers need to learn to comfortably exist in a "conflict zone" somewhere between unacceptable provider control and unacceptable risk by the individual and family. Objectives need to be selected with awareness of and sensitivity to this underlying dynamic. Most individuals learn and grow from taking risk and learning from both their successes and failures. In a person-centered approach, individuals and families on the road to recovery should not be unreasonably denied the same opportunities.

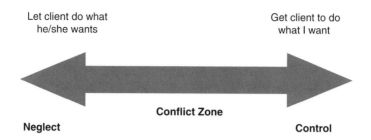

Let client do what
he/she wants

Get client to do
what I want

Conflict Zone
Neglect   **Control**

FIGURE 7.2

III. MAKING IT HAPPEN

As stated in the quotation at the beginning of this chapter, opportunities are not created by luck, they are built, step by step. Attaining goals is not a matter of luck. Goals are reached by pursuing objectives and building on each increment of success over time.

Objectives must be created in the context of each individual's assessment, reflect an understanding of their unique needs and challenges, and respond to their specific individual goals. Yet there are many resources—ranging from books and manuals to various software programs and service planning tools—designed to help providers create service plans that do not follow these basic principles. Instead, these training and practice guides are often organized and driven by a predetermined inventory of problems largely determined by diagnosis.

In such approaches, if the diagnosis is depression, then the problem is predictably described as low mood, the goal is to feel better, and the objective is to reduce symptoms on an established mood rating scale. There is nothing in this method that recognizes the unique needs, concerns, desires, and qualities of the individual. This is the antithesis of a person-centered approach. While these tools and resources may help providers meet regulatory and administrative requirements for planning, they are unresponsive to the unique needs and abilities of each individual. Objectives cannot merely be chosen from a pre-determined menu of diagnoses, problems, and goals. Rather, they must always be responsive to the unique attributes and challenges of each person.

Examples

The study examples provide an opportunity to examine how the ideas and values of a person-centered approach can be applied to developing object-ives for an individual plan.

Aaron

The objectives of Aaron Howard are clearly action-oriented, measurable, and in support of his goals. The first objective addresses his need to identify and appropriately express his feelings, since his aggressive behavior toward others has caused him many difficulties with peers, school, and foster placements. His second objective is geared toward obtaining bladder con-trol appropriate for his age. The narrative summary indicates that he is embarrassed by his enuresis and it is causing him substantial problems with his peers. Both objectives meet the general criteria of being behavioral, measurable, and time framed, and relate directly to his goals. In addition, both objectives clearly build on the specific identified strengths related to each objective. It is entirely likely that Aaron will be able to succeed in reaching these objectives.

Objectives related to trauma, abuse, or his parents' poor parenting skills could be developed, but the most immediate issue facing Aaron is his risk of being placed in residential care due to the incidents with the foster family as well as his school and peer difficulties. The focus in his plan is on behavior change and his immediate need to build skills for success. These two objectives address his barriers (i.e., lack of adequate bladder control, aggressive behavior, and inability to stay in school) to attaining his goals. If these two objectives are met, Aaron will be more likely to improve relationships with others, obtain friends, and stabilize his foster family placement.

Sally

Developing the plan for Sally Hewlett was a challenge because the goal is so narrow in scope and Sally herself has such a low level of motivation and investment; however, this is not an entirely atypical circumstance. While it is tempting to write that attendance or participation in the 10-week required educational classes is the objective needed to attain the goal, mere attendance at a class or learning new ideas does not necessarily translate into behavioral change. In this instance, the true measure of change is Sally's ability to abstain from the use of alcohol, as required by the court and as measured by a breathalyzer test administered prior to each class. The objective selected is her avoidance of alcohol during a critical period of scrutiny. In this approach, the class becomes one of the interventions to support her sobriety. This is actually consistent with the court order and the implicit expectation that Sally changes her behavior by participation in the program.

Sam

At this time there is no need for more than one objective to help Sam Hewlett meet his goal of wanting his own home. One of the key strengths and resources he has to draw upon towards meeting this goal is his time-limited Section 8 voucher. Helping him to secure housing with the voucher in the next 60 days will help Sam to achieve his life goal as well as to meet the treatment/service goals and transition/discharge criteria.

The stated objective, "Sam will be living in his own Section 8 apartment within 60 days," meets all of the criteria of being an observable and measurable change in status, function, or behavior within a specified time frame, and it is immediately relevant to the goal. It builds upon his strengths and is reasonably attainable within the specified time frame.

In this case, the objective itself does not immediately address the barriers. Instead, as the purpose and intended impact of the various services and interventions are specified, barriers to securing housing, as identified on the goals sheet, will be addressed. There are times when it is more appropriate or effective to immediately translate barriers into objectives, but the circumstances of Sam's needs and his resources do not make this an efficient approach. Nor would this plan be better served by having more objectives; in fact, it might be weakened or diluted.

Instead, the approach to planning modeled in this book emphasizes the importance of specifying the purpose or intent of the interventions; in some circumstances, like Sam's, this is how the barriers can be best addressed. When this is done, the objectives can be fewer and more straightforward, and the interventions and services can be more powerful and effective. Chapter 8 will consider the interventions in Sam's plan in greater detail. If there are too many objectives, it is often difficult to specify all of the interventions necessary to meet each objective and there is an enormous amount of unnecessary paperwork.

Carmen

The objective for Carmen Suarez is to attend school all day for 2 weeks without any absences. This is directly tied to her goal of wanting to graduate from high school, and addresses the barriers of social anxiety and symptoms of depression that inhibit her academic success. The assessment information is clear in identifying Carmen's primary aim: to finish high school and attend college. Her objective reflects that goal.

While Carmen's story is rich with psychodynamic themes and psychological underpinnings to her grief, loss, and depression, these issues are not an immediate focus of treatment. They do help to clarify the diagnosis and explain some causative precipitants. But the focus of the plan is not on furthering that understanding or on a process of resolving her grief. Instead the emphasis is on behavioral and functional change and attainment of her goals. Psychotherapy, which brings an opportunity to resolve some of those feelings, is one of several interventions, not an end unto itself.

REFERENCE

1. www.intentionalcare.org.

## CHAPTER 8

Interventions

Never confuse movement with action.

Ernest Hemingway

I. STATING THE CASE

Interventions are the activities and services provided by the members of the team—including professional and/or peer providers, the individual and family themselves, or perhaps other sources of support within the community—that help the individual achieve their goals and objectives. Interventions may be synonymous with treatment, care, services, therapy, support, medications, programs, and so on. They are different than objectives but are also closely linked. While an objective describes desired changes in status, abilities, skills, or behavior for the individual, the interventions detail the various steps taken by the team to help bring about the changes described in the objective.

The elaboration of the interventions is simply a description of the methods of the plan. If the individual plan is a contract between the provider, individual, and family, the goals are the ultimate deliverable, the objectives are the intermediate products, and the interventions are the methods used to fulfill the agreement. This contract should be viewed by the individual and family, as well as the provider, as a mutual commitment to a series of actions designed to cause change.

In the road map analogy, interventions can be thought of as tools to support completion of the journey. Interventions can be compared to having the tires changed, adding fuel, stopping to get directions along the route, or any sort other assistance and guidance the individual and family need to keep striving towards the destination. Interventions as described in an individual plan are the proposed resources and services to be delivered and should specify who will do what, when, where, and how often. Interventions are not entirely about "doing for" or "doing to" the individual and family. Instead, they describe how assistance can be provided to individuals so that they can achieve their desired outcomes. In a person-centered planning approach, natural supports (those people/agencies in the community who can become part of the recovery support system for the individual) should be considered and included as interventions.

The entire individual plan documents the medical necessity of services and supports billing along with other utilization review functions. However, possibly nowhere is the statement of medical necessity made more clear or succinct than in the interventions. If the objective is properly conceived, then the description of the intervention and its intended impact or purpose related to the objective makes the indication, appropriateness, and efficacy of the service clear. This provides an unassailable justification of the medical necessity.

There are five key elements to the specification of an intervention in the individual plan. It is not unlike the proverbial 5 Ws of journalism: *what, who, when, where, and why.* For purposes of developing an individual plan, the elements include

- describing the modality or type of service or activity
- identifying who is responsible for the activity by name, role, function, or discipline
- specifying the frequency, intensity, and duration of the interventions
- specifying the location, as appropriate
- stating the purpose, intent, or impact of the intervention in support of the objective

What

Specificity about exactly what is the proposed activity or service is extremely important, and the more specific the better. It is not sufficient to merely write "individual therapy." The interventions should specify as much as possible the type of therapy. Is it individual, family, or group therapy? Is it psychodynamic or cognitive-behavioral? In some settings these service descriptions may be tied to billing codes and other documentation of provider activity.

Sometimes it is challenging to be this specific, but it is an important component of a person-centered recovery oriented approach. To a degree, this attention to detail distinguishes this model from other methods for creating plans. There is real concern, especially in the mental health and addictive disorders fields, that individuals and families seeking services do not necessarily get what they need, but rather what the provider is able and willing to deliver. From the perspective of the individual, it can be compared to the old joke about Ford's Model T—you could get any color you wanted, as long as it was black. From the provider perspective, it is the risk that if all one has is a hammer, everything begins to look like a nail. Being able to be clear and specific in the description of the service makes elaboration of the other details much easier, more accurate, far more effective, and person-centered.

Who

There is some latitude in specifying *who*; it may require adaptation from setting to setting. For example, in a traditional outpatient private-practice treatment setting, specifying who may seem superfluous. However, in a multi-disciplinary team, specifying who, not only by professional discipline but also by name, may be critically important in ensuring that every member of the team knows exactly who is responsible for what activity. In some settings, this specificity also helps to assure that providers are working within their scope of practice and are not being expected to do things beyond their capability, role, or credentialing.

When the activity or service is the responsibility of the individual, family, or other supports within the community, specifying who is responsible may take on another level of significance or importance. Being explicit and ensuring that everyone on the team knows their role helps to ensure follow-through and completion. For the purposes of record audits (either conducted internally by the organization or externally by utilization reviewers, accreditation and licensing entities, funding sources, and so on), it is helpful for these auditors to have an understanding of who the team members are (by either credential, title, discipline, organization, or association). Merely identifying a name does not inform the reviewer. In some settings, it may be useful to divide those activities for which the individual, family, or other natural supports, have direct responsibility from those of the provider. When review of the individual plan for documentation of medical necessity and billing is a consideration, making this distinction may reduce confusion.

When

There are three components to describing the time elements of an intervention. These include the following:

- *Frequency:* This should include a description of how often the service is to be provided within the time frame of the objective. For example, is it a one time event, twice a week, weekly, once a month, or quarterly.
- *Intensity:* Is the service provided for 30 minutes or 1 hour?
- *Duration:* Is the service provided over 1 month or 2 months, or for a more extended time?

There are some services or interventions for which this level of specificity is difficult to achieve, particularly activities such as case management/coordination and others that are often provided on an as needed basis. For the purposes of medical necessity documentation, specifying either upper or lower limits of service frequency, intensity, and duration can satisfy this requirement as well clarify expectations and help organize team resources.

Where

In some situations, this item may be unnecessary to specify and may well be assumed to be at one location or in one setting. However, in a rehabilitation model, the provision of *in situ* or on-site services in a number of different locations in the community, such as at home, school, or work, is increasingly becoming the norm. In such circumstances, there may be value in specifying the location of the intervention. Providing services in sites away from a clinic or facility often enhances the efficacy of the interventions.

Why

While all five elements specifying an intervention are important, the description of the intended purpose, impact, or outcome of the service is perhaps the most critical. This description should closely relate to the *what* of the intervention and describe the role of this service or activity in support of the desired change specified in the objective. A clear statement of the intended purpose or impact of each intervention is probably the most explicit statement of medical necessity for each service provided. When there is a close linkage between what is expected to occur as a result of the service and the outcome or objective, the medical necessity of the service is beyond question. In contrast, when the intended purpose or impact of the service is not made explicit, it can be difficult to justify the service as part of a change strategy. This clarity helps the provider as well as the individual and family to understand the expectations and values of each intervention and service. In turn, this understanding promotes engagement and change.

For example, it is not sufficient to simply specify group psychotherapy as the intervention. Rather, a brief phrase that describes how group therapy will help that individual or family meet their objective should also be included. In other words, it is conceivable that everyone in the group therapy session may be working on a different issue and objective, each of them gaining from the experience of group therapy unique and relevant information for their own plan and stated objective.

The link between the objective and the intent of the intervention should have "face validity" efficacy. Whenever possible, evidence-based interventions should be used. However, it is not required, *per se*, that there be strong evidence linking the intervention to the desired change—in many cases such evidence does not exist. Rather, there should be a reasonable link between the desired changes and the service. The statement of purpose or impact that is part of specifying an intervention should make the efficacy—the likely effectiveness of the intervention—clear to the individual as well as the provider.

The Number of Services

Although not included in the 5 Ws, the question of how many services or interventions should be provided is a closely linked issue to also consider. Unfortunately, there is no magic number or easy guideline. It is similar to the story of the Three Bears and their porridge—not too many and not too few is just right. Neither the individual and family, nor the provider members of the team, should feel overwhelmed with too much to do. By the same token, neither should there be so little activity that change is not likely to occur in the specified time frame.

Determining the optimal array of services and interventions is highly dependent on a number of factors beyond the needs of the individual and family, including the objective itself, the extent or complexity of their challenges, and their strengths. This said, the risk of having either too few or too many interventions needs to be considered. In general, every member of the team is likely to contribute in helping the individual and family achieve their objective. Accordingly, over time, the interventions and services should include and reflect the rich resources of the team and the natural supports of the community. The more complex and challenging the objective, the greater the number and range of services that are likely to be necessary to achieve the objective.

Choice

Possibly nowhere is the issue of choice by the individual and the family more critical or essential than in the decisions made about interventions. There may be indicated services or treatments that are simply not acceptable to the individual and family, based upon their past experiences, preferences, culture, and a wealth of other factors. The choice and preference of the individual must reign supreme in making decisions about what can be provided to help them attain their objectives and goals. Choice is one of the central features of a person-centered, recovery oriented approach to providing mental health and addictive disorders services.

At the same time, there may be requests for services from the individual and family that the provider is unable to address. This may be due to a lack of resources or access, but may also result from a request that the provider feels is likely to be ineffective or perhaps even harmful. While a commitment to individual and family preference is the driving force in creating the individual plan, providers should not agree to activities that they believe will result in the wasteful use of limited resources or negative outcomes. At the same time, caution must be taken to ensure that providers do not inappropriately use these concerns as an excuse to avoid going beyond usual practice and failing to respect the preferences and choice of individuals.

In some settings and for some groups, there have been recent service innovations that have placed an emphasis on a "whatever it takes" approach to providing services—albeit within some boundaries of reasonableness and legality. The success of programs such as California's AB 2034 initiative to help homeless mentally ill people, and a host of supported housing programs by the Corporation for Supported Housing, are only a few examples of flexible, humanistic, and compassionate approaches to providing services driven by individual needs rather than proscribed program menus. This is the essence of person-centeredness and requires a significant re-thinking of service provision to succeed, on the part of direct-service providers as well as administrators and policy makers. Flexibility can promote recovery and foster significant creativity in person-centered problem solving and innovative approaches to meeting the needs of individuals and families. Hopefully there will be further opportunities for such flexibility and changes in service-delivery systems. Unfortunately, most providers still work within systems that are far more constrained and limited in terms of what is acceptable and what is reimbursable.

The commitment to culturally competent care should always be a consideration in deciding upon and selecting interventions. There may be instances when individuals and families desire services consistent with their cultural beliefs and experience. Sometimes these preferences extend beyond what the traditional service-delivery system can readily provide. Acknowledgment, support, and creative problem solving can help individuals and families obtain services consistent with their expressed preferences and values. Services should be sensitive to culturally determined choice as much as possible. Providing services that are culturally alien or dystonic will not likely be effective and may result in driving the individual and family away. Interventions that are consistent with cultural values and experience will foster engagement and success.

While making every effort to respect and honor choice and preference, providers cannot reasonably be expected to deliver a substantial amount of services for which they cannot be reimbursed, particularly if those interventions are of questionable value from the provider's perspective. In these circumstances, a respectful acknowledgment of the differences must be made. In many instances, a workable resolution is for the provider to help the individual and family find access to those desired services and activities that the provider is unable to deliver. Again, the caveat must be clear; providers cannot facilitate activities that they believe present a significant risk of harm to the individual. Rather, they have an important obligation to make their concerns clear to all.

On the other hand, some providers at times have adopted an almost slavish commitment to the values of preference and choice. In the face of what appears to be problematic and risky actions by the individual and family, providers may take a *laissez faire* approach believing that individuals need to suffer the "natural consequences" of their choices and decisions. While this is true to some degree, and an individual seeking services deserves the same right to try and fail as anyone, there comes a point at which such a stance by a provider borders on abandonment or neglect.

What is the right balance between choice and control? There is no easy answer to this question, but thoughtful attention and awareness can help to assure safety while supporting the recovery journey.

Decisions by individuals and families to refuse a particular intervention or to decline services entirely can be equally problematic. If the individual and family have been able to successfully identify a goal, then motivational interviewing and enhancement techniques might be helpful in fostering engagement and promoting participation. Regardless, mindfulness of the process as well as the willingness by the provider to discuss and negotiate as differences emerge can help to ensure that services and plans are effective while at the same time preserving individual rights, dignity, and respect.

The Use of Natural Supports

A person-centered approach to planning should include and involve resources beyond the professionals and paid providers working with the individual and family. The professional provider does not always have all the answers or resources that are needed to help individuals and families meet their goals. Yet, at the same time, there are many people in the person's life or other resources within the community that may be a source of help and assistance. One component of identifying strengths for each individual should be identifying these natural supports and resources. This is, in part, why strengths are specified and tied to each objective—they are part of the building blocks and resources available to help create a menu of services and activities in support of the objective.

Natural supports include those individuals, organizations, institutions, and resources available to the individual and family, which are not part of the formal mental health and addictive disorders service-delivery system. Natural supports in the community can include extended family, neighbors, friends, volunteers, other individuals in recovery, clergy, and traditional healers (e.g., tribal elders, curanderos, and so on), as well as representatives of community agencies or any other resources acceptable to the individual and family. The individual and family themselves are often aware of and highly knowledgeable about resources in their own community, and should be encouraged to identify and consider these supports and assistance.

The value and attraction of natural supports is that, over time, they can become a part of the individual's and family's strengths and resources and help to lessen their dependence on professional services. The connections with these individuals and organizations can help promote recovery and wellness; they further support community integration, reduce isolation, expand interests, help to overcome stigma, increase motivation for recovery, and promote friendship and social networking. In considering a possible transition away from a dependence on the provider, access to these supports and non-specialized services can be critical to success and long-term community stability.

The use of natural supports is not intended to replace the provider, but rather to augment and enhance the team and success of the individual plan. The individual and family are still in need of the provider's assistance, skills, knowledge, and expertise, but may need less professional time if they have access to community resources and supports. There is ever-increasing evidence of the value and effectiveness of peer-based consumer-operated services for individuals seeking mental health as well as addictive disorders services. A well-developed plan should appropriately include access to such services as part of an overall strategy to meet the individual's goals and objectives.

Stages of Change and Phases of Recovery

Interventions need to be person-specific, not diagnosis-specific. One aspect of being person-centered is the recognition of each individual's and family's stage of recovery and their current status in a stage-wise approach to understanding change. Matching interventions to the phase of recovery requires assessment of the stage and the individual. For example, individuals who have co-occurring substance abuse and psychiatric issues might benefit most from interventions that are small, incremental, and concrete. For an individual who is in a pre-contemplative stage of recovery, the most appropriate interventions might include motivational enhancement strategies and educational opportunities which help them progress into the contemplation stage. On the other hand, if the person is actively seeking treatment for substance dependence, then interventions could be appropriately geared towards learning new skills and supports in order to achieve abstinence and to improve stability and sobriety.

Evidence-Based Practices

A person-centered approach should strike an appropriate balance between the application of evidence-based interventions at all stages of the recovery process and the unique needs, preferences, and values of the individual and family. Typically, "evidence" includes scientific studies as well as professional consensus regarding promising approaches and efficacious services. However, the ultimate demonstration of evidence is the fit between the intervention and the individual at a particular point in time as judged by the participation and response of the individual (i.e., the difference between efficacy and actual effectiveness).

There is an inherent tension in the commitment to person-centered care and the increasing emphasis placed on providing evidence-based services. There is little in the literature that speaks to reconciling the differences and discrepancies that can exist between what science predicts as being most efficacious and the variability of personal choice and preference. While most individuals and families want the very best care and service, this does not always mean they are prepared to accept, without question, the recommendations of providers.

Brent James, MD,[1] of Intermountain Health Systems, has attempted to resolve this problem in an approach that he describes as "mass customization." Using the proverbial 80/20 split, he posits that all humans share about 80% of their genetics and characteristics with everyone else—we are all part of the *mass*. But the other 20% is what makes each person truly unique and individual. This idea can be applied to *customize* evidence-based practices to meet individual preference and honor a commitment to person-centered services. The 80% core should help to organize the bulk of the practice; it contains what is probably most effective most of the time. In the remaining 20%, the provider and individual need to consider how to make changes and accommodations so that personal preference is respected without unduly compromising the value of services with demonstrable benefit.

Ideally, the mental health and addictive disorders fields will evolve to a point where matching individuals' needs and objectives to the most effective interventions is a standard and routine procedure. There is some data now to suggest the merit of using evidence-based research to specify interventions in the plan. *The Journal of Studies on Alcohol*[2] notes that persons who are appropriately matched to treatment will show better outcomes than those who are unmatched or mismatched.

Despite the intense interest in evidence-based practices, there has been little research done on how to best include them in individual person-centered plans. This is partly due to the very nature of the practices themselves. Evidence-based practices, such as assertive community treatment (ACT), supported employment, or integrated dual diagnosis treatment, are not discrete interventions that can readily be identified in a service plan. For the most part there is no billing code attached to any of these practices or services. Rather, they reflect a set of values and principles, the availability of an array of services, an approach to understanding individual needs, and the organization of service-delivery systems. Much of the effort to implement these practices is required at a systems and organizational level.

For example, supported employment appears to be a very effective approach to helping individuals with severe mental illness who are motivated to return to work succeed in attaining and maintaining employment. It involves a complex mix of case management, supports, and rehabilitative skill development in coordination with other services as each person's individual barriers to successful employment are addressed and resolved. The real success in the implementation of supported employment at an individual level lies in the ability of providers to develop objectives and organize interventions both consistent with the model and responsive to the unique needs of each person. The clear articulation of interventions and services is where the real implementation of evidence-based practices occurs.

Level of Care

Although it may seem perfectly obvious, interventions also need to match the level of care needed and chosen by the individual. For example, if the assessment process, including the use of tools such as the American Society of Addiction Medicine-Patient Placement Criteria (ASAM-PPC2) and Level Of Care and Utilization Scale (LOCUS) (described in detail in Chapter 4), determines that the individual needs outpatient care, then developing interventions that are unattainable or unavailable within that setting is unrealistic. Recently, the Texas Department of Mental Health and Mental Retardation has developed the Adult-Texas Recommended Authorization Guidelines (Adult-TRAG).[3] These guidelines blend level of care criteria with disease management and benefit or service packages in a unique and effective way so that providers, individuals, and families can better understand the linkage between an assessment of their needs and the array of services available.

It is surprising how often there is a mismatch between the individual's needs, the level of care assigned, and the services provided. This is another example of the problem of providing services simply because they are what is available and offered by the provider rather than what is needed by the individual and family. The LOCUS, ASAM, and TRAG level-of-care tools, as well as others, can be helpful in describing the range of services and interventions that should be available at each level of care. These systematic approaches to matching need with level of care can be a useful resource in designing systems of care as well as individual plans. Although frequently a challenging task for providers, the specification of interventions should not be that difficult. If the objective is clearly stated and the individual's and family's strengths are identified, then deciding upon the activities to help promote the desired change should be rather straightforward. There are a few simple guidelines that can help all of the members of the team properly complete this important part of the planning process.

II. CREATING THE SOLUTION

Following an assessment and narrative summary, the essential components of the person-centered plan are:

- Goals: *what the individual wants to change or accomplish*
- Objectives: *how the individual will accomplish the goals*
- Interventions: *what the individual needs in terms of services and community resources to meet the objectives*

These three elements should always be found in some fashion on individual plan forms and documents. Some care systems have developed individual service plan forms that are structured with the italicized phrases as headings, instead of the traditional goals, objectives, and interventions.[4] The challenge to successful individual person-centered planning goes well beyond forms, but for many providers having such prompts can help to structure the task and support the development of a plan that is more responsive to individual needs and concerns.

There are four basic strategies for providers to consider in developing interventions for individual person-centered, recovery-oriented plans. Providers should approach the task of identifying interventions and services to meet specific objectives with:

1. an understanding of the individual from a strengths-based, cultural, recovery stage, and other perspectives as identified in the narrative summary
2. complete knowledge and understanding of the full scope of services available within the organization that can be provided directly

3. extensive knowledge of the resources available in the community that extend beyond the formal care system and scope of practice
4. an accurate understanding of the preferences of the individual and family for the types of services and levels of care that they find acceptable

Matching Interventions to Stages

Table 8.1, developed for the California State Hospitals by Nirbhay Singh, Ph.D., can be a useful tool for providers in trying to match interventions with the individual's and family's stage of change. Knowing the stage is important because when interventions are not matched, they are likely to be inappropriate and ineffective. Engagement and participation in the intervention is critical for its success, and not all interventions are appropriate at a particular stage. Individuals who are in the precontemplative stage need a very different approach than those that are actively involved in their own recovery. More than prescribing specific services, as these must be determined by the objective, Table I provides recommendations and suggestions for how best to approach the individual and family and how to frame or structure an intervention or service.

Throughout the entire process of developing a plan, dialog, participation, and meaningful involvement are all essential—and this is particularly true in making decisions about action steps to promote change. As with most things, it is not just about what is done but also about *how* it is done. The conversation and engagement with an individual and family in precontemplation are necessary and can be different from the discussions at later stages. Recognition of this continuum, and the proper adjustment of strategies to promote involvement and participation, can be the keys to success in helping the individual and family move from one stage to the next.

Service Array

Individuals' and families' needs and challenges should be understood from a broad bio-psycho-social perspective. *Bio* should include concerns related to physical status and well-being, *psycho* is related to the individual's internal emotional and cognitive functioning, and *social* is associated with the surrounding external milieu. Services and interventions should ultimately

TABLE 8.1   Stages of Change Continuum and Matching of Interventions

Stages of Change Continuum	Approaches to Person-Centered Planning
Stage 1: Precontemplation	
<ul><li>Denial</li><li>Unwillingness to change</li><li>Unaware of having a disease, disorder, disability or deficit</li><li>Unaware of the causes and consequences of the disease, disorder, disability or deficit</li><li>Unaware of the need for treatment and rehabilitation</li><li>Lack of motivation to engage in treatment and rehabilitation</li></ul>	<ul><li>Consciousness-raising interventions, e.g., sharing observations, confronting the individual with specific consequences of their behavior</li><li>Therapeutic alliance or relationship building with the provider; understanding and emotional relationship</li><li>Nonpossessive warmth—the provider relates to the person as a worthwhile human being; shows unconditional acceptance of the person (as opposed to the behavior, e.g., addiction, offense)</li><li>Empathic understanding—extent to which the provider understands what the individual is experiencing from the individual's frame of reference</li><li>Catharsis—expression of emotion; provider engages in active listening skills, empathic observations, and gentle confrontation (reality checks)</li><li>Motivational Interviewing—a person-centered, directive method for enhancing intrinsic motivation to change by helping the individual to explore and resolve his or her "issues"; provider facilitates the individual to resolve his or her ambivalence with regard to change. Based on four general principles for providers: express empathy, develop discrepancy, roll with resistance, and support self-efficacy</li><li>The Intervention—confronting the individual in a nonjudgmental, caring, and loving manner</li><li>Provider approaches–authoritarian approaches to behavior change lead to greater resistance to engage in change</li><li>Promote emotional well-being—poor emotional well-being inhibits an individual's progress, positive well-being facilitates positive intervention outcomes</li></ul>

(Continued)

TABLE 8.1   *(Continues)*

Stage 2: Contemplation	
• Aware of their issues ("problems") • Know the need for change • Not yet committed to change	• Continue with precontemplative stage consciousness-raising interventions and slowly introduce new interventions • Receptive to bibliotherapy interventions • Receptive to educational interventions • *Pre-suppositional Questions*—used to encourage individuals to examine and evaluate their issues, situation, or predicament. Providers can use pre-suppositional questions to think about change in a non-threatening context. As an example, consider an individual who thinks he does not have a problem. The provider's pre-suppositional question could be, "Let's agree that what you are saying is true … 'How would you know when you are ready to be discharged?" • *Circular Questions*—used in a non-threatening manner to ask a question about the individual's issues, situation or predicament from the perspective of an outsider • *Miracle Questions*—used as a method to assist an individual in imaging change and with goal setting. Classic example: "Suppose you go to bed tonight, and while you are asleep a miracle happens and all your issues, situations, or predicaments disappear. Everything is resolved to your liking. When you wake up in the morning, how will you know that the miracle happened? What would be the first thing you would notice that is different?"
Stage 3: Preparation	
• Ready to change • Need to set goals and priorities for future change • Receptive to treatment plans that include specific focus of interventions, objectives, and intervention plans	• Continue with contemplative stage awareness enhancing interventions and slowly introduce new interventions • Providers encourage the individual's sense of "self-liberation" and foster a sense of personal recovery by taking control of his or her life

(Continued)

TABLE 8.1 *(Continues)*

Stages of Change Continuum	Approaches to Person-Centered Planning
	• Discrimination Training and Stimulus Control interventions can be introduced at this stage. The provider enhances the individual's awareness of the conditions that give rise to his issues, situations or predicaments. Focus is on the presence or absence of antecedents, setting events, and establishing operations.
	• *Scaling Question*—used as a tool by the individual to "buy into" the treatment planning process. Providers can use it to obtain a quantitative measure of the individual's issues, situation or predicament, as perceived and rated by the individual and then assist the individual to think about the next step in the change process. Example: "On a scale of 1 to 10, with 1 being totally not ready and 10 being totally ready, how would you rate your current readiness to be discharged?" If the individual self-rates as a 4, the provider can follow this up with, "During the next month, what steps can you take or what can you work on to get from 4 to 5?" Scaling questions can be used to (a) obtain a quantitative baseline, (b) assist the individual to take the next step in the process of recovery, and (c) encourage the individual to achieve recovery by successive approximations (i.e., in incremental steps—one point at a time, one month at a time).
Stage 4: Action	
• Make successful efforts to change • Develop and implement strategies to overcome barriers • Requires considerable self-effort • Noticeable behavioral change takes place • Target behaviors are under self-control, ranging from a day to six months	• Cognitive–behavioral approaches • Explore and correct faulty cognitions—catastrophizing, overgeneralizing, magnification, excessive responsibility, dichotomous thinking, selective abstraction • Learning-based approaches • Action-oriented approaches • Skills that support rehabilitation

(Continued)

TABLE 8.1   (*Continues*)

Stage 5: Maintenance	
• Meet discharge criteria • Be discharged • Maintain wellness and enhance functional status with minimum professional involvement • Live in environments of choice • Be empowered and hopeful • Engage in self-determination through appropriate choice-making	• Adapt and adjust to situations to facilitate maintenance • Develop personal wellness recovery plans • Utilize coping skills in the rhythm of life, without spiraling down (i.e., if substance use is a problem, cope with distressing or faulty cognitions without using drugs) • Learn about mindfulness, especially unconditional acceptance, loving kindness, compassion for self and others, and letting go

Stage 6: Evaluation	
• Assess personal outcomes • Obtain social validation and feedback from significant others	• Continue with dynamic change process • Preempt relapse by engaging in personal wellness recovery plan • Accept that change is a spiral rather than a linear process • Practice and use mindfulness strategies

reflect the same broad and holistic approach to supporting change. Although not every individual and family will have needs and challenges in each of these three domains, thinking about biological, psychological, and social interventions can be a useful construct for contemplating the task of specifying an intervention.

- *Biological interventions*: In general, biological interventions will involve providers such as physicians, dentists, chiropractors, nurses, nutritionists, laboratory personnel, and so on. In some cases, alternative approaches such as biofeedback, physical therapy, and acupuncture may also be included.
- *Psychological interventions*: This includes the broad range of psychotherapies that range from traditional psychodynamic individual therapy to multi-family psychotherapy; therapy is provided by psychologists, social workers, marriage and family therapists, counselors, pastors, and peers, among others. The focus on such interventions is generally on the affective and cognitive functioning of the individual but may

also address other needs such as behavior and impulse control, inter-personal relationships, and family dynamics.

- *Social interventions*: This range of services and activities often involves case managers and others related to care coordination at the interface of the individual and family, the community, and the formal care system. Facilitation, linkage, brokerage, and monitoring are all within the scope of these activities. These services are often provided in the community or in the home as compared to an office or facility setting. Many times these services will focus on helping the individual and family develop and apply skills that help to promote their recovery and sustain them in the community. Occupational therapy and other rehabilitation providers can also play an important role.

The aforementioned list is by no means intended to be comprehensive or complete. Rather, it is intended to provide some prompts for considering a broad array of services, interventions and activities. This multi-dimensional approach should be considered in specifying interventions, and developing an effective array of services to help the individual and family achieve their objectives and goals.

Community Resources

Providers do not have to do everything! If services are not directly available within the provider organization, then referrals should be made to appropriate resources. The scope of available services may or may not encompass all of the needs of any one individual and may not be culturally appropriate for all individuals and families. In such instances it is critical that providers be creative, open-minded, able to utilize natural and peer supports, etc.

Community resources for potential natural supports for adults and children may include the following:

- family members
- church and affiliated religious programs
- indigenous healers and alternative providers
- neighbors
- community colleges
- YMCA, youth groups, sports leagues, and so on
- health departments
- local hospitals

- mentorship programs, self-help groups, peer support
- volunteer agencies
- library reading programs
- day camps
- social clubs
- teachers
- governmental services, e.g., Department of Labor, Aid to Families, etc.

There is a tendency when writing plans to include only those services and activities for which the provider is responsible, which will generate billing and document medical necessity. Oftentimes those natural supports that the individual or family has identified or taken are not included in the plan. Both types of interventions are important and contribute to the plan's success in an integrated and holistic manner and should be included. A practical solution to some of the administrative concerns about confusion between billable and non-billable services being commingled in one list of interventions is to break out and document non-billable individual and family activities in a separate list. This sometimes has the advantage of making even clearer the responsibilities and obligations of the individual and family in their own recovery.

III. MAKING IT HAPPEN

As in the preceding chapters, the following section discusses the move from the theoretical and didactic to the practical. The concepts, values, and principles are all well and good, but what it actually looks like and how it is done need to be demonstrated and explained. For each of the individuals, Aaron, Sally, Sam, and Carmen, examples of services and interventions are provided that are linked tightly to the identified objectives.

Previous caveats about the limitations of examples need to be reiterated. In specifying interventions, questions about the clinical appropriateness and correctness of the services will inevitably arise. There is no claim or assertion intended in these examples that they are the only or even optimal response. Rather, the criterion for their inclusion is that they are reasonable. Regardless, the focus should be on considering the key elements of a properly constructed and documented intervention:

- Is the service or activity clearly described?
- Does the intervention build on the strengths of the resources of the individual and family?

. Is the provider or role of the individual included?
. Is there an array of service interventions and types of activity?
. Are natural supports utilized when appropriate?
. Are the frequency, intensity, and duration of the intervention specified?
. Does each intervention include a description of the intended purpose, impact or outcome related to the objective?

Examples

Aaron

Aaron Howard's plan includes a wide range of activities: case management; coordination of the family, school, and referrals; play therapy; medication management and evaluation; neurological evaluation; skill building; and family therapy. Some will argue that there are too many interventions in this plan. However, returning to the narrative summary and the goals and objectives on the plan, one can see that Aaron's needs reflect a complicated, long-standing situation that requires multiple types and levels of interventions. Most importantly, each intervention includes a statement of purpose or intention that helps to make the plan a coherent, relevant, coordinated, and assertive effort to help him and his foster family meet the stated goals.

It seems that virtually all of his interventions are of a professional nature, with no natural or peer supports. With his current challenges and his risk of placement outside the foster family, it is presumed that at this point in time he needs a high intensity of professional intervention. However, it may be learned over time that Aaron could benefit most from a peer therapy group experience, instead of individual therapy. Perhaps some interventions may not work as well as others or Aaron may become overloaded with activities. The interventions can then be discontinued or modified as discussed in the following chapter on review and evaluation.

Sally

The interventions for Sally Hamilton clearly relate to the court order and are within the parameters of the state-mandated program. Instead of merely listing the activities the addiction counselor will provide, the statements describe the intended impact of the service as it relates to the objective of abstinence during the program. Providing the breathalyzer test, educational classes, motivational counseling, and an exit interview are all activities designed to help Sally develop tools she can utilize to refrain from drinking during the program period. If she is unable to utilize the tools and begins to drink alcohol, the exit interview will provide an opportunity for reassessment and further discussion of her immediate needs.

Sam

The first objective of Sam Hewlett is a straightforward derivative of his goal and translates his hope for independent living and housing into the practical objective of securing housing using his time-limited Section 8 voucher. There are five interventions listed for Sam's first objective. They are all reasonable and meet the key criteria for a well-described intervention: each service includes a description of the intended impact or purpose as it relates to the objective. In doing so, they address some of the barriers identified in the goal statement, while others address needs and challenges identified in the integrated summary but not necessarily immediate barriers to fulfilling the objective.

The interventions also reflect the rich and diverse mutlidisciplinary inputs of the team—ranging from the psychiatrist to the occupational therapist and the addictions counselor—and draw upon the benefit of peer input and support. Taken together, it is a credible package of services that are mutually enhancing and offer a greater likelihood of success than any one intervention alone; everything is focused on one outcome—helping Sam get his Section 8 housing.

Carmen

The interventions for Carmen Suarez are a combination of professional assistance as well as the engagement of natural supports at the community center group for teens. It is clear that her first priority is to attend school so that she can graduate; therefore, multiple interventions need to be applied in order for her to be able to meet her immediate objective. As with Aaron and Sam, the multi-disciplinary team plays an important role in providing a variety of services. Providing these wrap-around services, ranging from psychiatry and case management to family therapy, psychotherapy, and peer group support, is all designed to give Carmen the supports she needs to succeed in her recovery.

REFERENCES

1. James, B. *American College of Mental Health Administration Summit.* Santa Fe, NM: 2002.
2. Matching Alcoholism to Patient Heterogeneity. *Journal of Studies on Alcohol,* 1997.
3. http://www.mhmr.state.tx.us/archive/20060413bhsbdtrag.html.
4. *ISP Training Manual.* The Department of Behavioral & Developmental Services (BDS), State of Maine, October 2002.

Journey's End: The Destination

The odd thing about traveling is that sometimes you end up in places that you never intended—for better or for worse. It is a mystery how it happens despite following the map.

Sometimes the destination is exactly as planned—it is just not what was envisioned or expected—or perhaps you arrived at the wrong time of year expecting warmth and sun only to find cold rain instead. But the inevitable question is: what is next? Do we keep on moving? Is this really just another spot on the road to take a rest, or is it more of a final destination, a new place to put down roots and stay settled for a while?

Arrival is a time for reflection and reconsideration—a chance to look back and reminisce about the trip, experiences enjoyed, and lessons learned along the way, and to dream about what opportunities and distant lands might lay ahead.

Chapter 9 focuses on review and reconsideration—reflection is as much a part of the journey as the preparation and travel itself.

Evaluating the Process

It is good to have an end to journey towards; but it's the journey that matters in the end.

Ursula K. LeGuin

I. STATING THE CASE

Chapter 4 asserted that "assessment is initial and ongoing," but what does this really mean? Evaluation should be a continual activity rather than an event that marks the beginning and conclusion of a service episode. The work of supporting an individual and family in their journey towards recovery and wellness involves a process of assessment and reassessment; but when and how should that occur? Continual review is needed so that goals, objectives, and interventions are matched not only to the unique needs of each individual but also to the stage-specific needs of each person as they evolve through the process of recovery. And there is the proverbial $64,000 question: Did the individual reach the destination? Was the goal achieved? Was it where they really wanted to go? Do they want to stay? Where do they want to go next? The answers to these questions essentially lie in revisiting the individual plan with a fresh look and focus. The task is to review and evaluate the team's progress towards achieving the individual's and family's identified recovery goals.

Treatment Planning for Person-Centered Care
179

Update and Review

Assessment and reassessment should, at minimum, occur at several key points in the overall service-delivery process or recovery journey. The information gathered can help to evaluate the trip, monitor progress, and direct mid-course corrections or even possible detours to points of interest. In other words, based upon the information gathered in reassessment, there may be an update of the plan including modifications of the integrated summary, goals, objectives, and/or services. This helps to ensure that at all times the plan is:

- a dynamic, current, accurate, relevant, working, person-centered document
- an up-to-date reflection of the individual's and family's challenges and needs
- actually used by the treatment team to direct services, guide outcomes, and support medical necessity

There are key points in the service-delivery process when some level of update, review, and reassessment of the individual's and family's needs, status, and plan is indicated. These include

- the time each service is provided
- the target date specified in the objective
- at intervals specified by licensure, certification, accreditation, policy, payer, or other requirements
- at transition or discharge
- at some period following transition or discharge to evaluate the extended benefit and outcome of services

The last item in this list clearly goes beyond the scope of this book. While studies of the extended impact of service outcomes are important, they require system-level responses, are resource intensive and difficult to conduct, and are not the focus of the individual plan. This chapter will focus on the first four items in the list, although some discussion about the issue of monitoring and system re-entry is provided later in this section.

Reassessment should not be assumed to mean a start-from-scratch repeat of an original assessment. Instead it is meant to be a targeted, strategic, and more specific update focused on details that are relevant and meaningful for that individual and family. In reassessment, the focus is on these questions, as appropriate to the individual and family, and their circumstances:

- Is there new information to inform *any* of the plan's elements?
- Has anything of significance changed in the individual's and family's life, within key domains such as: health, mental health, substance use, employment, relationships, living environment and other psychosocial factors?
- Have goals or transition/discharge criteria changed in any way?
- Have new strengths or resources emerged?
- Are there new or different barriers? Are there new concerns or needs?
- What has been the impact of the services provided? Have they helped? Are there other things that should be done? Should target dates be changed? Is the intensity and frequency of services appropriate?
- Are there new or different objectives?

In a properly written and prepared plan, there will always be an update and something to document: without exception, there must be at least a transition or discharge criterion, a goal and objective with a time frame or target date. When that date is reached, there must be a determination of the status of that objective—either it has been met or it has not. If it has not, there should be some consideration as to why and that should inform the following steps. If the objective has been met, what is the next stop in the individual's and family's journey?

What is the process for obtaining input concerning progress toward goal achievement? There is not one uniform approach that necessarily works well across all settings, providers, or individuals. What is important is that the process is a conscious and visible activity. At the very least, the provider members of the team are accountable to the individual and family for monitoring the time frames specified in the objectives. At those key dates, the individual and family should be involved in some meaningful determination of whether or not the objectives have been met and what should be the next steps in the plan.

Quality of Care

The following vignette, extracted from a community mental health center record, emphasizes how critically important a proper plan and ongoing review is to the lives of individuals and families receiving services.

An adolescent girl, living with her grandmother after both her parents have died, has recently been suspended from school. She is using drugs, has been charged with auto theft, and has been diagnosed with attention deficit disorder (ADD). Because of her multiple problems, she has been assigned a social worker through the local

child welfare agency and has been referred for mental health services. Her treatment
plan goals are that "she will express her anger in an appropriate manner" and "she
will become skilled in DBT [Dialectical Behavioral Therapy]". The progress
notes indicate she is deteriorating rapidly, violating probation, smoking marijuana,
and exhibiting hypersexual and defiant behaviors. Her individual plan review
documentation indicates "she will continue working on anger management skills,
attend the intensive outpatient program and continue with the individual plan."

Unfortunately, this example is not uncommon. At minimum it represents a failure of assessment, planning, and review at multiple levels. Without conducting a detailed analysis, it is immediately clear that these are not the individual's and family's goals and that they are written more like objectives—and quite poorly at that. Perhaps most importantly, there is a disturbing disconnect between the individual's deterioration and the interventions specified in the plan update. It is shocking to see how often plans perpetuate ineffective treatments! There is no better argument to be made for the value and importance of time well spent in assessment, planning, review, and update of the plan than the need to ensure effective services and progress.

In addition to a person-centered focus on reviewing the process of services and the recovery/wellness journey, it is also important for providers to look inward from time to time and evaluate their own performance in serving individuals and families. While one could legitimately argue "it's all about outcomes," the preceding chapters have made a strong case that the process of how assessments are conducted, how plans are developed and implemented, the quality of services provided, and how outcomes are achieved are also critically important. In other words, an important part of any review and evaluation of the individual plan is some consideration of the team's performance, ranging from its actual work process to the documentation of the plan and services in the clinical record. This type of review should be part of the ongoing quality improvement and peer review activities of any provider organization, ranging from the solo practitioner to highly complex and organized systems of care.

Documentation is inevitably an important aspect of the evaluation, review, and update portion of the individual plan and service-delivery process. Essential elements of the review and reassessment process are tied to actual service provision that for a variety of reasons, ranging from billing to legal liability and continuity of care, must be recorded. However, it is often problems in documentation that make it difficult for providers to demonstrate their work in service planning and service delivery. Once again the old adage, "if it isn't written down, it didn't happen" applies. Recognizing that providers frequently complain about the burden of paperwork and how it keeps them from performing their "real job," the following section will examine, in part, how documentation issues are closely linked to clinical processes and can actually support a person-centered, recovery-oriented individual plan and service system.

II. CREATING THE SOLUTION

In *Stating the Case,* four key points in the planning and service-delivery process necessitating a review and update of the plan were identified. These included service provision, target dates, mandated intervals, and transition or discharge. Each of these points or phases carries with it special considerations in terms of provider responsibilities, involvement with the individual and family, impact on the plan, and service delivery and documentation. Accordingly, each point is a subsection of *Creating the Solution.* The last subsection addresses strategies for assessing provider performance in individual planning.

When Service Is Provided

Historically, there has been a range of documentation standards for recording the provision of services, commonly referred to as progress notes, service notes, case notes, and so on. These entries should be used to document services and should reference the specific objectives under which the service is provided. Notes can include unstructured narratives, as well as highly structured formats such as:

PIE: **P**roblem identification, **I**ntervention, **E**valuation
SOAP: **S**ubjective, **O**bjective, **A**ssessment, **P**lan
DAP: **D**escription, **A**ssessment, **P**lan

These three formats share some important elements in common beyond the fact that they are structured, which is in and of itself important. They all require *assessment* to be part of the note.

The DAP format is effectively the same as the SOAP and collapses subjective and objective into one category or field (i.e., description). *Subjective* was meant to capture the individuals' own words while *objective* was to include the provider's data or observations, but often the subjective report was forced and inaccurate, which is why the SOAP format drifted into DAP. The *description* section should include what is also found in the *P* part of the PIE format: a combination of the individual's self-report of his or her status, feelings, and symptoms, and the provider's observation of the same. The *I* in PIE should include a description of the service or intervention delivered.

The *assessment* section of DAP and SOAP, equivalent to *evaluation* in the PIE, should include the provider's impressions of the impact of the intervention, the individual's overall progress to date, the apparent effectiveness of the service and plan, and other related thoughts and observations that inform the decision-making process. These could be considered "microassessments" as they are generally very specific, narrow in focus, and for the most part tied to the intervention and the objective.

In the *plan* section, the next steps should be described. If progress is being made that is consistent with what had been anticipated in the individual plan, then simply a notation referring to the plan is sufficient. However, if progress is significantly lagging, then rethinking the strategy and possible next steps should be included.

The PIE, SOAP, and DAP formats have often been referred to as a part of a "problem-oriented record" but can just as well be used in a recovery model to support an *objective-oriented* or *recovery-oriented* record. If an objective is properly developed and created, and a service or intervention is written that specifies the provider, modality, and most importantly the intended purpose or impact as it relates to the objective, then a formatted structured note greatly simplifies the obligation to document services, substantiate the medical necessity, and satisfy the expectation that there be a reassessment at the point of service.

Writing a formatted note that includes a mini-assessment is beneficial for a few important reasons. One is that it keeps the provider clear and focused on what the task is for each individual, and the purpose or relevance of the intervention and service is apparent. With this approach, it is difficult to provide ineffective services for an extended period of time; the lack of progress becomes too apparent for all, and the provider and team are compelled to re-evaluate. At the same time, if the service is proving to be an effective intervention and helping to support the change identified in the objective, then this approach to documentation, review, and reassessment generates enthusiasm and support for moving forward and maintaining momentum. This is the proverbial win–win approach. Hopefully the efficiencies in service delivery, documentation, and accountability in this approach are clear and compelling. It makes it clear that assessment is both initial and ongoing, both real and valuable.

At the Target Date Specified in the Objective

As stated earlier, the individual plan can be considered a contract between the provider and the individual and family, so that the objectives become the equivalent of the short-term or interim deliverables, the sum of which is the goal. The provider has an obligation to honor the target dates on the objectives and to conduct a review and update of the plan when the target dates on the objectives occur.

In some settings, there may be external mandates to review individual plans or conduct plan updates within specified time frames appropriate to the level of care. This can range from weekly for acute care to monthly for short-term care and between quarterly to semi-annually for more long-term care. While the target dates on objectives should always be determined by what is most appropriate for the individual and their needs, the provider is often able to satisfy externally imposed requirements by setting objective target dates below those thresholds. It is often better to have more short-term and modest but attainable objectives that are reviewed more frequently than to have "larger" longer-term objectives that default to the mandated timeframes for review. Regardless, these target dates should prompt a team meeting to review the plan and make modifications as necessary.

When the review occurs, the essential questions are: Have the deliverables been produced? Has the objective been met? If the answers are yes, the process is in many ways relatively simple. There are a number of further questions to be considered: Has anything of significance changed for the individual or family, for better or for worse? Is the overall goal the same? With the current objective accomplished, what is next? What lessons were learned in the process? How does this success inform the selection of the next objective? What was learned about what works best in terms of services and interventions that promote and support change? What did not help? What, if anything, seemed to hinder the process? All of these questions are effectively a form of reassessment, but they are rather targeted and specific to the circumstances. The focus is on understanding a recent success and accomplishment, appreciating what there is to learn from it, and deciding how to build upon it to support the individual and family in pursuit of their goal.

Another approach is to reconsider the individual's stage of recovery and any significant changes. For individuals addressing substance abuse problems, the six dimensions of the American Society of Addiction Medicine (ASAM) placement criteria, the American Association of Community Psychiatry (AACP) Level Of Care and Utilization Scale (LOCUS) tool, the Texas Recommended Authorization Guidelines (TRAG), or Procheska's stages of motivation can all be useful frameworks. Together, this information can help to re-inform the planning process.

On the other hand, if the objective was *not* met, the focus of the review and update needs to be on understanding why. Was it partially met? Would more time make a difference? Was it the right objective? Did other circumstances change? Were the interventions helpful? Were the services provided in the right location with the necessary frequency and intensity? Should the objective be scrapped or modified? What should the objective be? What steps can be taken to assure success in this next interval? Perhaps it is simply a matter of extending the time; perhaps it is a matter of bringing new services and interventions to bear, or providing the services with greater intensity or frequency.

The insights gained in this process often help to further inform both the provider as well the individual and family about strengths, as well as challenges and barriers that need to be overcome. This in turn, may well cause some discussion about formulations, priorities, and even goals. All of these factors need to be taken into consideration when reviewing the plan at target dates, particularly for objectives that were not met.

In considering this review process, it should become more apparent that setting relevant and attainable objectives with reasonable time frames—not too short and not too long—is beneficial. The setting of objectives is not a paper exercise to be filed in the record and forgotten. Rather, the objectives are the documented agreement for change between the provider and the individual and family. They should be reviewed regularly and serve as a point of short-term accountability which is all part of making the process meaningful and effective. It is much more satisfying for everyone to see a pattern of meaningful progress than recurrent failures. Asking the tough questions when an objective is not met can help to assure success in the next interval. And nothing succeeds like success!

At Mandated Intervals

It is not unusual to review a record for an individual or family with a long service history in a community mental health center or an addiction recovery program and find that there is one formal assessment completed some 10 years ago without current documentation of any formal reassessment or update. Oftentimes there have been multiple staff transitions and changes over those years and one is left to wonder exactly who knows what about this individual. What are his or her strengths and needs at this point? What information serves as the basis for the development of any meaningful individual recovery plan? All too often there is none.

There is an emerging consensus that a formal annual reassessment, following the domain-based approach for the initial assessment, is a reasonable practice standard to follow for those individuals and families requiring services over extended periods of time. Certainly a full reassessment on a more frequent basis can be done, but this may not yield enough benefit to justify the effort and expense. However, if there are significant unanticipated or unexplained changes in the appearance, presentation, status, health, or function of the individual, then reassessment is clearly indicated.

In some cases this expectation of a formal annual reassessment has been written into code, regulation, accreditation standards, licensure requirements and the like. Sometimes it is merely a matter of organizational policy. In some settings, it is more frequent, while in others it is less and yet in others the requirements do not exist at all. Obviously, providers must meet those requirements where they exist. However, the temptation to default to the lowest possible standard should be resisted. While reassessment and review can appear to be burdensome, timeliness is an essential component of quality care. When periodic reassessments become a routine component of care, both the provider and the individual are handsomely repaid for their investment with improved outcomes and satisfaction.

The focus in reassessment should be on building upon the existing clinical database and understanding what, if anything, has changed in each of the domains—accomplishments, improvements, and the acquisition of new abilities and strengths as well as losses, setbacks, new challenges, and barriers since the last evaluation was completed. It does not need to be a complete recantation of the entire original assessment. Instead, highlighting those significant and relevant details describing changes that are meaningful in support of the individual's and family's recovery goals and journey is sufficient.

In a paper record system, this reassessment can potentially be recorded on a single page that is tacked on to the original assessment. This way, each year another page is added on to the assessment and its evolution can be followed progressively through the years. Many of the systems for electronic clinical records have the ability to update an assessment, by automatically populating fields with data, so that current facts and narrative do not have to be re-typed, and only new information has to be entered. Care should be taken to ensure that new information which changes the formulation and fundamental understanding of the individual and family, their strengths, and their needs, is included in a revised and updated version of the narrative summary. The possibility that out of these processes new goals may emerge or that current goals may have changed also needs to be considered. Attention should also be paid to changes in priorities, barriers, and strengths, all of which may need to be reflected in the individual plan.

While some level of reassessment is occurring through the course of the year in the "micro-assessments" that are tied to the service notes, and assessments that are part of reviewing the objectives, neither of those is intended to be comprehensive. In contrast, the annual reassessment is intended to provide a formal, thorough, and comprehensive review. In this way there is some assurance that important concerns, which may not have been a particular focus in the recovery process over the proceeding year, are not overlooked or neglected. It is an opportunity to ensure that while there is a focus on specific issues and change strategies, the importance of recognizing the whole person is not forgotten. Annual reassessment provides an opportunity to reconsider a holistic approach to understanding the individual and family, their strengths, their needs, and the remainder of the journey yet to be traveled.

Along with a formal reassessment, some providers and organizations may want to consider a formal and comprehensive review of the entire individual plan on an annual basis. Other reviews and updates discussed in this section have focused on particular elements of the plan, the objectives, and the services. The risk is that over time, drift occurs. There is always the possibility that in the course of events the individual has actually shifted their goal and it is no longer reflected in the plan or in the discharge and transition criteria. As a result, the integrity and coherency of the plan can be lost and objectives may no longer relate to the goal as they once did. One strategy is to consider a thorough and comprehensive review of all of the elements of a plan for those individuals and families whose length of service significantly exceeds that which is typical for the provider or setting.

At Transition or Discharge

A true commitment to recovery means fostering the independence of the individual and the family, not fostering dependence on service-delivery systems and professionals. This means that planning for and anticipating transition or discharge must be a part of every individual plan. Where do people who have received services go once their goals have been met? Hopefully they develop coping skills and other resources and learn to rely on themselves, family, friends, church, peer support, and civic groups—the natural supports and resources within the community. Providers have an obligation to repeatedly re-evaluate the individual's and family's readiness to discontinue services entirely or to transition to a lower level of care. Sometimes some individuals do need ongoing professional services and supports, but can preserve their gains and/or make continual progress with a mix of community, family, and peer-based support, along with limited professional services, as compared to dependence on a full menu of comprehensive care.

Providers will frequently ask how to write an individual plan and demonstrate the medical necessity of "maintenance." Admittedly, this is difficult. Although the idea of maintenance has long been a part of at least the mental health lexicon, it is a concept that is effectively foreign to the notion of recovery. In recovery, individuals and families are always working to the point where they are self-sustaining, living beyond the challenges of mental illness and addictions, and relying on the natural supports of the community. Perhaps they have need for limited and specific professional services, such as medications, but that is a far cry from the idea of being "maintained" in a state of illness.

As much as possible, individual plans should reflect the individual's recovery goals and not foster dependence and promote disability and maintenance. There is little question that many individuals are impacted by the disincentives of disability benefits as well as a legacy of misinformation about mental illness and addictive disorders and their potential for recovery. The obligation of the provider is to educate and encourage; the review, update, and reassessment can be seen as yet another opportunity for providing hope and encouragement.

When individuals have reached a point of readiness for transition or discharge, a final review and reassessment is in order. Ideally, all case or episode-of-care closures and transitions are anticipated and consistent with the individual plan. Regrettably, people all too often leave mental health and addiction recovery services by simply never returning, either celebrating their success or expressing their frustration and disappointment with their feet. This is something to be avoided as much as possible. A planned and thoughtful transition is an opportunity for the members of the team to share their experiences in working together for the success of the individual and family. It provides closure and a chance to wish them well as they continue on their recovery journey—perhaps to return at some point in the future, perhaps never to be seen again.

Some of the questions to consider at transition or discharge include: Is their discharge or transition planned or precipitous? Are they ready? Have the goals been achieved to the individual's and family's satisfaction? Have they received the services and help they were hoping for? Do they have the skills they need in order to succeed? Are they ready for the next leg of the journey?

Do they have a map? Do they have their provisions? Do they know the way back if they need to return? What barriers exist to their re-entry?

Ensuring that the needs of the individual and family at transition or discharge are met is critical to their success. Much of this should have been anticipated long prior to the actual time of transition. However, at the moment of transition, it is important to re-assess the individual's and family's readiness and the availability and appropriateness of post-transition arrangements and resources—either professional, community, and/or peer-based. Ensuring that the individual and family fully understand what they need to do, and how to access the resources that they need, is all part of the process.

Assessment of ongoing service needs is highly individual and somewhat setting-specific. Individuals leaving an inpatient or residential setting will likely have fairly immediate needs for some sort of outpatient follow-up; someone completing a brief course of individual psychotherapy may have no anticipated future needs; and many of the persons completing drug rehab counseling will need to be participating in community-based 12-step programs as part of their recovery promotion plan. Involving the individual and family in this planning process is essential, and their preferences and choices must be the guide. The availability of resources will also inevitably play a role in shaping the plan.

Arrangements for follow-up and continuing care need to create a continuum of services for individuals that may include linking individuals and families with relevant supports in the community, follow-up with the person at regular intervals, access to peer or aftercare groups, and educating individuals about continuing care options, such as pharmacotherapy. For many individuals and families, part of the journey of recovery is accepting the risk of relapse or recurrence and the possibility that mental illness and addictive disorders may require additional treatment or supports at some future point in time. Systems must be designed so that individuals do not face barriers to reassessment, re-entry into services, and re-activation of service plans should that become necessary.

A person-centered approach, focused on a long-term view of recovery, should consider including a mechanism for providing on-going monitoring, feedback, and encouragement. This should also include linkage to natural supports in the community and, when necessary, re-engagement and early re-intervention monitoring, feedback and support. White et al.[1] propose a Behavioral Health Recovery Management model which calls for "sustained monitoring and recovery support services [which] contrasts with models that provide repeated episodes characterized by 'assess, admit, treat, and discharge,' as is traditional in the treatment of substance use disorders. It also contrasts with mental health programs that focus on stabilization and maintenance of symptom suppression rather than on recovery and personal growth."

Another aspect of the review process at transition or discharge involves the preparation of a summary document. Whether this record of services and accomplishments attained by the individual and family is a document maintained in the clinical record, is given to the individual and family, or is transmitted to another provider, it is still very useful to have what is, in essence, a final integration of the plan. This summary should include at minimum:

- a brief description of the reasons that the individual and family initially sought services
- the formulation that guided the development of the plan
- the strengths that were recognized and built upon
- the discharge/transition criteria—the goals
- the major services or interventions provided
- the changes and growth that occurred as a result of the interventions and service
- current and anticipated future service needs

As appropriate, the transition or discharge summary may include additional information such as diagnosis, medications, health concerns, medical treatments, and so on. Accreditation standards all require that a "transition summary," "continuing care plan," or "discharge summary" be prepared and include essential elements such as those previously listed. This plan can then be utilized to facilitate continuity of services as individuals and families move from one provider and setting to another. These records are also helpful if an individual or family leaves services and then returns seeking help anew.

Evaluating Provider Performance

Not only is it essential to evaluate the progress of the individual and family in their journey towards wellness and recovery, from time to time it is important to evaluate how well the provider is doing in meeting the needs of those seeking services. Recovery is not only about the destination, it is also about the journey. Understanding the provider's role in helping individuals toward their final destination should be a part of the process of ongoing learning and quality improvement. In a sense, the provider is on a journey as well, to be the best possible coach and facilitator of others' recovery.

Providers have at least two masters to satisfy. In a traditional sense, their supervisor, agency director, and/or payer are their boss. However, in a recovery-oriented approach, the ultimate judges of the performance of the provider (and system) are the individual and family receiving of services. An evaluation process to assess provider performance should include these three components of feedback, evaluation, and accountability.

From the Individuals' Perspective...

Over the past 10 years there has been increasing use of formal consumer survey tools to gain feedback from the recipients of services and from their family members about their perception and experience of services. This is different from a mere evaluation of satisfaction and instead attempts an understanding of key or critical points in the service-delivery process.

The Mental Health Statistics Improvement Project (MHSIP) consumer survey has become a virtual standard in the field. The adult version, along with a children's and parent's version, has been used successfully with a wide range of service recipients in many different settings to obtain feedback from individuals and families. Tables 9.1 and 9.2, respectively, are samples of the adult and family versions of the MHSIP surveys. Many of the items pertain immediately to how the individual and family perceive and experience the process of treatment planning and the role that they as consumers play in determining their goals and treatment. These surveys are an excellent tool for providing feedback to providers about their performance at being person-centered.

From an Administrative Perspective...

Providers, either solo practitioners or members of large organized care delivery systems, should have some periodic ongoing and formal quality assessment and review of their work. This should include, at minimum, a review of records that not only considers the quantity and timeliness of record documents but also addresses the "quality" of the documentation. There are multiple purposes to such reviews, including efforts to improve the quality of services provided to each individual, assess appropriateness and patterns of utilization of services, and identify training needs.

TABLE 9.1   MHSIP Adult Consumer Survey

	Strongly Agree	Agree	I am Neutral	Disagree	Strongly Disagree	Not Applicable
1. I like the services that I received here.						
2. If I had other choices, I would still get services from this agency.						
3. I would recommend this agency to a friend or family member.						
4. The location of services was convenient (parking, public transportation, distance, etc.).						
5. Staff were willing to see me as often as I felt it was necessary.						
6. Staff returned my call in 24 hours.						
7. Services were available at times that were good for me.						
8. I was able to get all the services I thought I needed.						
9. I was able to see a psychiatrist when I wanted to.						
10. Staff here believe that I can grow, change and recover.						
11. I felt comfortable asking questions about my treatment and medication.						
12. I felt free to complain.						

(Continued)

TABLE 9.1   (*Continued*)

	Strongly Agree	Agree	I am Neutral	Disagree	Strongly Disagree	Not Applicable
13. I was given information about my rights.						
14. Staff encouraged me to take responsibility for how I live my life.						
15. Staff told me what side effects to watch out for.						
16. Staff respected my wishes about who is and who is not to be given information about my treatment.						
17. I, not staff, decided my treatment goals.						
18. Staff were sensitive to my cultural background (race, religion, language, etc.)						
19. Staff helped me obtain the information I needed so that I could take charge of managing my illness.						
20. I was encouraged to use consumer-run programs (support groups, drop-in centers, crisis lines, etc.).						

In order to provide the best possible mental health services, we need to know what you think about the services you received during the last [specify time period], the people who provided it, and the results. There is space at the end of the survey to comment on any of your answers.

TABLE 9.1 (*Continued*)

	Strongly Agree	Agree	I am Neutral	Disagree	Strongly Disagree	Not Applicable
As a direct result of services I received						
21. I deal more effectively with daily problems.						
22. I am better able to control my life.						
23. I am better able to deal with crisis.						
24. I am getting along better with my family.						
25. I do better in social situations.						
26. I do better in school and/or work.						
27. My housing situation has improved.						
28. My symptoms are not bothering me as much.						

TABLE 9.2   Youth Services Survey for Families (YSS-F)

Please help our agency make services better by answering some questions about the services your child received **OVER THE LAST 6 MONTHS.** Your answers are confidential and will not influence the services you or your child receive. Please indicate if you **Strongly Disagree, Disagree**, are **Undecided, Agree**, or **Strongly Agree** with each of the statements below. Put a cross **(X)** in the box that best describes your answer. Thank you!!!

1 = *Strongly disagree*; 2 = *Disagree*; 3 = *Undecided*; 4 = *Agree*; 5 = *Strongly Agree*.

	1	2	3	4	5
1. Overall, I am satisfied with the services my child received.					
2. I helped to choose my child's services.					
3. I helped to choose my child's treatment goals.					
4. The people helping my child stuck with us no matter what.					
5. I felt my child had someone to talk to when he/she was troubled.					
6. I participated in my child's treatment.					
7. The services my child and/or family received were right for us.					
8. The location of services was convenient for us.					
9. Services were available at times that were convenient for us.					
10. My family got the help we wanted for my child.					
11. My family got as much help as we needed for my child.					
12. Staff treated me with respect.					
13. Staff respected my family's religious/spiritual beliefs.					
14. Staff spoke with me in a way that I understood.					
15. Staff were sensitive to my cultural/ethnic background.					

TABLE 9.2   (*Continued*)

	1	2	3	4	5
As a result of the services my child and/or family received:					
16. My child is better at handling daily life.					
17. My child gets along better with family members.					
18. My child gets along better with friends and other people.					
19. My child is doing better in school and/or work.					
20. My child is better able to cope when things go wrong.					
21. I am satisfied with our family life right now.					

22. What has been the most helpful thing about the services you and your child received over the **last 6 months**?

23. What would improve the services here?

Please answer the following questions to let us know how your child is doing.

24. How long did your child receive services from this Center?

☐ a.   Less than 1 month

☐ b.   1–2 month

☐ c.   3–5 months

☐ d.   6 months to 1 year

☐ e.   More than 1 year

25. Is your child still getting services from this Center?   ☐ Yes   ☐ No

26. Is your child currently living with you?   ☐ Yes   ☐ No

27. Has your child lived in any of the following places in the **last 6 months**? (CHECK ALL THAT APPLY)

☐ a.   With one or both parents   ☐ g.   Group home

☐ b.   With another family member   ☐ h.   Residential treatment center

☐ c.   Foster home   ☐ i.   Hospital

☐ d.   Therapeutic foster home   ☐ j.   Local jail or detention facility

☐ e.   Crisis Shelter   ☐ k.   State correctional facility

TABLE 9.2   (*Continued*)

☐ f.   Homeless shelter   ☐ l.   Runaway/homeless/on
                                          the streets
                                  ☐ m.   Other (describe): _____

28. In the last year, did your child see a medical doctor (or nurse) for a health check up or because he/she was sick? (Check one)

☐ Yes, in a clinic or office   ☐ Yes, but only in a hospital   ☐ No   ☐ Do not
                                       emergency room   remember

29. Is your child on medication for emotional/behavioral problems?   ☐ Yes   ☐ No

   29a. If yes, did the doctor or nurse tell you and/or your child what side effects to watch for?   ☐ Yes   ☐ No

30. In the last month, did your child get arrested by the police?   ☐ Yes   ☐ No

31. In the last month, did your child go to court for something he/she did?   ☐ Yes   ☐ No

32. How often was your child absent from school during the last month?

        ☐ 1 day or less
        ☐ 2 days
        ☐ 3 to 5 days
        ☐ 6 to 10 days
        ☐ More than 10 days
        ☐ Not applicable/not in school
        ☐ Do not remember

Please answer the following questions to let us know a little about your child.
Child's Race: (Check two if needed)
___ American Indian/Alaskan Native   ___ White (Caucasian)   ___ Black (African
                                                                                      American)
___ Asian/Pacific Islander   ___ Other: Describe _____
Are either of the child's parents Spanish/Hispanic/Latino?   ___ Yes   ___ No
Child's Birth Date:_____
Child's Gender: ___ Male   ___ Female
Does your child have Medicaid insurance?   ___ Yes   ___ No

Thank you for taking the time to answer these questions!

This instrument was developed as part of the State Indictor Project funded by the Center for Mental Heath Services (CMHS). It was adapted from the Family Satisfaction Questionnaire used with the CMHS Comprehensive Community Mental Services for Children and their Families Program and the MHSIP Consumer Survey.

Accreditation standards typically require that records be reviewed in an ongoing manner to determine if:

- the psychosocial assessment is comprehensive
- the written plan follows the assessment conclusions
- goals and objectives are based on active input from the individual and are understandable to the individual
- objectives are measurable and appropriate
- services delivered relate to the goals and objectives
- co-occurring disorders are addressed
- progress is documented and relates to the plan
- the plan is regularly reviewed and updated

Records may be reviewed for a whole host of other reasons or concerns, including documentation of service provision for billing and medical necessity. Rather than being prescriptive or comprehensive, the above list is meant to suggest at least some quality-of care-concerns that should be reflected and documented in the record.

Some organizations have gone so far as to quantify the record review by assigning points to the different elements and then arriving at a total score for that record (and provider). Other organizations have developed automated databases that capture the findings of a record and prepare reports that can be easily given to providers and their supervisors. No matter the methodology, the goal is to give providers feedback about their performance and to continually improve the quality of documentation and services delivered to the individual.

Ideally, record reviews should be tied directly into the organization's information management system and should be used to improve the quality of services. Regular reports of overall results should be made available to key staff responsible for quality improvement and management. Typically such reports are analyzed for trends and are reported in aggregate form to a larger audience. Findings should also be shared with individual providers so that they have an opportunity to make necessary corrections and improvements. Examples of organizational changes that can occur as a result of quality records review may include additional training or the allocation of funding for staff training, program design and implementation, personnel assignments, evaluation of staff competencies, and improved outcomes.

A quality record review may also be organized as a peer-review effort and involve direct-care staff. By involving the actual providers in the review, direct learning occurs through the process of understanding and reviewing a set of criteria that reflects appropriate documentation of quality services. If the organization is truly recovery-oriented, then it may also include "recovery coaches" (staff who are in recovery who may or may not be providing direct services) in the peer-review process. No matter who the peer reviewers are, they all need to receive training on how to evaluate records from a quality perspective. When training does not occur, the strength and purpose of the peer-review process is at risk of being devalued by the recipients of the review. Initially, staff members may be somewhat resistant to a peer-review process, as they are hesitant to examine and comment upon their colleague's work, and equally reluctant to have their own work evaluated. However, if presented as a learning tool for overall program improvement, the process is usually accepted and becomes a dynamic method for staff to support each other in improving their skills, knowledge, and abilities. Additionally, it is important to educate staff that the process provides aggregate information to assist management in making decisions related to the organization's staff education and training.

Another approach is to utilize supervisors in the review system or to engage external reviewers such as contract quality improvement organizations or consultants. If the process is a supervisory one, then it usually becomes part of the employee's annual job performance review, and may take the form of a *compliance* or *quality assurance audit*, instead of a *continuous quality improvement* focus. Often the purpose of such reviews is to assure that there is adequate documentation to support the medical necessity of all billed services—ranging from assessments and services plans within specified time frames to notes documenting each service provided.

Regardless of exactly how such a review is conducted, or the specific objectives, ranging from quality improvement to compliance assurance, it is essential that the expectations and values implicit in the review be consistent with the principles of a person-centered approach to planning and providing services. Few things are more maddening and demoralizing for staff than to be taught one set of values and expectations only to find that in reality they are held to another set of standards. In organizations attempting to shift from earlier practice approaches to a recovery-oriented, person-centered model, inconsistencies between training expectations and performance review findings can seriously undermine staff spirit and ultimately erode quality of care. There must be an alignment of expectations and standards throughout the system; providers (especially those working in organized systems of care) cannot effect the necessary changes on their own, no matter how committed to the principles and values they may be. Real change must occur at all levels of a system in order for the vision and hope of person-centered recovery-oriented care to be a reality for all individuals and families served.

Table 9.3 includes a sample review tool that provides an example of how a record review can be organized and the review points highlighted. This particular sample is a combination of both quantitative and qualitative measures which are derived from a range of sources including licensure and certification requirements along with accreditation standards. The required "due dates" for completing the various elements of the record are arbitrary and only meant to be illustrative. An organization should determine the elements of a record review form that best meets its needs in order to support conformance to internal policies and procedures, billing documentation, external accountability, and regulatory demands.

Outcomes

No matter how well written standards are, how well designed the system is, or how well trained the reviewers may be, standards and criteria are always open to interpretation. Determining the quality of documentation and the fidelity of a person-centered approach to planning will always be seen through the eyes of the beholder! Each evaluator, despite using the same set of standards, will bring their own set of values and experiences into the process and might view the same criteria differently. The most important consideration overall is to remember that the ultimate evaluator of quality is the individual receiving services, based on the *outcomes* for each individual.

Table 9.4, *Milestones in Recovery From Mental Illness,* presents an integrated set of outcomes or milestones developed by individuals, families, and providers from Stanislaus County, California.[2] This is an excellent example of identifying outcomes from the perspective of adults with mental illness. The eight clear milestones described in the recovery process are all components of successful person-centered outcomes. These milestones, similar in thought and process to the Alcoholics Anonymous 12 Steps to Recovery, are also aligned with the stages of change model. In addition, subjective and objective indicators make explicit what one could expect to experience within the eight milestones. There are successes for each person's milestone, not a finite end to the individual's journey.

Historically, outcome measurements have tended to focus on predefined social goods, such as employment, housing, school attendance, reduced hospitalization, incarceration, and so on. There is no question that these are, for the most part, desirable benefits from services, but they

TABLE 9.3   Recovery Record Review Form

Indicator	Criteria	Frequency	Critical Value	Reviewer's Comments
1. Initial Intake/ Screening	Intake form is completed	Same day as admission		
2. Medical exam	History and physical form is completed	Within 5 days of admission		
3. Preliminary Recovery Plan	Form is completed and filed in the record	Within 5 days of admission		
4. Orientation completed	Orientation checklist is signed and filed in the record	Within 7 days of admission		
5. Complete and thorough psychosocial assessment	Includes all domains and the person's strengths, needs, abilities and preferences	Within 10 days of admission and annual update		
6. Interpretive summary	Includes the person's strengths, needs, abilities and preferences, level of care, duration of treatment, co-occurring diagnoses	Within 10 days of admission		
7. Complete Recovery Plan	Includes documentation of a planning meeting, the person's signature, and filed in record	Within 15 days of admission		

Critical Value = points on a scale of 1–3, with 3 representing full compliance, 2 partial compliance, and 1 no compliance. Highest possible score is 51.

TABLE 9.3   (*Continued*)

Indicator	Criteria	Frequency	Critical Value	Reviewer's Comments
8. Goals on plan follow the assessment summary	Goals relate to the assessment summary information			
9. Goals are understandable to the person and are based on his/her input	Goals are expressed in the words of the person			
10. Goals are broad, long term, written positively	They represent the person's needs and are not deficit based			
11. Objectives are on the plan	They relate to goals, are action oriented, steps to achieving the goal(s)			
12. Objectives are measurable and under standable	It can be identified when they are achieved and the person is actually able to do them			
13. Objectives are time framed	Each objective has an anticipated time frame to be accomplished			

(*Continued*)

TABLE 9.3 (*Continued*)

Indicator	Criteria	Frequency	Critical Value	Reviewer's Comments
14. Interventions are identified	These can be services provided by the staff, others, natural supports, family members			
15. Interventions are provided by...	Identification of who is providing services, including credential, title, or affiliation			
16. Interventions happen when and how often	Frequency of services is identified			
17. The plan is reviewed and updated	Progress notes indicate a planning meeting has occurred, the plan itself is revised, a quarterly report is written	At least quarterly		
		TOTAL		

TABLE 9.4   Milestones in Recovery from Mental Illness

There are many paths to recovery. The following key milestones in the recovery process were developed by consensus groups involving individuals, families and providers. They were developed from the individual's point of view and identify those key accomplishments that are commonly part of the progression in the recovery process. There are many other accomplishments in numerous life domains that may be part of the breadth of an individual's recovery that are not included in this table.

	Subjective	Objective
R	I begin to **Recognize** my inner distress but may be unable to identify what it is.	Beginning awareness of problem(s) within oneself.
E	I begin to **Examine** my distress with the help of others.	Willingness to discuss problems and accept help.
C	I **Choose** to believe that hope exists.	Begin to believe that hope and recovery is possible.
O	I start **Overcoming** symptoms that keep me from examining what is important to me.	Coping with symptoms and examining life circumstances.
V	I **Voluntarily** take some action toward recovery.	Take action step(s) directed towards recovery.
E	I start to **Enjoy** the benefits of mutual recovery.	Actively participates in mutual aid, peer support and experiences benefits of recovery.
R	I am **Responsible** for my own recovery.	Takes ownership and responsibility for one's own recovery.
Y	**Yes**, I am helping others strengthen my recovery.	Being of service to others strengthens one's own recovery.

are not necessarily person-centered. For the individual who, for whatever reasons, is *not* interested in working, measures of employment do not match well and are not a meaningful assessment of outcome. The eight milestones offer an alternative approach to evaluating outcomes that focuses on the individual and family and their recovery process, as well as their capacity to make choices and manage their own lives. There is more work and research needed in the mental health and addictive disorders field in developing meaningful and relevant approaches to outcome measurement. The challenge is to rethink past approaches and to create outcome measurement tools that are consistent with person-centered approaches to services and individual self-defined recovery goals. The Stanislaus milestones are only one example of how this could be accomplished.

III. MAKING IT HAPPEN

In this final section, the review and update of the plans for Aaron, Sally, Sam, and Carmen are considered. For Aaron, this review is but a rest stop in his journey; for Sally it is a vista point with a new understanding and view of the road that lays ahead. Sam's update is an example of the unexpected detours and change of course that can happen while traveling, and the new opportunities and challenges that can arise. For Carmen, her review describes the satisfaction, re-evaluation, and transition planning that occurs when the destination is reached. Taken together, these four examples provide illustrations of the various functions and impacts of the review process and its importance to person-centered planning and recovery. No plan is complete without it.

Aaron

Ninety days later, Aaron Howard's plan review notes that he has reduced his aggressive behaviors; however, he is still experiencing difficulty with wetting himself. The foster family would like to see services continued and Aaron is feeling some measure of success so he is willing to carry on.

No new goals are identified and continuing to focus on the existing goals and objectives are appropriate to the situation. However, two new interventions are introduced and the plan is updated to reflect the completion and termination of previous interventions. The psychological evaluation has been completed and there is no evidence of any significant neurocognitive problems that might impact Aaron's treatment or his progress. However, Aaron has not yet shown significant response or benefit to date from the sand tray therapy, and it has been suggested that perhaps peer support/therapy might be more effective. Accordingly, peer therapy group once a week for 120 days was added as a new intervention. In addition, as an example of the use of natural supports within the community, the plan is for Aaron to join a sports team so that he has additional structured and supervised opportunities to interact with peers and work on developing prosocial and adaptive skills in expressing his anger and controlling his aggressive behavior.

The neurological evaluation has indicated there is no physical explanation for Aaron's continued problems of enuresis. The urologist and the psychologist believe his bladder control problems are "functional" and the result of a post-traumatic stress reaction related to trauma and separation from his birth family. He is being treated with imipramine and DDAVP nasal spray which is possibly beginning to show some benefit. There is the possibility that the imipramine may be also be helping to relieve some underlying depressive symptoms which may also play a role in his aggression.

Sally

Sally Hamilton has satisfied all of her legal obligations by completing the 10-week educational program and the four motivational counseling sessions. As a result of what she has learned from the experience, Sally is now more aware of how her use of alcohol over the years has caused repeated problems in her life. During the required exit interview, it became apparent that she has moved from the pre-contemplation stage to the contemplation stage of change. Sally was able to acknowledge that she was in need of some changes in her life and some help to achieve them. She was able to articulate a new goal of learning more about addiction and how to reduce her use of alcohol.

For the next 8 weeks Sally is willing to explore altering her drinking behavior and to invite her daughter to the family educational sessions. In addition, she will continue the motivational counseling sessions on a weekly basis, increasing the intensity from a 1/2 hour to 1 hour. Therefore, her plan has changed to reflect a new goal, a new objective, and new interventions. Sally is still not committing to total abstinence or a life of recovery; instead, the door has been opened to look at the impact of her drinking on herself and others, via education and exposure to some new ideas that she is willing to consider and learn more about.

The interventions continue, on balance, to be more didactic than introspective in nature, with more motivational counseling to enhance her knowledge base and to challenge some of her old beliefs. This approach is consistent with her contemplation stage of change. At the conclusion of the 8 weeks, she and her addictions counselor will re-evaluate her status and progress using the Stages of Change Readiness and Treatment Eagerness Scale (SOCRATES) standardized assessment tool to help determine any further service needs.

Sam

Sam Hewlett's individual plan is reviewed 60 days from the initiation of the first objective, which was the time frame for him to secure Section 8 housing. Sam's story takes a somewhat unexpected turn at this point in that what was initially a life-enhancement goal has now come to figure more prominently. As described on the update and review page, after little success in the rental market and with time on the voucher running low, his case manager approached Sam's family about the possibility of renting a vacant in-law unit on their property to Sam under the Section 8 voucher.

The family agreed, but with some caveats, cautions, and clear expectations, especially given their past history with Sam and his struggles with mental illness, substance abuse, and treatment. Sam was willing to accept their conditions for a number of reasons: he wanted to be closer to his ill mother, he wanted to begin to repair his relationship with his family, he was starting to feel better as a result of his treatment, he was more motivated to address his substance dependence issues, and he did not want to lose his Section 8 voucher. Although somewhat ambivalent and anxious about making a commitment to sobriety, Sam was willing to accept this requirement from his parents along with their expectation that he keep the apartment neat, clean, and safe. Sam was quick to acknowledge that he would need help with both of these expectations and challenges.

The second objective was created at the plan review session and proposes the expectation that Sam will maintain his living situation in his parent's in-law unit for the next 6 months. While 6 months is a somewhat extended interval, it is consistent in terms of Sam's goals and recent progress, and in no way precludes a quarterly interval review of the plan to ensure his continued progress.

The original goal and discharge/transition criteria have remained the same; in a well crafted plan, that should often be the case. The goal is stable until the discharge/transition criteria are met, and it is the objectives that change more frequently. The barriers to his goal have perhaps shifted—it is more a matter of emphasis than having new barriers surface. It is arguable that the barriers section of the original plan should be updated and changed, but this is a matter of judgment. His parent's new requirements for Sam to live in the in-law unit are unequivocally defined in the barriers section of the update page.

The additional interventions in support of the new objective are clearly responsive to the parent's expectations and are consistent with Sam's expressed motivations. Once again, a caveat is warranted: these are not the entirety of interventions and services that would likely be needed to help Sam achieve his objective and goal, and providers with different philosophies and different approaches might choose a somewhat different course. For the purposes of demonstrating the individual plan process, it is clear that all of the interventions are in support of Sam meeting his objective, and the contribution of each intervention is clearly stated.

Carmen

Following a series of successful interventions, Carmen Suarez is ready to be discharged from the mental health center and a discharge/transition summary has been prepared. Although her life goal and life enhancement goal are not resolved, her service goal of returning to school has been achieved—she is now attending classes regularly. It may be tempting for a caring provider to want to intervene and further engage Carmen. Clearly she still needs to more fully address her family issues, her grief over her abortion, and her newly discovered binge alcohol use. However, Carmen has benefited significantly from the services she received and she has been able to focus on resolving her immediate needs. In addition, she has found support in the community via Alcoholics Anonymous and the peer group at Barrios Unidos. Carmen now knows that she can seek help from professionals without shame and stigma, and she is aware of the services available should she decide to return and address those other issues.

REFERENCES

1. White, W., Boyle, M., Loveland, D., Corrington, P. *The Behavioral Health Recovery Management Project: A Brief Primer.* Peoria, IL: Fayette Companies and Chestnut Health Systems.
2. Carroll, A. Personal communication. Modesto, CA: Stanislaus County Behavioral Health and Recovery Services.

Epilogue

The following true stories about individual success help to prove the value of person-centered planning in support of recovery and wellness in a way that no amount of teaching, preaching, or theory ever can.

The first vignette about Ms. E. L. is written by a provider, Frances, who approached the whole idea of the developing person-centered recovery management plans with skepticism about their value and utility for the individual as well as for the provider. Frances believed that she was already "doing it," and believed that she routinely allowed individuals seeking help make their own decisions about goals and services. In retrospect, this provider now realizes that learning new skills in developing person-centered plans has taught her how to do a better job of facilitating rather than being the decision maker for the individual.

Frances now realizes that many times in the past she worked to protect the individual and unwittingly discouraged the individual's real goals. Inevitably she would act on behalf of the individual instead of promoting recovery and empowerment—and in doing so she was not truly being person-centered. By adopting a person-centered approach to developing recovery management plans, this provider has learned that working to establish a true collaborative partnership with the individual is a far more effective approach.

Pete, a service recipient, writes the second vignette. His story speaks for itself.

Treatment Planning for Person Centered Care
Copyright © 2005 by Elsevier Inc. All rights reserved.

Ms. E. L.

Ms. E. L. is a 49-year-old woman who has been diagnosed with bipolar disorder and severe substance use disorders for over 25 years. She had experienced numerous traumatic events in her youth and young adulthood and often complained of high levels of anxiety, including fear of abandonment, difficulties interacting with other, and a preference for avoiding others.

Since Ms. E. L. began receiving services in 1989, she had undergone either psychiatric hospitalization or inpatient treatment for substance dependence on an average of four times annually. Ms. E. L. was viewed as a difficult client by many providers who appeared to be caught in a vicious cycle of repeated episodes of substance use and worsened bipolar symptoms that in turn increased her likelihood of further substance abuse. Typically her treatment plan focused on goals that were suggested by her provider over which she felt she had little input or control: stopping her substance use, taking medications, and staying out of the hospital. Throughout her treatment, Ms. E. L. had always expressed a desire to attend college but she was convinced that she would fail due to her psychiatric disability and substance abuse. Ms. E. L. had some limited encouragement to pursue this goal, but it seemed that whenever she truly entertained this possibility she became overwhelmed and typically had to be re-hospitalized.

Several years ago, Ms. E. L. changed providers and had the opportunity to develop a person-centered recovery management plan. Her initial recovery goals were to improve her relationships with others, and to develop assertiveness skills in order to avoid allowing others to take advantage of her. What had been an overwhelming goal in the past somehow now seemed more manageable. Building on her plan, Ms. E. L. began to report feeling more empowered in her relationships and more confident about her ability to achieve her goals.

Soon she established new goals related to academic and career pursuits. Ms. E. L. recognized that if she wanted to attend college she would have to stay out of the hospital. She also realized that much of her symptoms and problems could be managed, when given the tools, knowledge, and skills for making choices in her everyday life. The most important choice she made for herself was to discontinue her substance use. She decided to involve herself in a Dual Disorder Treatment Program, and, in addition to her psychiatric and individual therapy, she attended groups to address substance-abuse issues.

Ms. E. L. also determined that it was important to recognize the signs suggesting that her bipolar disorder might be worsening and learn how to take preventive action to re-stabilize herself. During the year that Ms. E. L. worked on these goals, she reduced the number of times she required inpatient treatment from four to one. Encouraged further by her treatment successes, Ms. E. L. sought admission to college and was accepted.

Ms. E. L. was understandably anxious about her ability to perform at the college level. Rather than falling back on old habits of substance abuse to cope with this anxiety, she devoted therapy time to addressing these anxieties and learning how to use relaxation and hypnotic procedures to remain calm.

Ms. E. L. attributes her success to the recovery process and the support and understanding of her provider. The process of developing a plan that Ms. E. L. felt reflected her own concerns, understanding, hopes, and dreams made a huge difference. The therapist encouraged Ms E. L. to set goals that she viewed as important and then helped her to outline the steps (objectives) that she needed to take to in order to accomplish those goals. As Ms. E. L. took increasing self-responsibility for the recovery process, she also took ownership of the service planning process with increasing involvement in both her treatment services as well as community activities. Her success spurred her to attempt goals that, while important to her, had previously been seen as unattainable.

Pete

I am a 50-year-old white male, who was a heavy drug user, unemployed most of most my adult life, and was diagnosed with manic depressiveness. I slept only 2 to 3 hours a night, and did not stay on my medication because of the side effects. When I did take the medication I would sleep 13 to 14 hours a day and I would be sexually impotent. I could not tolerate these side effects so I would just stop taking my medications. I would continually get into trouble with the law and would be in and out of jail. I would move from place to place. I was actually homeless, even though I would find people who would let me stay with them for short periods of time. I was also at times hospitalized in an inpatient setting rather than in jail.

In 2001, the court system forced me into a mental health center for services. This time the case worker that was assigned to me asked if I wanted to be a part of a project using a recovery model. As I realized that

I had hit bottom and recognized that I had a problem, I knew I needed to try something and if it was about recovery then I was willing to try. The recovery model gave me the choice of what I wanted to work on.

I decided that I wanted a job, even though at that time I was not substance free. My rationale was that I needed some money in my pocket so that I could get housing, which would assist me from walking away from the people in the drug culture whose places I could "crash in," which would assist me in becoming drug free.

The worker did not agree with my choice but respected that I needed to try this my way. He is now not only my therapist but a mentor and a partner with me in my recovery. He assisted me in finding employment. At first I worked part-time and now I am working full-time. I have regained driving privileges (a driver's license). Soon after that I got my own place and I have been drug-free for three years.

I have become more active in the community and am not as isolated as before. When setbacks surface, I work the plan. I am able to deal with them and see them as part of the process of recovery.

Wilma Townsend

Appendix A
Child Diagnostic Assessment

Name Aaron K. Howard	**Age** 11 years 5 months	**Client #** 1234

I.   Needs and Challenges Requiring Assistance

Child's Description of Problem

Aaron says: "I just want to live with my mother and brother and sister. Everyone is making a big deal out of things that happened at my house."

Referral Source and Reason for Referral

Referred by the Department of Social Services, who is his guardian, for assistance in managing behavioral and emotional problems that are jeopardizing placement. He was hospitalized several weeks ago for threats to harm others. Aaron is currently in foster care due to physical/emotional abuse by his parents and is having difficulties adjusting to the separation from his biological family. He was removed from his first foster home placement after two months because of bedwetting and anger outbursts with destruction of objects and threats to his foster family. He also has problems with general self care and hygiene.

Family/Guardian Perceptions of Problem

The foster father, Mr. Hosea Sumi, accompanied Aaron to the interview. He states Social Services asked him to call the mental health center for an appointment. He does not know much about Aaron since he has only been living with him for two weeks following his hospital discharge.

Aaron himself seems to have difficulty acknowledging the problems described by his foster mother and Social Services.

Strengths/Capabilities

Aaron says that he likes to play sports. He showed an interest in improving his relationship with others and seems motivated to be able to return home.

Activities of Daily Living

Aaron has problems with bedwetting and toileting. The foster father noted that he does not know how to wipe himself after a bowel movement.

Friendship/Social Peer Support/Relationships

He has difficulty getting along with his peers, particularly in an unstructured play situation. He can be aggressive toward them and demand to get his way.

Meaningful Activities (Community Involvements, Volunteer Activities, Leisure/ Recreation, Other Interests)

Attends Boys' Club 2 days/week.

Community Supports/Self Help Groups (AA, NA, etc.)

Has a Big Brother from a local agency for the past 2 months.

Client Name   Aaron K. Howard   Age   11 years 5 months   Client #   1234

I.   Needs and Challenges Requiring Assistance (*cont*)

Religion/Spirituality

No issues noted. He has not had a religious upbringing, nor does he express any interest in religion or spirituality.

Cultural/Ethnic Issues/Information/Concerns

Aaron is African-American. His foster family is Japanese-American.

Communication Needs   ☐ TDD/TTY Device   ☐ Sign Language Interpreter

☑ None Reported   ☐ Assistive Listening Device(s)   ☐ Language Interpreter Services Needed

☐ Other Spoken Language _____

☐ Preferred language_____

II.   Description of Needs/Preferences

In order to describe the age-appropriate needs and preferences for the identified child/adolescent, the provider should have a meaningful focused dialogue about recovery and wellness with the child. This should help identify individual needs and preferences as well as challenges.

1. Behavioral Health Clinical and Rehabilitative Services Needed

Mr. Sumi reported that his wife has recently said she is afraid of Aaron because of his outbursts, and he wants help so that Aaron can stay in their home. He hopes for some support and advice to better manage Aaron's behavior, and for some help in knowing how to talk to Aaron about "old problems" that he might have so he can learn ways to handle his feelings. Aaron stated that he would like to get along better with other children.

2. Environmental Supports Needed

Aaron has been placed on a half-day school schedule because of his behavior. He misses the opportunity to participate in school activities, including team sports and wants to be able to play soccer at school. He has been excluded from school sports because of aggressive and disruptive behavior.

3. Goals

Aaron and his foster parents agree that they hope that as a result of services Aaron will remain safe, succeed in his current foster home, and work towards reuniting with his mother and siblings.

4. Barriers

Aaron needs to gain better control over his feelings of anger and frustration and find non-violent ways of expressing his feelings. He also needs to improve his self care.

5. Priorities

Help Aaron maintain current foster placement.

Client Name Aaron K. Howard	**Age** 11 years 5 months	**Client #** 1234

III. Pertinent Developmental Issues

Mother's Pregnancy History

Alcohol and other drug abuse are suspected.

☐ no problems reported

Infancy (age 0 – 1)

Reportedly met developmental milestones within expected age ranges.

☐ No problems reported

Preschool (age 2 – 4)

Did not attend.

☐ No problems reported or not pertinent

Childhood (age 5 – 12)

Some problems in toileting and self care.

☐ No problems reported or not pertinent

Adolescent (age 13 – 17)

☑ No problems reported or not pertinent

Pertinent Sexual Issues/ Concerns

☑ No problems reported or not pertinent

IV. Living Situation/Social Information

Living Situation   ☐ Parent's Home   ☐ Relative's Home   ☐ Friend's Home
☑ Foster Home   ☐ Respite Care   ☐ Group Home   ☐ Homeless

Primary Household

Household Members (Name)	Relationship to Client	Age	Occupation/Level of Education	Quality of Relationship
Client – Aaron	self	11	student	
Onika Sumi	foster mother	46	homemaker	fair
Hosea Sumi	foster father	47	engineer	fair
Lee Sumi	foster brother	10	student	good

Additional Family Members (i.e., Parents or Siblings not living in primary or secondary households)

Mother, father, sister age 6, brother age 3 (both the sister and brother are in other foster homes). His father is currently in jail. His mother is currently in clean and sober housing after a 30-day rehab program for treatment of her crack-cocaine dependence.

Pertinent Family History

Aaron's biological father reportedly has a history of paranoid schizophrenia and his mother is reportedly of borderline intellectual functioning (per Social Services). According to Social Services' documentation, Aaron's parents abused and neglected him and his siblings, and both parents have a history of mental health and substance problems. The father was also physically abusive to Aaron's mother. He is currently incarcerated for attempted homicide involving a former landlord. His mother is reportedly motivated to regain custody of her children.

Name Aaron K. Howard	**Age** 11 years 5 months	**Client #** 1234

V. Family Environment/Relationships

Parent–Child Relationship(s) *Identify either Primary (P) or Secondary (S) Household*   Foster Family

Parent–Child Conflict	☑ None-mild	☐ Moderate	☐ Severe
Parent Supervision and Monitoring of Child	☑ Always	☐ Usually ☐ Inconsistently	☐ Rarely
Cooperation Between Parents Regarding Child-Rearing	☐ Always	☑ Usually ☐ Inconsistently ☐ Rarely	☐ Not Pertinent
Parent Positive Activities with Child	☑ Frequent	☐ Occasional	☐ Infrequent
Parent Satisfaction with Relationship	☑ Satisfied	☐ Neutral	☐ Dissatisfied
Child Satisfaction with Relationship	☐ Satisfied	☑ Neutral	☐ Dissatisfied

Comment *Describe further, if needed*

Initially, Aaron was well behaved, although he appeared sad and would get up and wander in the house during the night. In the last 2 months, Aaron has been more oppositional and irritable, and this is creating tension in the household. His foster father reports that he has a hearty appetite and his sleep patterns are stable. Although he becomes easily agitated when he is engaged in unstructured play activities with his foster brothers or peers and starts calling people names, his foster father reports that Aaron accepts redirection when given by the foster parents. Aaron was fidgety, but cooperative during the interview with his foster father.

Sibling–Child Relationship(s)   ☐ No Siblings

Child-Sibling(s) Conflict	☐ None-mild	☑ Moderate	☐ Severe
Sibling(s) Positive Activities with Child	☐ Frequent	☐ Occasional	☐ Infrequent
Sibling(s) Satisfaction with Relationship	☐ Satisfied	☐ Neutral	☐ Dissatisfied
Child Satisfaction with Relationship	☐ Satisfied	☐ Neutral	☐ Dissatisfied

Comment *Describe further, if needed*

He states he wants to reunite with his biological brother and sister, and he often asks when he can visit with them. According to the foster mother he has difficulty getting along with the foster siblings at both placements with problems in conflict resolution and aggressive behavior.

Other Family Concerns

Family Member Alcohol Abuse	☐ No	☑ Yes	If **YES**, Indicate ☑ Parent	☐ Sibling	☐ Other
Family Member Substance Abuse	☐ No	☑ Yes	If **YES**, Indicate ☑ Parent	☐ Sibling	☐ Other
Family Member Mental Health Problems	☐ No	☑ Yes	If **YES**, Indicate ☑ Parent	☐ Sibling	☐ Other
Family Member Health Problems	☑ No	☐ Yes	If **YES**, Indicate ☐ Parent	☐ Sibling	☐ Other
Family Member Disability	☐ No	☑ Yes	If **YES**, Indicate ☑ Parent	☐ Sibling	☐ Other
Family Member Legal Issues	☐ No	☑ Yes	If **YES**, Indicate ☑ Parent	☐ Sibling	☐ Other
Family Financial Concerns ☑ No	Yes				

Other (Describe) Biological mother may have some developmental disabilities.

Comment *Specify problems that impact client's needs*

Aaron's mother has relapsed twice before from attempts at drug rehab. She has not tried clean and sober housing before and understands that she needs a minimum of 6 months drug-free before any reunification plan can be initiated.

Name Aaron K. Howard	**Age** 11 years 5 months	**Client #** 1234

Medical History

Aaron was born at 32 weeks gestation after a pregnancy during which mother had only one prenatal visit. Apgars 5 and 8; he required initial stimulation and was placed in the newborn intensive care unit. He had jaundice and mild respiratory problems in the newborn period. He was treated for colic with multiple changes of formula. He had a febrile seizure at age 8 months, and was treated with Dilantin for 1 year. He has been hospitalized for bronchiolitis in his first year, for chelation of an elevated lead level when he was 2 years old, and for asthma when he was 4 years old. He is allergic to penicillin.

VI. Mental Health Treatment History

Outpatient Mental Health Treatment ☑ None Reported

Agency	Current	Past (Date)	Clinician Name

Psychiatric Hospitalizations/Residential Treatment Facilities ☐ None Reported

Facility	Date of Service	Reason (Suicidal, Depressed, Etc.)
Greenfield Psychiatric	5/17/03–5/22/03	Threatened to kill foster family members

Previous or Current Diagnoses (if known) Unknown

Current Medications (Prescription/OTC/Herbal)   ☐ None Reported

Current Medication	**Rationale**	**Total Daily Dosage**	**Compliance**			
			Yes	No	Partial	Unk
Risperdal	Outbursts	5 mg bid	×			
Trazadone	Sleep problems	50 mg	×			
Ritalin	Hyperactivity	40 mg	×			
DDAVAP	Eneuresis		×			
Alupent Inhaler	Asthma	2 puffs prn				×

Primary Care Physician (Name, Phone Number, and Address)

County Health Clinic

Other Prescribing Physician(s)

Past Psychotropic Medications   ☐ None Reported

Psychotropic Medications	**Reason for Discontinuation**
Valproic Acid (temper outbursts)	Ineffective
Adderal (ADHD)	Worsened sleep problems
Strattera (ADHD)	Gastric upset
Imipramine (ADHD—"moodiness")	Constipation, "fainting spell"
Tenex (ADHD—sleep problems)	Daytime drowsiness, worsening behavior

Client Name Aaron K. Howard	**Age** 11 years 5 months	**Client #** 1234

VII. School Functioning

Educational Classification

☐ Regular education classroom, no special services. (If no to this, check all that apply below)

☐ 01 Multiple Disabilities (Not deaf-Blind)	☐ 06 Orthopedic Impairment	☐ 12 Autism
☐ 02 Deaf-Blindness	☑ 08 Emotional Disturbance (SBH)	☐ 13 Traumatic Brain Injury
☐ 03 Deafness (Hearing Impairment)	☐ 09 Mental Retardation (DH)	☐ 14 Other Health Impaired (Major)
☐ 04 Visual Impairment	☐ 10 Specific Learning Disability	☑ 15 Other Health Impaired (Minor)
☐ 05 Speech or Language Impairment	☐ 11 Preschoolers with a Disability	☐ 16 Other

Comments

Grades   He receives mostly C and D grades.

Schools attended

School	Comments
Greenfield Elementary	Completed 4th grade with C grade, required help in the Resource room, multiple behavioral problems noted
Greenfield Middle	Currently in 5th grade

Other test results (IQ, achievement, developmental) ☑ No other tests results reported

Aaron has not had an I.E.P.

Attendance   ☑ Not a problem

Previous grade retentions   ☐ None Reported

Aaron had an extra year of kindergarten "to mature" and because his birthday is late in the year.

Suspensions/expulsions   ☐ None Reported

He has been removed from the after school program (see below).

Other academic/school concerns   ☐ None Reported

He has had repeated behavioral problems at school. He has been verbally and physically aggressive with his peers. He also reportedly exhibited self-injurious behavior at school by trying to cut himself with a ruler, and scratched and pinched himself in the after-school program. The administrator for the after-school sports program asked for his removal because he posed a threat to the other children and also did not accept redirection.

Barriers to learning   ☐ None Reported

Impulsivity, short attention span, inability to stay on task or complete work. Poor fine-motor coordination and handwriting.

Peer relationships/Social functioning   ☐ None Reported

Poor – see above

Name Aaron K. Howard	Age 11 years 5 months	Client # 1234

VII. Alcohol/Drug History

Illegal Drug Use/Abuse Past 12 Months ☑ No ☐ Yes	Prescription Drug Abuse Past 12 Months ☑ No ☐ Yes
Non-Prescription Drug Abuse Past 12 Months ☑ No ☐ Yes	Alcohol Use/Abuse Past 12 Months ☑ No ☐ Yes
Toxicology Screen Completed ☑ No ☐ Yes	Toxicology Screen Results
Presenting with Detox Issues? ☑ No ☐ Yes	Symptoms

Check All That Apply ☐ IV Drug User ☐ Pregnant

Drug/ Substance/ Alcohol	Age of 1st Use	Date of Last Use	Frequency	Amount	Method

Alcohol/Drug Treatment History

AoD Treatment

☑ None

☐ Current – List provider and services received

☐ Past ☐ OP ☐ IOP ☐ Residential ☐ Hospital ☐ Detox ☐ Other

Agency	Date of Service

Other Comments Regarding Substance Abuse/Use *Include AOD use/abuse by other family members/significant others, AOD related legal problems, SAMI stage of treatment (for providers using Dual Disorders Integrated Treatment approach)*

There is some concern that Aaron is at risk as his mother is apparently addicted to cocaine and his natural siblings have used marijuana as well; he has expressed a curiosity about drugs.

IX. Abuse History

☐ No Self Reported History of Abuse/Violence	☑ Physical Abuse	☑ Domestic Violence/ Abuse
☐ Community Violence	☑ Physical Neglect	☑ Emotional Abuse
☐ Elder Abuse	☐ Sexual Abuse/Molestation	☐ Other

Name Aaron K. Howard	**Age** 11 years 5 months	**Client #** 1234

IX.   Abuse History (*cont*)

Comments *Identify if client served as a victim of abuse, or a perpetrator, or both*

Aaron's mother rejected him at birth as he was the product of an unwanted pregnancy and there is some question about his paternity. Since then his mother has been inconsistent with her affection. Aaron has been a victim of physical and emotional abuse and neglect. He has seen his mother abused by his father. He stated that he tried to protect his mother one time from his father by hitting him with a plastic baseball bat when his father was beating her. Due to both of the parents' mental health and substance abuse issues, Aaron and his siblings were often left alone for long stretches of time. He is afraid of the dark and he reports that he has nightmares. He has also been self-injurious as reported in another section of this document.

X.   Employment   ☑ Not Pertinent—Skip this Section

Currently   ☐ Yes   ☐ No   **If YES, Name of Employer**
Employed

Job Title

Employment Interests/Skills/Concerns

XI.   Legal History

Current Court Status   ☑ None Reported   ☐ On Probation   ☐ Detention
                           ☐ On Parole   ☐ Awaiting Charge   ☐ AOD Related
                                                              Legal
                                                              Problems
                           ☐ Court Ordered to Treatment   ☐ Other

History Of Legal Charges   ☑ No ☐ Yes If yes, (check and describe)
                           ☐ Status Offense (e.g., Unruly)   ☐ Delinquency Name of
                                                              Probation/Parole
                                                              Officer (if applicable)

Adjudications   ☑ No   ☐ Yes If YES, describe

Detentions or Incarcerations   ☑ No   ☐ Yes If YES, describe

Civil Proceedings   ☑ No   ☐ Yes If YES, describe

Domestic Relations Court Involvement   ☐ No   ☑ Yes If YES, describe

He is in custody of Social Services due to abuse and neglect by his parents

Juvenile Court Involvement *Related to Child Abuse, Neglect or Dependency*

Current ☑ No   ☐ Yes   Comment_____

Past   ☑ No   ☐ Yes   Comment_____

Name Of Case Worker (If Applicable)

Children's Protective Services Involvement with Family ☐ No ☑ Yes   If YES,
                                                                          describe

Aaron is currently in "Permanency Planning" status. CPS has a tentative or preliminary reunification plan which is dependent on mother's success in drug recovery and Aaron's success in anger management

Name of CPS Caseworker(s) assigned to family *If applicable*

☐ None Reported   Brenda Williams

Name Aaron K. Howard	**Age** 11 years 5 months	**Client #** 1234

XI.   Legal History (*cont*)

Name of Guardian *ad litem* or Court Appointed Special Advocate (CASA) assigned to family

☐ None reported   Onika Sumi

Additional Comments

Aaron's current caseworker has been assigned for 1 month. The previous caseworker was involved for 1 year.

XII.   Inventory of Strengths and Needs by Functional Domains

Check all areas requiring assistance or attention and describe strengths and needs

✓ **Interpersonal relationships**
Despite problems of aggressive behavior, Aaron has one friend at school. Aaron can be very affectionate at times and tries hard to be helpful.

✓ **Motivation**
Aaron is highly motivated to return home to his mother.

✓ **Mood/sad**
Being separated from his biological family saddens him.

✓ **Losses**
Loss of biological family and removal from first foster family home.

✓ **Anxiety**
Mild irritability, anxiety, and some vigilance noted during the assessment interview. History of nightmares, ongoing.

✓ **Traumatic Stress**
Victim of physical and emotional abuse and neglect.

✓ **Anger/Aggression**
He is angry over being separated from his family. He has been aggressive with his peers and with his first foster family members.

✓ **Oppositional Behaviors**
Some mild defiance reported by foster parents.

✓ **Inattention**
Requires further assessment to evaluate poor academic performance. Recommend psychoeducational testing and an I.E.P.

✓ **Impulsivity**
Aaron shows poor impulse control and great oppositionality, by demanding to have his way no matter the circumstances.

Disturbed Reality Contact (Psychosis)
No evidence of symptoms.

Name Aaron K. Howard	**Age** 11 years 5 months	**Client #** 1234

XII.   Inventory of Strengths and Needs (*cont*)

✓   **Mood Swings/Hyperactivity**
Seems moderately sad and depressed when not engaged.

Check All Current Problem Areas

Substance Use/Addictive behaviors
None

Sleep Problems
None

✓   **Enuresis/encopresis**
Aaron wets his bed several times a week and also loses bladder control when he is anxious.

✓   **Psychosocial stresses**
Aaron needs a medical evaluation for possible neurological/urological basis for bladder control problems.

Pertinent Health Issues (Include any Allergies)
None

Client's family needs education to be able to *Describe areas of family education needs. Family education must be directed to the exclusive well being of the client.*

✓   **Client needs other environmental supports** *Describe areas where environmental supports are needed to support the client in community living and possible sources of that support.*

School, team sports.

✓   **Other**
Aaron's biological mother may need home-based services, parenting training and other supports as part of a reunification plan.

Skills Training/Community Support Needs *Check age-appropriate skills training and/or community support needs identified*

☐ Needs symptom and disability management skills   ☑ Needs enhancement of social/personal skills

☐ Needs residential supports to develop skills necessary for community living   ☐ Needs education related services to develop

☑ Needs enhancement of social support skills and recreational activities

As evidenced by *Describe the specific age-appropriate skill areas where improvement is needed*
Aaron needs to better demonstrate his ability to do the following:

1. respond to redirection from adults,

2. get along with his peers, and to handle unstructured play activities.

3. care for himself and his personal hygiene.

XIII. Mental Status Summary

Mental Status Examination *Complete Mental Status Assessment Form or provide a thorough written narrative below.*

Aaron is a rather handsome 11-year-old African-American who appeared his stated age. He was cooperative throughout the interview process. He was appropriately and casually dressed, however, his pants were noticeably damp which he tried to conceal by pulling down the tail of his shirt. He admitted that he had wet his pants, and appeared very embarrassed about this.

Aaron spoke rapidly but clearly and stated that he felt fine and that he was happy. However, his affect was incongruent in that he appeared to be anxious and sad. He said that he sometimes feels anger towards his peers at school because they tease him. He finally admitted feeling sad because he is separated from his family. At the same time he is genuinely hopeful that he and his family will be reunited.

Aaron was anxious and mildly agitated as the interview progressed and had difficulty sitting. When asked to retake his seat he at first became angry but was able to calm himself quickly.

His thought processes were clearly focused on his issues of separation and placement. Associative processes were intact and there was no evidence of any delusional thinking or hallucinations. He denied any obsessive patterns of thinking or compulsive behaviors. He reports he sleeps well and only occasionally experiences nightmares. His interpretation of proverbs was poor and overall his thinning was fairly concrete with little insight.

No extensive cognitive testing was done at this time but his general fund of knowledge was appropriate for his age; he could recall 2 out of 3 items at 5 minutes and do serial 7 subtractions correctly to 93. His judgment was assessed as fair.

Current Risk of Harm to *Self* □ None Reported ☑ Low □ Moderate □ High
Comment

Although Aaron has a history of minor cutting and scratching, he denies any suicidal or self destructive ideation, impulses, or plans at this time.

Current Risk of Harm to *Others* □ None Reported ☑ Low □ Moderate □ High
Comment

Aaron denies any thoughts or feelings about hurting others at this time.

XV. Diagnosis *Check Primary*

	Narrative Description	Code ☑ DSM □ ICD-9
Axis I	Depressive Disorder NOS	311
	✓ Post-traumatic stress disorder	309.81
	Attention Deficit/Hyperactivity disx	
	Comb type	314.01
	Enuresis not due to a medical condition	307.6
Axis II	No diagnosis on Axis 2	V71.09
Axis III	r/o Bladder or neurological disorder	
Axis IV	Problems with primary support group	
	Educational problems	
Axis V	**Current GAF** 40	
	Highest in Past Year GAF *(If Known)*	40

Name Aaron K. Howard	Age 11 years 5 months	Client # 1234

XVI.   Cultural Formulation

Cultural identity

Aaron did not express any feelings related to his ethnicity/race. He refers to himself as black.

Possible cultural explanations of illness

None at this time.

Cultural factors related to psychosocial environment and levels of functioning

Aaron is currently living with a first-generation Japanese American family who has a high level of cultural identity with Japanese culture and traditions. It will be important to monitor the family for issues of identity and culture that might arise.

Cultural elements in the client provider relationship

Mother's fears about a well-published recent expose of racism and discrimination against African-American families may impact her ability to trust and work with the system.

Overall cultural assessment in diagnosis and service plan

While present to a degree, cultural factors do not appear to be a major factor in understanding this child's needs or in developing a treatment plan at this time but have the potential to become a more significant issue in the future.

XVII.   Clinical Summary/Formulation

This clinical summary is based upon information provided by (*Check All That Apply*)

☑ Client   ☐ Parent(s)   ☑ Guardian(s)   ☐ Family/Friend   ☐ Physician   ☑ Records
☐ Law Enforcement   ☑ Service Provider   ☐ School Personnel   ☐ Other Specify

Formulation/Summary

Pertinent History

Aaron is an 11-year old African-American boy, removed from parents for abuse/neglect at age 9. He has failed one foster placement. He has had two medical and one psychiatric hospitalization. He is experiencing school failure and has been restricted from school activities because of behavior.

Predisposing Factors

Genetic loading for major mental disorder. Possible intrauterine drug exposure. Premature birth with neonatal problems. History during infancy of febrile seizure, nutritional difficulties, and hospitalization. History of attachment problem with mother.

Aaron has a long standing history of physical and verbal abuse as well as rejection and emotional neglect from his biological parents, along with observing physical violence between his parents. He has also experienced the behavioral effects of their mental illness and substance abuse patterns. The dynamics of this family experience has left him with a deep sense of loss, hurt, and fear.

Precipitating Factors

His current aggressive and impulsive behavior is jeopardizing his current placement.

Name Aaron K. Howard	**Age** 11 years 5 months	**Client #** 1234

XVII.   Clinical Summary/Formulation *(cont)*

Previous Treatment

Multiple pharmacological attempts to address ADHD, but not meaningfully combined with a psychosocial treatment plan, and not addressing MDD or PTSD. No I.E.P. or evaluation of his cognitive abilities, which would be important for developing a psychotherapeutic plan.

Perpetuating factors

Symptoms of MDD, ADHD, possible PTSD, and possible learning disorder (no work-up to confirm) present continuing strain for Aaron in his attempts to adjust and succeed in school. Multiple out-of-home placements, also necessitating change of schools, and disruption of peer relationships. Ongoing asthma treated with stimulant inhaler that may exacerbate ADHD symptoms and anxiety.

He also has difficulty discussing the past abusive behavior of his parents as well as his own out of control behavior. He has had one psychiatric hospitalization that was the result of a crisis intervention when he threatened to kill his first foster family resulting in the recent hospitalization that led to this referral and assessment. He reported having nightmares and enuresis, and he is fearful of the dark. This is consistent with individuals who have experienced significant trauma. His low self-esteem and poor impulse control resulting from troubled attachment and inconsistent parenting have made it difficult for him to tolerate and express frustration.

Present Condition

Strengths identified include his willingness to attend individual therapy and the support and encouragement of his foster parents. His hopefulness for a better future and return to his mother is an important strength to build on—without this hope, trying to help Aaron would be much more difficult. At the same time it is important that he remain realistic about the extent of his mother's problems and the possibilities that he will not be able to rejoin her.

Aaron appears to have a fair relationship with his new foster family. Although he appears sincere in wanting to make this situation work well, his foster mother is somewhat frightened by him. He has clearly demonstrated resiliency in terms of surviving an extremely dysfunctional family environment and upbringing. He has expressed interest in participating in school sports and this might be a good outlet for him, as well as an opportunity to learn how to interact with his peers in a more positive manner. With proper interventions, Aaron should be able to succeed in a family setting, socially, and at school.

Reunification with his biological mother is possible but it will depend upon her success in rehabilitation. Helping Aaron to accept and understand this will be a challenge that has the potential for setbacks and should be approached with care and caution.

Name Aaron K. Howard	**Age** 11 years 5 months	**Client #** 1234

CALOCUS Worksheet

Please check the applicable ratings within each dimension and record the score in the lower right hand corner. Total your score and determine the recommended level of care using either the Placement Grid.

I. Risk of Harm	**IV-B. Recovery Environment—Level of Support**
☐ 1. Low potential for risk of harm ☑ 2. Some potential for risk of harm ☐ 3. Significant potential for risk of harm ☐ 4. Serious potential for risk of harm ☐ 5. Extreme potential for risk of harm Score 2	☐ 1. Highly supportive environment ☑ 2. Supportive environment ☐ 3. Limited support in environment ☐ 4. Minimal support in environment ☐ 5. No support in environment Score 2
II. Functional Status	**V. Resiliency and Treatment History**
☐ 1. Minimal impairment ☐ 2. Mild impairment ☑ 3. Moderate impairment ☐ 4. Serious impairment ☐ 5. Severe impairment Score 3	☐ 1. Full response to treatment ☑ 2. Significantly resilient and/or response to treatment ☐ 3. Moderate or equivocal response to treatment and recovery management ☐ 4. Poor response to treatment and recovery management ☐ 5. Negligible response to treatment Score 2
III. Co-Morbidity	**VI-A. Acceptance and Engagement —Child/Adolescent**
☑ 1. No co-morbidity ☐ 2. Minor co-morbidity ☐ 3. Significant co-morbidity ☐ 4. Major co-morbidity ☐ 5. Severe co-morbidity Score 1	☐ 1. Optimal ☑ 2. Constructive ☐ 3. Obstructive ☐ 4. Destructive ☐ 5. Inaccessible Score 2
IV-A. Recovery Environment— Level of Stress	**VI-B. Acceptance and Engagement —Parent/Primary Caretaker**
☐ 1. Minimally stressful environment ☑ 2. Mildly stressful environment ☐ 3. Moderately stressful environment ☐ 4. Highly stressful environment ☐ 5. Extremely stressful environment Score 2	☑ 1. Optimal ☐ 2. Constructive ☐ 3. Obstructive ☐ 4. Destructive ☐ 5. Inaccessible Score 1
Total Score: **15**	Level of Care Recommended: **Outpatient**

CALOCUS Level of Care Determination Grid

Rating Dimensions	Level of Care					
	Health Management and/or Recovery Maintenance (Level I)	Home and Community Mental Health Services and Supports (Level II)	Intensive Community Mental Health Services and Supports (Level III)	Intensively Managed Home and Community-Based Services and Supports (Level IV)	Up to 24 Hour Intensively Managed Home or Residential (Group Home) Placement or Community-Based Service and Supports of Equal Intensity (Level V)	Medically Managed Secure Residential or Inpatient Placement or Community-Based Services and Supports of Equal Intensity (Level VI)
I. Risk of Harm	2 or less	2 or less	3 or less	3 or less	(4) 3	(5) 4
II. Functional Status	2 or less	2 or less	3 or less	3 or less	(4)* 3	(5) 4
III. Co-existing Conditions (Co-Morbidity)	2 or less	2 or less	3 or less	3 or less	(4)* 3	(5) 4
IVA. Stress	Sum of IVA + IVB is 4 or less	Sum of IVA + IVB is 5 or less	Sum of IVA + IVB is 5 or less	3 or 4	4 or more	4 or more
IVB. Support	2 or less	2 or less	3 or less	3 or less	4 or more	4 or more
V. Resiliency	2 or less	2 or less	3 or less	3 or 4	3 or more	4 or more
VI. Treatment, Acceptance, & Engagement	2 or less	2 or less	3 or less	3 or 4	3 or more	4 or more
Composite Rating	**10 to 13**	**14 to 16**	**17 to 19**	**20 to 22**	**23 to 27**	**28 or more**

MENTAL HEALTH AND ADDICTION RECOVERY PLAN

FOR

Aaron Howard

GOALS	Goals should be stated in the **individual's or family's own words** and include statements of dreams, hopes, role functions and vision of life. For each individual and family and/or setting, completion of all three sub-goals may not be necessary or appropriate.

Life Goals

Aaron states, "I want to live with my mother."

Service/Treatment Goals

Stabilize Aaron's current foster placement so that he can work with his biological family towards reunification.

Life Enhancement Goals

Aaron also states, "I want to have friends and get along better with others."

ANTICIPATED DISCHARGE/TRANSITION SETTING AND CRITERIA	Describe the setting in terms of location, level of care, length of stay and service needs. Describe changes in the individual's and family's current needs and circumstances that will need to occur in order to succeed in discharge or transition.

Aaron is able to continue in his current foster home by attending school regularly, managing his bladder functions, and expressing his feelings without aggression.

BARRIERS	Describe the **challenges as a result of the mental illness or addictive disorder** that stand in the way of the individual and family meeting their goals and/or achieving the discharge/transition criteria. Identifying these barriers is critical to specifying the objectives as well as services and interventions in the following section of the plan.

- Lack of adequate bladder control
- Aggressive behavior
- Inability to stay in school

Aaron Howard

Objective Worksheet #1

This objective is related to which goal(s) or transition/discharge criteria (i.e. treatment goal) or barrier?
This objective relates immediately to the service /treatment goal and indirectly to the life enhancement goal as children often reject peers who act angry and aggressive toward them.
Is there more than one *active* objective that addresses this goal?   ☑ Yes   ☐ No

OBJECTIVE	*Using action words, describe the **specific changes expected** in measurable and behavioral terms. Include the target date for completion.*
# 1	Aaron will be able to say when he is angry, sad, frustrated, and disappointed without aggression towards people or property as reported by his foster parents
TARGET DATE	within 90 days

INDIVIDUAL/FAMILY STRENGTHS	*Identify the individual's and family's past accomplishments, current aspirations, motivations, personal attitudes, attributes, etc. which can be used to **help accomplish this objective**.*
Supportive foster parents, has a "big brother," motivated to return to school and play sports	

INTERVENTIONS	*Describe the specific activity, service or treatment, the provider or other responsible person (including the individual and family), and the **intended purpose or impact as it relates to this objective**. The intensity, frequency and duration should also be specified.*

- Clinic psychologist to conduct comprehensive assessment to evaluate neuro-cognitive functioning within 3 weeks to help inform and support psychotherapeutic plan.
- Individual psychotherapy with child specialist 1 hour weekly for 12 weeks to help Aaron identify feelings associated with aggressive impulses and alternative means to express these emotions.
- Child psychiatrist to re-evaluate current pharmacotherapy for 30 minutes every 2 weeks to help reduce symptoms of depression, inattention, and impulsivity.
- Family therapist to meet with Aaron and foster family for 90 minutes in their home every 2 weeks to observe Aaron's functioning within the family and to provide skills training and insight to help Aaron develop adaptive skills and alternatives to aggression.
- Case manager to provide in-school support and skill building 1/2 hour a day 3 days a week for 2 months during recess to help Aaron develop alternatives to aggressive behavior and prosocial appropriate peer responses.

Aaron Howard

Objective Worksheet #2

This objective is related to which goal(s) or transition/discharge criteria (i.e. treatment goal) or barrier?
This objective relates immediately to the service /treatment goal and indirectly to the life enhancement goal as his continued incontinence threatens his placement and erodes his self esteem.
Is there more than one *active* objective that addresses this goal?   ☑ Yes ☐ No

OBJECTIVE	*Using action words, describe the **specific changes expected** in measurable and behavioral terms. Include the target date for completion.*
# 2	Aaron will be entirely free of wetting incidents as reported by foster mother, schoolteacher, and Aaron.
TARGET DATE	within 120 days

INDIVIDUAL/FAMILY STRENGTHS	*Identify the individual's and family's past accomplishments, current aspirations, motivations, personal attitudes, attributes, etc. which can be used to **help accomplish this objective**.*
Supportive foster parents. Aaron is aware of and embarrassed about this problem and therefore motivated to address the problem.	

INTERVENTIONS	*Describe the specific activity, service or treatment, the provider or other responsible person (including the individual and family), and the **intended purpose or impact as it relates to this objective**. The intensity, frequency and duration should also be specified.*

- Foster parents will arrange for evaluation by pediatric urologist within 3 weeks to rule out underlying undetected organic cause for and pharmacotherapy of childhood enuresis.
- Clinic nurse will provide counseling for 1 hour a week for 4 weeks on diet, fluid management, bladder training, and behavior therapy to reduce incident of nocturnal enuresis.
- Case manager to coordinate behavior plan with class teacher and school administration within 1 week and follow up every 2 weeks as needed thereafter to facilitate Aaron's regular access to bathroom facilities during school hours to prevent accidents.
- Clinic social worker to provide 30 minutes of weekly sand tray therapy for 12 weeks to explore the possible psychological connection between history of suspected abuse and neglect and lack of bladder control.

INDIVIDUAL PLAN

1st 90-Day Review

Aaron Howard

☐ **Objective Time Frame**   ☑ **Required Interval**   ☐ **Other**_____

CHANGE in ASSESSMENT DATA, FORMULATION, or DIAGNOSIS

The urological evaluation did not find any physiological or neurological basis for the incontinence. Imipramine 50 mg nightly and DDAVP nasal spray were started to treat the functional enuresis and there has been substantial improvement.

Psychological assessment did not reveal any significant neuro-cognitive deficits requiring modification of the plan. Aaron should be able to participate in and benefit from a wide range of therapeutic activities.

INDIVIDUAL'S/FAMILY'S COMMENTS and SELF-ASSESSMENT

The foster parents note that the situation at home and school has improved somewhat this past 90 days due to the new skills Aaron is learning in order to deal with his aggressive behavior. They say that improvement is still needed. They are happy to see less incidents of wetting himself and are finally feeling confident that he will be able to eventually control his bladder and improve his self-care.

CHANGE in GOALS, BARRIERS, or TRANSITION/DISCHARGE PLANS

No new goals have been identified.

New interventions added to both continued objectives.

INDIVIDUAL'S RESPONSE TO INTERVENTIONS

OBJECTIVE #	OBJECTIVE STATUS	OBJECTIVE CHANGED	INTERVENTION CHANGED
1	☐ MET ☑ PARTIALLY MET ☐ NOT MET	☐ YES ☑ NO	☑ YES ☐ NO
2	☐ MET ☑ PARTIALLY MET ☐ NOT MET	☐ YES ☑ NO	☑ YES ☐ NO
	☐ MET ☐ PARTIALLY MET ☐ NOT MET	☐ YES ☐ NO	☐ YES ☐ NO
	☐ MET ☐ PARTIALLY MET ☐ NOT MET	☐ YES ☐ NO	☐ YES ☐ NO

Individual Plan

1st 90-Day Review

Aaron Howard

NARRATIVE SUMMARY of TREATMENT PLAN UPDATE	*Changes since last review, and rationale for treatment or medication changes, if applicable*

Aaron has not yet been able to meet his objective of no wetting incidents 100% of the time. After 90 days of services he is not having any wetting incidents about 50% of the time. He has not been able to respond to the intervention of sand tray therapy. It is thought that the use of a peer support group might be more beneficial to him. Therefore, he will participate in peer therapy 1 time per week for the next 90 days (instead of the sand tray therapy intervention) to explore the possibility of a possible psychological link between being separated from his biological family and his lack of bladder control. The neurological evaluation conducted last month indicated that there is no physiological or anatomical reason causing the enuresis. The psychologist believes that his bladder control problem is the result of a post-traumatic stress reaction to being separated from his birth family.

His aggressive behaviors at home, school, and with peers have declined as he has learned some new skills according to the case manager's report. The consultation with the clinic psychologist has occurred and concluded that he does not have any neuro-cognitive dysfunction. It is recommended that the family therapy, individual therapy, and skill building activities continue during the next 90 days so that the gains made can be solidified. In addition, it is suggested that Aaron be allowed to join a sports team so that he can interact with his peers in another setting and continue to work on reducing his aggression.

Aaron Howard

Objective Worksheet #1

90-day review modification

This objective is related to which goal(s) or transition/discharge criteria (i.e. treatment goal) or barrier?
This objective relates immediately to the service /treatment goal and indirectly to the life enhancement goal as children often reject peers who act angry and aggressive toward them.
Is there more than one *active* objective that addresses this goal?   ☑ Yes ☐ No

OBJECTIVE	*Using action words, describe the **specific changes** **expected** in measurable and behavioral terms. Include the target date for completion.*
# 1	Aaron will be able to say when he is angry, sad, frustrated, and disappointed without aggression towards people or property as reported by his foster mother.
TARGET DATE	within 90 days

INDIVIDUAL/FAMILY STRENGTHS	*Identify the individual's and family's past accomplishments, current aspirations, motivations, personal attitudes, attributes, etc. that can be used to **help accomplish this objective.***
Supportive foster parents, has a "big brother," motivated to return to school and play sports.	

INTERVENTIONS	*Describe the specific activity, service or treatment, the provider or other responsible person (including the individual and family), and the **intended purpose or impact as it relates to this objective.** The intensity, frequency, and duration should also be specified.*

- Individual psychotherapy with child specialist 1 hour weekly for 12 weeks to help Aaron identify feelings associated with aggressive impulses and alternative means to express these emotions.
- Child psychiatrist to re-evaluate current pharmacotherapy for 30 minutes every 2 weeks to help reduce symptoms of depression, inattention, and impulsivity.
- Family therapist to meet with Aaron and foster family for 90 minutes in their home every 2 weeks to observe Aaron's functioning within the family and to provide skills training and insight to help Aaron develop adaptive skills and alternatives to aggression.
- Case manager to provide in school support and skill building 1/2 hour/day 3 days a week for 2 months during recess to help Aaron develop alternatives to aggressive behavior and prosocial appropriate peer responses.
- (New) Aaron's foster parents to arrange for Aaron to participate weekly in local youth soccer program for 4 months to provide him a healthy outlet for his energy and aggression while creating an opportunity to meet new friends.

Aaron Howard

Objective Worksheet #2

90-day review modification

This objective is related to which goal(s) or transition/discharge criteria (i.e. treatment goal) or barrier?
This objective relates immediately to the service /treatment goal and indirectly to the life enhancement goal as his continued incontinence threatens his placement and erodes his self esteem.
Is there more than one *active* objective that addresses this goal? ☑ Yes ☐ No

OBJECTIVE	*Using action words, describe the **specific changes expected** in measurable and behavioral terms. Include the target date for completion.*
# 2	Aaron will be entirely free of wetting incidents as reported by foster mother, schoolteacher, and Aaron.

TARGET DATE	within 120 days

INDIVIDUAL/ FAMILY STRENGTHS	*Identify the individual's and family's past accomplishments, current aspirations, motivations, personal attitudes, attributes, etc. which can be used to **help accomplish this objective.***
Supportive foster parents. Aaron is aware of and embarrassed about this problem and therefore motivated to address the problem.	

INTERVENTIONS	*Describe the specific activity, service or treatment, the provider or other responsible person (including the individual and family), and the **intended purpose or impact as it relates to this objective**. The intensity, frequency and duration should also be specified.*

- Foster parents will arrange for evaluation by pediatric urologist within 3 weeks to rule out underlying undetected organic cause for and pharmacotherapy of childhood enuresis.
- Clinic nurse will provide counseling for 1 hour a week for 4 weeks on diet, fluid management, bladder training and behavior therapy to reduce incident of nocturnal enuresis.
- Case manager to coordinate behavior plan with class teacher and school administration within 1 week and follow up every 2 weeks as needed thereafter to facilitate Aaron's regular access to bathroom during school hours to prevent accidents.
- ~~Clinic social workder to provide 30 minutes of weekly sand tray therapy for 12 weeks to explore the possible psychological connection between history of suspected abuse and neglect and lack of bladder control.~~ ⟨Deleted at 90-day review⟩
- ⟨New⟩ Aaron will participate in a staff facilitated pre-adolescent peer therapy/support group with other boys who have suffered trauma and loss, 45 minutes each session weekly for 4 months, to improve self-esteem and benefit from positive peer pressure to maintain bladder control.

APPENDIX B
ADULT DIAGNOSTIC ASSESSMENT

Client Name   First   **Sally**   MI   Last   **Hamilton**   **Client #**   123-45-6789

Presenting Problem

Presenting Problem/Circumstances

Include a description of symptoms, behavioral and functioning problems, precipitating factors, and referral source and reason for referral, services sought, and client expectation

Sally is a 49-year-old Caucasian female referred by the court for treatment due to a DUI (Driving Under the Influence) conviction. She was pulled over by the police for driving with a broken headlight. This is her first DUI conviction and she has been ordered to 10 weeks of the Level 2 program (education group). She had a BAC of .13% at the time of her arrest, but she reported that she had had 3 beers that day. She reported that she does not have a drinking problem because she is only a "casual" drinker and drinks alcohol, at most, one time per month, averaging 6–12 beers per episode. The ASAP program conducted an evaluation of her drinking use, utilizing the MAST (Michigan Alcoholism Screening Test) and it resulted in a score of 2.

Living Situation

Description: ❑ My Home (house, apt., room; with/without a roommate, subsidized or not)   ❑ Friend's Home ☑ Relative's Home   ❑ Foster Care Home   ❑ Residential Facility (Group Home)   ❑ Group Home/Transitional   ❑ Jail/Prison   ❑ Nursing Home   ❑ Hospital (psychiatric)   ❑ Homeless living with friend   ❑ Homeless in shelter/No residence   ❑ Other:

Household Members *Name*	Relationship to Client	Age	Quality of Relationship
Polly Jenkins	daughter	28	Good
Significant Family Members/ Others not listed above	**Relationship to Client**	**Age**	**Quality of Relationship**

Social Information

Primary/Family/Marital/Significant Other Support Systems:

She is a widow of 7 years who currently lives with her daughter. She has a good relationship with her daughter and is satisfied with this situation; however, she advises that she would like to have a significant relationship of her own at some point in time.

Sally says she has five close friends who are a support to her. She goes out with her friends after work to eat and maybe to have a "few drinks." She says she truly feels cared about from her daughter and friends. She spends most of her free time with her family (primarily her daughter) and friends.

Social Information (*cont*)

Pertinent Family History *Include family MH and AOD history*

Both her father and her uncle have had significant problems with their use of alcohol. Out of her three brothers and three sisters, two of her brothers are dependent on drugs and alcohol and one sister is an alcohol abuser/alcoholic. Another sister has had a psychiatric hospitalization. She is not entirely sure of everyone's status in terms of their current use of alcohol and/or other drugs. She reports that her daughter, Polly, does not use alcohol or other illicit drugs at all. She says that Polly was horrified by her arrest and that Polly had been urging her to cut down on her drinking for some time now.

She reports that she had a good relationship with her husband until his sudden death of a heart attack at age 45.

Strengths/Capabilities

Sally has a strong support network and loving relationships with family and friends. She is in the normal/average range of intellectual functioning. She has always maintained employment and is financially stable. She has good initiative and ability to complete tasks. Her daughter does not abuse alcohol or other drugs, therefore, she is living in a safe environment.

Limitations of Activities of Daily Living

None

Friendship/Social/Peer Support Relationships

As described above, she has a good support network and active friendships. She reports that her drinking has never changed/damaged any of her relationships and noted that in the past year she has reduced the frequency of contact with a girlfriend who drinks heavily.

Meaningful Activities *Include community involvements, volunteer activities, leisure and recreation, other interests*

Sally is not involved in any volunteer, community, or leisure activities.

Community Supports/Self Help Groups *Include AA, NA, NAMIO, etc.*

None

Religion/Spirituality

She says she is not involved at all with any religious organization or activities and that she does not see herself as a spiritual person.

Cultural/Ethnic Issues/Information/Concerns

None

Developmental Issues

None

Sexual History/Concerns

She has been sexually abstinent since her husband died 7 years ago. She reports no sexual abuse from family members or others in her lifetime.

Education, Employment, and Military Information

Education History (Check All That Apply): ❑ GED   ☑ HS Grad
❑ College—Number of Years _____ Degree/Major: ❑ Other Degree:
_____ Highest Grade Completed

History of Learning Difficulties ☑ None Reported	❑ Learning Disability - Type: ❑ Mental Retardation ❑ Special School Placement: ❑ Other:
Barriers to Learning ☑ None Reported	❑ Inability to Read or Write ❑ Other:
Special Communication Needs: ☑ None Reported	❑ TDD/TTY Device ❑ Sign Language Interpreter ❑ Assistive Listening Device(s) ❑ Language Interpreter Services Needed ❑ Other Spoken Language:

Employment: (Check all that apply)

Employed: ☑ Full Time (35 hours or more per week)   ❑ Part Time (< 35 hours per week)
❑ Non-Competitive   ❑ Unemployed
Date Last Worked: _____
Not in Labor Force: ❑ Disabled   ❑ Retired   ❑ Homemaker   ❑ Student
❑ Living in Institution   ❑ Other:

If Employed, Name of Employer:

She is a certified nursing assistant (CNA) for Shady Grove Nursing Home.

Job Performance History:

Number of Jobs in Last 5 Years ___2___

Attendance: ❑ Above average   ☑ Normal   ❑ Tardiness   ❑ Absenteeism
Performance: ❑ Exemplary   ☑ Good   ❑ Average   ❑ Below Average

Employment Interests/Skills:

Is client satisfied with job?   ❑ No ☑ Yes
Is client experiencing financial problems?   ☑ No ❑ Yes
(If not currently employed) - Client wants to work?   ❑ No ❑ Yes
Is client concerned that employment will affect benefits? ❑ No ❑ Yes

Comments on past or current skills/interests:

Education, Employment, and Military Information (*cont*)

Military History
☑ No ❑ Yes If yes, describe branch of service, any pertinent duties, and any trauma experienced during service as applicable:

Type of Discharge if other than General/Honorable:
Date of Discharge:

Mental Health Treatment History

Outpatient Mental Health Treatment   ❑ None Reported

Agency	Current	Past *Date*	Clinician Name
None			

Psychiatric Hospitalizations   ❑ None Reported

Hospital	Date of Service	Reason *Suicidal, Depressed, Etc.*
None		

Previous or Current Diagnoses (if known) ❑ Not known by client
None

Other Comments Regarding Mental Health Treatment ☑ No Comments

Current Medication Information *Include Medical, Psychiatric, OTC/Herbal*
❑ None Reported

Medication	Rationale	Total Daily Dosage	Compliance			
			Yes	No	Partial	Unk
None						

Primary Care Physician *Name, Phone Number, and Address* Dr. Sue Hill	Other Prescribing Physician(s)

Past Psychotropic Medications ❑ None Reported

Psychotropic Medications	Reason for Discontinuation
None	

Legal History

Legal Guardian/Custodian: ☑ None Reported   Phone:

Current Legal Status: ❑ None Reported ❑ On Probation ❑ Detention ❑ On Parole
❑ Awaiting Charge ☑ AOD Related Legal Problems ❑ Conditional Release
❑ Outpatient Commitment ☑ Court Ordered to Treatment ❑ Other:

History of Legal Charges: Juvenile ☑ No ❑ Yes If yes, ❑ Status Offense (e.g., Unruly)
                                        ❑ Delinquency
                        Adult ❑ No ☑ Yes If yes, ☑ Misdemeanor ❑ Felony

Date of most recent legal charges: 3 months ago

Legal History (*cont*)

Convictions   ❑ None Reported

DUI—first one, the presenting problem

Incarcerations   ☑ None Reported

Name of Probation/Parole Officer (*if applicable*):

Civil Proceedings   ☑ None Reported

Domestic Relations Court Problems (*i.e., Custody, Protective Services, Restraining Order*):

Juvenile Court Involvement (*Related to Child Abuse, Neglect, or Dependency*):

Current   ☑ No   ❑ Yes   Comment: _____

Past   ☑ No   ❑ Yes   Comment:_____

Name Of Case Worker (If Applicable):

Child Support Enforcement Orders: ☑ None Reported

Children's Protective Services Involvement With Family: ☑None Reported

Name of Children's Protective Services Caseworker(s) Assigned to Family (*if applicable*): ☑ None Reported

Alcohol/Drug History

Illegal Drug Use/Abuse Past 12 Months: ☑ No ❑ Yes

Prescription Drug Abuse Past 12 Months: ☑ No ❑ Yes

Non-Prescription Drug Abuse Past 12 Months: ☑ No ❑ Yes

Alcohol Abuse Past 12 Months: ❑ No ☑ Yes

Toxicology Screen Completed: ❑ Not Indicated ☑ No ❑ Yes If Yes, Results:

Presenting with Detox Issues: ☑ No ❑ Yes If Yes, Symptoms:

Check all that apply: ❑ IV Drug User   ❑ Pregnant

Drug/ Substance/ Alcohol	Age of 1st Use	Date of Last Use	Frequency	Amount	Method
Alcohol (beer)	13	2 days ago	1× per month	6–12	oral

Alcohol/Drug Treatment History

AOD Treatment

☑ None Reported

❑ Current – List provider and services received:

❑ Past: ❑ OP ❑ IOP ❑ Residential ❑ Hospital ❑ Detox ❑ Other:

Alcohol/Drug Treatment History (*cont*)

Other Comments Regarding Substance Abuse/Use

Include AOD use/abuse by other family members/significant others, AOD related legal problems

She first began using alcohol at age 13 with some friends. Her next drink was when she was 16 when she started drinking 2× weekly after her part-time job on the weekends, drinking 2–3 beers each time. This pattern continued until she graduated from high school at age 18, and increased her drinking to 3–4 times weekly, with 3–5 12 oz. beers each time. She said that she continued to drink fairly regularly, averaging 1–12 beers "every few weeks or so," until her husband died unexpectedly 7 years ago. Her drinking progressed for several years after his death until she was drinking 6–8 beers a day for about 1.5 years. She then reduced her intake when she started college for her certified nursing assistant degree. Now she reports she is able to control her drinking at "8–10 beers per month." She did note that her tolerance has increased in that it used to "take 6–8 beers to feel a buzz and now it's 8–10."

Sally stated that she does not have a drinking problem, but later in the interview said that she used to have a serious problem. She reported that she was able to quit drinking entirely during her pregnancy. She concluded by stating she no longer has any problems with alcohol and does "not really need treatment."

Abuse History

Describe in Comment Section Each Element Checked

☑ No Self-Reported History of Abuse/Violence	❑ Physical Abuse	❑ Domestic Violence/ Abuse
❑ Community Violence	❑ Physical Neglect	❑ Emotional Abuse
❑ Elder Abuse	❑ Sexual Abuse/ Molestation	❑ Other:

Comments Identify if client served as a victim of abuse, a perpetrator, or both:

Problem Checklist Including Functional Domains

Check All Current Problem Areas

Nutritional/Eating Pattern Changes/Disorders

Pain Management

Depressed Mood/Sad

✓ **Bereavement Issues**

Sally still is grieving the unexpected loss of her husband.

Anxiety

Traumatic Stress

Anger/Aggression

Problem Checklist Including Functional Domains *cont*

Oppositional Behaviors

Inattention

Impulsivity

Disturbed Reality Contact (Psychosis)

Mood Swings/Hyperactivity

✓ **Substance Use/Addiction**
Sally minimizes her use and involvement with alcohol and has never dealt effectively with the death of her husband, instead turning to alcohol. She has a current DUI and has been court-ordered into treatment.
Other Addictive Behaviors

Sleep Problems

Psychosocial Stressors:

Pertinent Health Issues (*Include any allergies*):

✓ **Client's family needs education to be able to** *Describe areas of family education needs. Family education must be directed to the exclusive well being of the client*
Sally has a family history of addiction and psychiatric issues; she has been living with her single daughter. Her daughter may need education about alcoholism and addiction, as well as the impact of addiction on the family.

✓ **Client needs other environmental supports** *Describe areas where environmental supports are needed to support the client in community living and possible sources of that support*
Although Sally has a job, and a support network consisting of her friends and daughter, it does not appear she is fully invested in the community in terms of any activities that do not involve drinking. This is a need identified by the clinician, not by Sally.

Skills Deficits/Skills Training/Community Support Needs *Check all applicable skills deficits, skills training and/or community support needs identified*

☑ Client needs symptom and disability management skills	❑ Client needs restoration or development of social/personal skills
❑ Client needs residential supports to develop skills necessary for community living	❑ Client needs employment related services to develop skills necessary for successful employment

Problem Checklist Including **Functional Domains** *cont*	
❑ Client needs education related services to develop skills necessary to enhance academic success	❑ Client needs restoration or development of social support skills and networks including recreational activities

As evidenced by *Describe potential needs for improved skills*
Sally might benefit by learning about alternatives to social activities that involve drinking, some skills/activities that would help her with intimate relationship building (without the use of alcohol).

Mental Status Summary

Mental Status Examination *Complete Mental Status Assessment Form or provide a thorough written narrative below*
She was appropriately dressed and groomed. Her interactions were appropriate; she was comfortable asking questions and relating information. Sally's speech was relevant and easily understood; there was no evidence of a thought disorder. Her affect and mood were appropriate, and she denied any recent mood swings or depressive symptoms. She was alert, well oriented, and cooperative. She demonstrated little insight into her need for substance abuse treatment, but understood the reasons for her referral. She appears to be in the normal/average range of intellectual functioning. Her adaptive functioning skills appear to be appropriate and she does not appear to be experiencing much distress related to her alcohol problems at this time.

Current Risk of Harm to Self or Others
☑ None Noted   ❑ Low   ❑ Moderate   ❑ High

Comment:

Client/Family/Guardian Expression of Service Preferences

The clinician and client (and/or primary support person) should have a meaningful recovery-focused dialogue to engage the client (and/or primary support person) about identified needs and preferences of client. Identify the indicated needs/preferences of client for the full range of behavioral health clinical and community-based rehabilitative services, and environmental support services available to them.

1. Behavioral Health Clinical and Rehabilitative Services Needed: Although Sally minimizes her drinking behavior, she does recognize that her most pressing need is to resolve the legal charges against her and to comply with the court order. She is willing to do "whatever it takes" to get the legal matter resolved. Therefore, she will attend the educational groups on substance abuse and addiction.

2. Environmental Supports Needed: None

Clinical Summary and Narrative

This Clinical Summary is Based Upon Information Provided By *Check All That Apply*

☑ Client   ❑ Parent(s)   ❑ Guardian(s)   ❑ Family/Friend   ❑ Physician   ❑ Records
☑ Law Enforcement   ❑ Service Provider   ❑ School Personnel   ❑ Other Specify:

Degree of Severity at Admission for the following Dimensions (AOD clients only)

Intoxication/ Withdrawal	Biomedical	Emotional/ Behavioral/ Cognitive	Treatment Acceptance/ Resistance	Relapse Potential	Recovery Environs	Family Function
None	None	Denied any problems/ no cognitive problems noted	Passive	Moderate	Home is alcohol-free; socializes with friends, which involves alcohol	

Diagnosis ☑ DSM Codes ❑ ICD-9 Codes

Check Primary		Narrative Description	Code
✓	Axis I	Alcohol Abuse—moderate—episodic	302.02
		r/o Alcohol Dependence	
		r/o Depression	
	Axis II	No diagnosis on Axis II	
	Axis III	None identified	
	Axis IV	Restricted driver's license	
	Axis V	Current GAF: 70	
		Highest in Past Year GAF (If Known): ____	

Narrative Summary *Etiology of presenting problem and maintenance of the problem; mental health history; AOD history; severity of problem; where problem occurs (functioning at home, at work, in community; onset of problem (acute vs. chronic); client motivation for treatment, whether problem is known to be responsive to treatment.*

Following her first DUI arrest and conviction, Sally has been referred by the court for attendance at 10 weeks of the Level II educational program. She admits to a history of alcohol use, but says she does not have a drinking problem and feels that her referral for treatment is an over-reaction to an isolated case of poor judgment.

Clinical Summary and Narrative *(cont)*

Per the order of the court, Sally is willing, albeit reluctantly, to attend 10 weekly substance abuse group sessions, and agrees to refrain from the use of alcohol during the course of the treatment sessions, and have an alcohol breath test before each group. At this point in time, Sally is motivated for treatment almost solely by her desire to resolve her current legal difficulties, and does not appear to have a significant internal need to address her substance use, grief issues, loneliness, or lack of intimacy since her husband's death.

Using a variety of assessment tools, including the ASAM dimensions of severity, the court report (which includes the MAST results), and a personal interview with Sally, the court's request for educational services concerning substance abuse seems to be an appropriate intervention. These results are consistent with short-term outpatient treatment that focuses on education and further assessment.

However, given Sally's risk factors, additional interventions are also recommended at this time. She appears to be in the precontemplation stage of recovery as evidenced by a number of factors including: 1) minimization of the extent of her use of alcohol (despite a BAC of .13% at the time of arrest), and 2) belief that she is not dependent nor at risk because she was able to successfully reduce the amount and frequency of her use while pregnant and while attending school. At the same time, Sally does acknowledge that she used to have a "serious drinking problem" before she started college. She has been drinking since age 13 and comes from a family history of addiction and mental health issues.

Therefore, in addition to the regular program, 4 sessions of motivational counseling are also recommended to help Sally better understand the stages of change in addictions model. Prior to completion of the program and per court order, Sally should have an exit interview to identify any further treatment needs. From a prevention perspective, it is hoped that Sally will at that time have better information to support future life choices and treatment decisions.

Anticipated length of stay overall is 12 weeks.

INDIVIDUAL MENTAL HEALTH
AND ADDICTION RECOVERY PLAN
FOR

Sally Hamilton

GOALS	Goals should be stated in the **individual's or family's own words**, and include statements of dreams, hopes, role functions and vision of life. For each individual and family and/or setting, completion of all three sub-goals may not be necessary or appropriate.

Life Goals

Treatment Goals

To satisfy the legal requirements of the court order.

Life Enhancement Goals

ANTICIPATED DISCHARGE/ TRANSITION SETTING AND CRITERIA	Describe the setting in terms of location, level of care, length of stay and service needs. Describe changes in the individual's and family's current needs and circumstances that will need to occur in order for them to succeed in discharge or transition.

1. Completion of the 10-week Level II educational program
2. Sobriety during the class time period
3. Participation in an exit interview

BARRIERS	Describe the **challenges as a result of the mental illness or addictive disorder** that stand in the way of the individual and family meeting their goals and/or achieving the discharge/transition criteria. Identifying these barriers is critical to specifying the objectives as well as services and interventions in the following section of the plan.

- Does not think she has a problem with her alcohol consumption
- May be tempted to drink alcohol during the course of the program and fail her breathalyzer test.

Sally Hamilton

Objective Worksheet #1

This objective is related to which goal or transition/discharge criteria (i.e. treatment goal) or barrier?
To satisfy her legal requirements
Is there more than one *active* objective that addresses this goal? ☐ Yes ☑ No

OBJECTIVE	Using *action words, describe the **specific changes expected** in measurable and behavioral terms. Include the target date for completion.*
# 1	Sally will be abstinent while attending the 10 weeks of classes, as demonstrated by self-report and the results of a breathalyzer test administered prior to each class.
TARGET DATE	10 weeks

INDIVIDUAL/ FAMILY STRENGTHS	Identify the individual's and family's past accomplishments, current aspirations, motivations, personal attitudes, attributes, etc. which can be used to **help accomplish this objective.**
Supportive daughter who does not drink. Sally has some awareness of the difficulties alcohol use has/is causing her. Sally is living in a drug-free environment, has natural supports and is working full-time. She appears to be task-oriented.	

INTERVENTIONS	Describe the specific activity, service or treatment, the provider or other responsible person (including the individual and family), and the **intended purpose or impact as it relates to this objective.** The intensity, frequency and duration should also be specified.

- The addiction counselor will conduct a breathalyzer on Sally each week before class to assure she is alcohol-free for 10 weeks.
- Sally will participate in the court-required educational program for 10 weeks to increase her coping skills in support of her abstinence.
- The addiction counselor will conduct a 1-hour exit interview at the completion of the program to assess Sally's status, risk of relapse, and possible additional service needs.
- The addiction counselor will provide 4 1/2-hour sessions of motivational counseling in conjunction with the 10-week program to help Sally understand the stages of change in alcohol recovery.

INDIVIDUAL MENTAL HEALTH
AND ADDICTION RECOVERY PLAN

1st 90-Day Review

Sally Hamilton

□ **Objective Time Frame**   ☑ **Required Interval**   □ **Other** _____

CHANGE in ASSESSMENT DATA, FORMULATION, or DIAGNOSIS
Sally has moved from pre-contemplation to the contemplation stage of her drinking

INDIVIDUAL'S/FAMILY'S COMMENTS and SELF-ASSESSMENT
Sally reluctantly acknowledges that her use of alcohol has interfered with her life at times over the years and that she is feeling increasingly out of control.

CHANGE in GOALS, BARRIERS, or TRANSITION/ DISCHARGE PLANS
Sally has met her initial goal of satisfying her legal requirements. She attended all of the educational groups, had a weekly breathalyzer test, completed all 4 motivational counseling sessions and has had an exit interview.
Sally now feels that she at least needs to cut back or stop drinking entirely but remains ambivalent about giving up alcohol. She is asking for help over the next 8 weeks to try and reduce her alcohol intake to a limited amount on weekends only and is willing to reconsider any additional treatment needs in 2 months.
There is a new goal and a new objective developed.

INDIVIDUAL'S RESPONSE TO INTERVENTIONS

OBJECTIVE #	OBJECTIVE STATUS	OBJECTIVE CHANGED	INTERVENTION CHANGED
1	☑ MET □ PARTIALLY MET □ NOT MET	□ YES □ NO	□ YES □ NO

NARRATIVE SUMMARY of TREATMENT PLAN UPDATE	*Changes since last review, and rationale for treatment or medication changes, if applicable*

During the exit interview, Sally admitted that she had not been honest and was unable to maintain sobriety during the 10 weeks of class, oftentimes drinking on the weekends. She learned some things during the classes and is now worried that alcohol may truly be a problem for her. She recognizes that she needs help from a counselor and her family to face this problem but still wants to try and reduce her use rather than commit to sobriety. She wants to better understand the process of recovery, where she is at, and what she can do to regain control of her life and alcohol use.

Revised Individual Mental Health
and Addiction Recovery Plan
for

Sally Hamilton

 **GOALS**

Goals should be stated in the **individual's or family's own words**, and include statements of dreams, hopes, role functions and vision of life. For each individual and family and/or setting, completion of all three sub-goals may not be necessary or appropriate.

Life Goals

Treatment Goals
"I want to cut back on my drinking."

Life Enhancement Goals

ANTICIPATED DISCHARGE/ TRANSITION SETTING AND CRITERIA

Describe the setting in terms of location, level of care, length of stay and service needs. Describe changes in the individual's and family's current needs and circumstances that will need to occur in order for them to succeed in discharge or transition.

1. Sally will achieve abstinence from alcohol or will substantially reduce the amount she drinks.
2. Sally will have a viable relapse prevention or harm reduction plan.

BARRIERS

Describe the **challenges as a result of the mental illness or addictive disorder** that stand in the way of the individual and family meeting their goals and/or achieving the discharge/transition criteria. Identifying these barriers is critical to specifying the objectives as well as services and interventions in the following section of the plan.

- Still has some ambivalence about her problem with her alcohol consumption.
- Lack of sober support system.
- Lacks insight and skills necessary to support her recovery.

Sally Hamilton

Objective Worksheet #2
Based on review

This objective is related to which goal or transition/discharge criteria (i.e. treatment goal) or barrier?
Treatment goal to reduce or eliminate alcohol use
Is there more than one *active* objective that addresses this goal?   ☐ Yes   ☑ No

OBJECTIVE	*Using action words, describe the **specific changes expected** in measurable and behavioral terms. Include the target date for completion.*
# 1	Sally will reduce her consumption of alcohol to no more than one glass of wine on the weekend for 4 consecutive weeks and will otherwise abstain from alcohol.
TARGET DATE	8 weeks

INDIVIDUAL/FAMILY STRENGTHS	*Identify the individual's and family's past accomplishments, current aspirations, motivations, personal attitudes, attributes, etc. which can be used to **help accomplish this objective.***

- Supportive daughter who does not drink.
- Increased awareness of the difficulties alcohol use is causing her.
- New level of motivation.

INTERVENTIONS	*Describe the specific activity, service or treatment, the provider or other responsible person (including the individual and family), and the **intended purpose or impact as it relates to this objective.** The intensity, frequency and duration should also be specified.*

- The addiction counselor will formally evaluate Sally's stage of change/recovery using the SOCRATES scale within 1 week and then again in 8 weeks to monitor her status and progress.
- Staff psychologist will meet with Sally for 1 hour /week × 4 weeks for motivational counseling to enhance current level of engagement in recovery process.
- Multi-family psychoeducation sessions every other week for 2 hours, ongoing, for Sally and her daughter to help build on family support for sobriety/harm reduction.
- Sally agrees to attend a minimum of 3 AA meetings a week for the next 8 weeks to try and resolve her ambivalence about abstinence.

Appendix C
County Mental Health—Multidisciplinary Intake Assessment (Re-Admission)
March 4, 2004

Last Name   *Hewlett*   **First Name**   *Sam*   **Dob** *7/9/50*

Data Sources ☒ **Client interview** ☒ **Record review** ☐ **Other** *(specify)* _____

Identifying Information

Sam Hewlett is a 53-year-old heterosexual, English-speaking, divorced, Caucasian male. He has no children. Sam is disabled as a result of a chronic and severe mental illness and receives SSI and Medicaid benefits. In the past he has been diagnosed with schizophrenia, schizoaffective disorder, bi-polar disorder, and anti-social personality disorder. In addition, he has had a long-standing pattern of alcohol, cocaine, and amphetamine abuse.

Sam is now retuning to the mental health center requesting services. He was discharged from clean-and-sober supported housing 6 months ago due to recurrent drug use. At that time he requested that his case be closed and he discontinued all services. He is temporarily living with another client. He has a Section 8 housing voucher that must be activated soon or it will be lost; this is part of his motivation in seeking readmission at this time. Although Sam has a history of legal involvement and probation he is not currently involved with the court system.

Sam was previously under the psychiatric care of Dr. Johnson at Community Support Services where he had been receiving regular pharmacotherapy. He was last seen in June 2003 and at that time was prescribed Haldol decanoate.

Consumer's Identified Concerns, Needs, and Recovery Goals

Sam is requesting services at this time because he is highly motivated to secure his own housing. However, Sam feels that he cannot manage the Section 8 process on his own as a result of a recent recurrence of symptoms including poor sleep, occasional voices, low energy, and difficulty in thinking clearly. He has been off meds for about 4 months and worries that he is relapsing. He also reports a recent increase in his drinking after a recent pattern of relatively controlled alcohol use. He states that he is tired of the chaos in his life.

Psychiatric Evaluation *completed by Christine Harris, MD*

History of the Present Illness

Currently, Sam seems to be struggling with feelings of anxiety and depression, which have been intensifying over the past 3-4 weeks. He states that he feels worthless much of the time and is tired of all his ups and downs. He wants attention from others, but when he receives it his feelings of self-blame, loneliness, and sadness persist. He is seeking the approval of his parents, particularly his father, but they are unwilling to engage with him at all because of past problems. He reports hearing dim, faint, voices that he cannot make out and is fearful of the return of more intrusive auditory hallucinations. He denies suicidal ideation but reports feeling that he cannot function daily and is overwhelmed by the problems of trying to find Section 8 housing.

Sam has not been taking any antipsychotic or antidepressant medications for the past 4-6 months although he has been able to get some Ativan from his PCP and on the street. He is returning to the clinic at this time because he feels that he needs to get back on meds before "something bad happens" but is not sure he wants to take monthly shots because of the side effects and he has some mild lip and tongue movements consistent with a diagnosis of Tardive Dyskinesia. Sam states that he is willing to "trade" taking medications for some help with his housing.

Past Psychiatric History

Sam has been hospitalized or jailed at least 7 times over the past 25 years. He has lived in various board and care homes and has been treated primarily at North County Mental Health. His treatment has been complicated by poor compliance and ongoing poly-substance abuse.

Sam describes having substance abuse problems and problems with the law since high school. At that time LSD was his drug of choice and he used it heavily. His first psychotic break occurred at age 17 in the jail. He was hallucinating, had not slept in 3 weeks, and was beaten up in jail as a "snitch."

He says he has been hospitalized at least 4 times but is unable to recall "the particulars." He says they were not all drug-related and recalls one instance where he believed a book he was reading was coming true. He was placed in Eastern State Hospital after taking off his clothes in a farmer's field.

He says his symptoms typically involve hearing voices, racing thoughts, inability to "shut up," and talking to himself. He denies that he has ever been suicidal. He has been assaultive and apparently broke someone's arm, although he has no recollection of these events.

Few details of past hospitalizations are available. Records indicate Sam was first hospitalized in 1973 with symptoms of extreme paranoia as well as auditory and visual hallucinations. During other hospitalizations, complaints of severe depression have also been reported.

Sam was last hospitalized on 2/8/01 at the County Hospital on an emergency detention order. He was brought in from clean-and-sober housing, after a roommate called stating he was stabbing a refrigerator with a knife. He told the police that the devil was trying to kill him and he had the knife to protect Jesus Christ. He was found to be highly agitated, religiously preoccupied, with presumed self-inflicted abrasions and singed hair, delusional ideation, and he required restraints. Drug screen at that time was positive for amphetamines. He was known to have been abusing cocaine into 12/2000 and occasionally self-medicating with Haldol.

During Sam's hospitalization, his informal probation for drug paraphernalia possession was revoked and he was placed on formal probation for 2 years through 3/03. Continued residence in a supervised clean-and-sober board and care was a condition of his probation as was participation in the county mental health program and random urine screens for drug use. Sam was reasonably compliant with the rules of the home, met weekly with his case manager, and saw the psychiatrist monthly. During this time he expressed a desire to live on his own and he completed a Section 8 application. However, when his probation expired he was frustrated and angry that his Section 8 was not approved, began to refuse to meet with his case manager and eventually refused all services, began drinking, and was evicted from the board and care.

Sam has been given several diagnoses in the past and his symptom presentation has always been confounded by his substance use history and withdrawal. There has been repeated speculation about the possibility that not only does he have an affective component to his illness, but that perhaps a more accurate Axis I diagnosis is major depression with psychotic features and not schizophrenia.

Substance Abuse History

Sam began drinking at age 8. His father was a liquor salesman, who stored alcohol in the garage. He says he has never been an alcoholic, but has only been able to refrain from alcohol use when incarcerated or on probation. During his 20s and 30s Sam used a number of different drugs including marijuana, amphetamines, cocaine, hallucinogens, and others. He denies any history of IV drug use. Cocaine has been his drug of choice since 1998. In 1996, Sam was jailed for cocaine possession and put on probation. He violated his probation in 1997 for using marijuana while living in a group residences. In 1998, he was arrested again for marijuana use.

Family Psychiatric History

Sam denies that there is a history of substance abuse or mental illness in the family. A review of the past record reveals, however, that both Sam's father and two brothers have had problems with alcohol and drugs and a younger brother died of an apparent suicide.

Medical History

Allergy

He is allergic to bee-stings.

Medications

He takes no medications other than psychiatric meds except occasional Tylenol.

General Health

Sam reports that he is in general good health although currently he complains of a cold. Overall his appetite has been poor but his weight has been relatively stable. His height is 5'10" and his weight is 170 lbs. He denies that he has ever used IV drugs, and denies any history of hepatitis or HIV. His last physical exam was by Dr. Richards in Westville, 11/2 years ago. He had a crown placed in 1999 but has not received cleaning or regular dental care. He has not had an eye exam for years.

Sam has been tobacco free for 5 years. He reports that he drinks about 2 cups of coffee and 3-5 colas a day.

Past Illnesses, Treatments, and Trauma

He has had two episodes of concussion: one at age 11, after flipping into the side of a swimming pool, and again following a MVA in '71. There is no history of seizures. He has limited motion in his right wrist.

Mental Status Exam

Sam is casually dressed and somewhat unkempt with uncombed hair and dirty clothes but appears to have bathed within the past few days. He is friendly and cooperative. His nose is running and he complains of it being sore. He denies this is cocaine related. Physically he is quiet. He complains of feeling depressed and anxious. Affect is blunted but congruent with a tense, tired look on his face and he is somewhat fidgety. Thoughts are organized and there is no apparent loosening of associations but he seems to have some trouble tracking and is easily derailed. There are no apparent delusions or other psychotic symptoms. He denies visual hallucinations but does report hearing some non-descript noises that he knows are not real. He denies recently talking to himself. Sam has some insight into his problems and needs but remains overall guarded, defensive, and reluctant to talk about the role of substance use in his life. No abnormal movements were noted. He denied paranoia, and suicidal or homicidal ideation.

He was oriented × 3, recalled 4 recent presidents, and 3/3 objects at 5 minutes. He was able to spell "world" backward and to abstract simple proverbs, i.e., let sleeping dogs lie was translated "forget about trouble." His answers to judgment questions were marginal (i.e., "See if there is a fire, look for an extinguisher" in a crowded theater).

Psychosocial History

Sam was born in Alaska. He moved to Westville at age 4. Sam says he no longer has a good relationship with his parents but wants to find a way to make amends for the past. This is an important step towards sobriety, as he wants to regain their trust. His mother was diagnosed 2 months ago with a malignant bone tumor in her leg. His father is fairly distrustful of him. He has a brother in Southville and another in Northdale. A sister lives in Centerville.

Sam was an above average student through grade school and into junior high. He was not in special classes. However, Sam began to have problems with his family and juvenile authorities at age 15 and he was sent to the Youth Authority ranch for 8 months during the 11th grade following repeated violations of probation and recurrent truancy. He did poorly in school but eventually received a GED in 1972.

Sam was married for about 5 years in his mid-20s but feels that his mental illness and drug problems destroyed his marriage. He has had no contact with his ex-wife in 20 years. There were no children in the marriage. Since that time, Sam has had difficulty in maintaining any relationship of significance although he talks of wanting to remarry.

Since his early 20s Sam has worked a variety of unskilled jobs, including fieldwork, warehousing, and janitorial work. He has been on SSI since 1993. He has no structured daily activities, and spends the day either wandering the downtown streets or visiting friends.

Sam has had some success in the past with 12-step involvement. At this time he has not attended a meeting of the local Dual Recovery group in about 3 months and is ashamed to go and have to admit to his recent setback and failures.

Psychosocial Skills / Needs Inventory

General Life Management Skills

Grooming and personal hygiene are always relaxed, that is, without much attention or concern. He manages to get what he needs in the way of basic food and clothing without aid. He uses public transportation well. He does not follow through with appointments or agreements. He has limited abilities in household management skills and no money management skills. He has been the suspected cause of two kitchen fires in the past.

Social Skills

Sam has generally appropriate social skills. He is quite self-effacing and non-threatening. He has the ability to make friends but has a hard time maintaining relationships. For the most part he prefers to be alone.

Community Participation Skills

He is not participating in any community activities and has had poor follow through in the past with any suggestions, ideas, or referrals. He denies any interest in employment, education, or volunteerism at this time. He makes no connection between his lack of activity and his mental health and addiction problems.

Housing

He now resides with another MH client who has given him a month to make other arrangements. He has just received a Section 8 voucher that must be used soon. Even if he secures housing, his ability to maintain a residence is at risk because of his history of poor judgment and behavior. While living in a supervised residence he has been known to bring in people off of the street (against the rules of the house) and has been evicted on several occasions.

Legal Issues

He has a long history of legal difficulties (see the psychiatric evaluation). He is free of all charges and probation at this time.

Summary, Analysis, and Formulation

Sam's return and request to resume services at this time may mark a turning point in his life-long struggle with mental illness and substance dependence. He has come to seek help at this time without coercion or requirement and seems genuinely motivated to make some changes and achieve some stability. Having his own place to live has long been a dream of his and the Section 8 voucher may be a once in a lifetime chance for him to finally obtain housing. Although Sam's insight is limited, he is aware that he is unable to meet his current challenges and that he is in need of help in managing his life and his mental health and substance dependence problems if he is to succeed.

Sam has a number of strengths to draw upon, ranging from his endurance and survival skills to his social skills and a past history of varying degrees of relational and occupational skills. Perhaps at this time his greatest asset is his housing voucher, his motivation, and willingness to seek help and pursue change. In addition, Sam has good knowledge of the mental health and the addictions treatment system, has SSI benefits and Medicaid, and access to transportation. His easygoing personality is a source of strength for him since people seem to enjoy his company for the most part. His interest in restoring his relationship with his family is another potential source of support.

Using a stage-wise approach to understanding Sam's needs at this time, he seems to have moved into "contemplation" and is potentially on the threshold of active treatment. Helping him to stabilize his immediate needs may well be a critical first step to any future change.

The greatest threats or barriers to Sam's success are the perennial challenges of his Axis I disorder and the disruption in his functioning which result from the symptoms, his poor adherence to treatment by history, his continued alcohol use and risk of relapse to a pattern of poly-substance dependence, and his lack of life skills management which need to be addressed if he is to succeed in securing and maintaining independent housing. However, if Sam can succeed in meeting his housing needs, the likelihood of additional gains in recovery remains a possibility.

Using the AACP LOCUS, Sam appears to be at Level 3—high intensity community-based services. This level of care provides treatment to clients who need intensive support and treatment, but who are living either independently or with minimal support in the community. Service needs do not require daily supervision, but treatment needs require contact several times per week. Accordingly, Sam will be assigned to the dual disorders treatment team and linked with a care manager who can help him to develop an individual recovery plan consistent with his stated goals and objectives.

Sam's current symptoms suggest that he is suffering from a depressive disorder although he could be in the early stages of a psychotic decompensation. However, it is noteworthy that he has done reasonably well over the past several months without antipsychotic medication. Helping him to better manage his stresses and pharmacologic re-evaluation should all be a part of his individual plan.

Sam will meet the criteria for discharge or transition to a lower level of care when he has sustained clinical stability, is at low risk of relapse for his substance use disorder, and has a stable housing situation. If he can be engaged in services, his anticipated length of stay is a minimum of 1 year.

DSM-IV Diagnosis		**Code**
Axis I	Schizophrenia, chronic undifferentiated type	295.90
	R/O major depression	
	Alcohol abuse	305
	Cocaine dependence in sustained partial remission	304.20
	Cannabis dependence in remission	304.30
Axis II	No diagnosis	V71.09
	R/O personality disorder	
Axis III	S/P head injury 1971	
	Right arm injury with decreased ROM in wrist	
	Allergic to bee-stings	
Axis IV	Problems with primary support group	
Axis V	**Current GAF** 31 **Highest GAF in past year** 45	

LEVEL OF CARE DETERMINATION GRID

Level of Care / Dimensions	Recovery Maintenance Health Management	Low Intensity Community Based Services	High Intensity Community Based Services	Medically Monitored Non-Residential Services	Medically Monitored Residential Services	Medically Managed Residential Services
Dimensions						
I. Risk of Harm	2 or less	2 or less	3 or less	3 or less	☐ 3	☐ 4
II. Functional Status	2 or less	2 or less	3 or less	3 or less	☐* 3	☐ 4
III. Co-Morbidity	2 or less	2 or less	3 or less	3 or less	☐* 3	☐ 4
IV A. Recovery Environment "Stress"	Sum of IV A + IV B is 4 or less	Sum of IV A + IV B is 5 or less	Sum of IV A + IV B is 5 or less	3 or 4	4 or more	4 or more
IV B. Recovery Environment "Support"	2 or less	2 or less	3 or less	3 or less	4 or more	4 or more
V. Treatment & Recovery Hx	2 or less	2 or less	3 or less	3 or 4	3 or more	4 or more
VI. Engagement	2 or less	2 or less	3 or less	3 or 4	3 or more	4 or more
Composite Rating	10 to 13	14 to 16	17 to 19	20 to 22	23 to 27	28 or more

☐ indicates independent criteria – requires admission to this level regardless of composite score

*Unless sum of IV A and IV B equals 2

MENTAL HEALTH AND ADDICTION RECOVERY PLAN
FOR

Sam Hewlett

GOALS	*Goals should be stated in the **individual's or family's own words**, and include statements of dreams, hopes, role functions and vision of life. For each individual and family and/or setting, completion of all three sub-goals may not be necessary or appropriate.*

Life Goals

"I want my own place to live."

Service/Treatment Goals

Sam demonstrates the necessary skills to be able to live independently with minimal ongoing support or supervision from the treatment team.

Life Enhancement Goals

"I want to have a better relationship with my parents."

ANTICIPATED DISCHARGE/ TRANSITION SETTING AND CRITERIA	*Describe the setting in terms of location, level of care, length of stay, and service needs. Describe changes in the individual's and family's current needs and circumstances that will need to occur in order to succeed in discharge or transition.*

- Sam has maintained independent housing for at least 6 months.
- Sam has not had any behavioral or functional problems related to drug and/or alcohol abuse.

BARRIERS	*Describe the **challenges as a result of the mental illness or addictive disorder** that stand in the way of the individual and family meeting their goals and/or achieving the discharge/transition criteria. Identifying these barriers is critical to specifying the objectives as well as services and interventions in the following section of the plan.*

- Continued psychiatric symptoms.
- Difficulty in completing Section 8 housing process on his own.
- Needs additional life-management skills.
- Risk of alcohol or other drug abuse.

Sam Hewlett

Objective Worksheet #1

This objective is related to which goal(s) or transition/discharge criteria (i.e., treatment goal) or barrier?
This objective relates immediately to Sam's life goal and the service/treatment goal.
Is there more than one *active* objective that addresses this goal?   ☐ Yes   ☑ No

OBJECTIVE	*Using action words, describe the **specific changes expected** in measurable and behavioral terms. Include the target date for completion.*
# 1	Sam will be living in his own Section 8 apartment.
TARGET DATE	within 60 days

INDIVIDUAL/ FAMILY STRENGTHS	*Identify the individual's and family's past accomplishments, current aspirations, motivations, personal attitudes, attributes, etc. which can be used to **help accomplish this objective**.*
Section 8 voucher, motivation, past history of independent living	

INTERVENTIONS	*Describe the specific activity, service or treatment, the provider or other responsible person (including the individual and family), and the **intended purpose or impact as it relates to this objective**. The intensity, frequency and duration should also be specified.*

- Psychiatrist to meet with Sam every 1–2 weeks for the next 2 months to clarify diagnosis and prescribe medications to reduce acute symptoms so that Sam can think clearly and pursue housing options.
- Case manager from the Dual Recovery treatment team to meet with Sam up to 4 hours per week for next 8 weeks to provide him support, direction, monitoring, and linkage to local housing resources and assist him as necessary with relocation.
- Occupational therapist to provide life skills management training, 30 minutes per session, twice a week for 4 weeks, for basic household safety so Sam has skills necessary to move in and maintain his apartment.
- Addictions counselor to provide motivational therapy 1 hour a week for 2 months to help Sam maintain current engagement in recovery process and support harm reduction strategies for current EtOH use.
- Sam to attend Dual Recovery group meetings 2 times per week for the next 8 weeks in order to re-engage with supports in the community, to provide some social interaction for him, and to assist in managing his substance dependence problems.

INDIVIDUAL PLAN
90-Day Review
Sam Hewlett

☑ Objective Time Frame   ☐ Required Interval   ☐ Other _____

CHANGE in ASSESSMENT DATA, FORMULATION, or DIAGNOSIS

Sam has responded well to a combination of citalopram and low-dose olanzapine with improvement in mood and overall function further supporting a primary diagnosis of depression. He was not been able to secure Section 8 housing in the community but his case manager was able to negotiate with Sam's parents for him to rent their in-law unit under the Section 8 voucher.

INDIVIDUAL'S / FAMILY'S COMMENTS and SELF-ASSESSMENT

Sam and his family are pleased with his improvement and the restoration of a healthier relationship, but there is a great deal of tension and anxiety about the arrangement and Sam's ability to meet his parent's expectations. Sam has sought a sponsor at the local DRA chapter.

CHANGE in GOALS, BARRIERS, or TRANSITION/DISCHARGE PLANS

Sam's parents have established a zero-tolerance policy for his drug and EtOH use and his ability to adequately maintain the apartment in order for him to keep his housing

INDIVIDUAL'S RESPONSE TO INTERVENTIONS

OBJECTIVE #	OBJECTIVE STATUS	OBJECTIVE CHANGED	INTERVENTION CHANGED
1	☑ met ☐ partially met ☐ not met	☐ yes ☐ no	☐ yes ☐ no
	☐ met ☐ partially met ☐ not met	☐ yes ☐ no	☐ yes ☐ no

NARRATIVE SUMMARY of TREATMENT PLAN UPDATE

Changes since last review, rationale for treatment or medication changes, if applicable

During a team meeting—when it looked like the Section 8 voucher would expire before Sam could find housing—the case manager and social worker decided to approach Sam's parents based upon conversations with Sam and his expressed grief over the alienation he has had from his parents—especially because of his mother's recent cancer and surgery. His parents were delighted to hear about Sam's progress and commitment to change, and felt they wanted to do what they could to help but did *not* want to fall into past patterns of co-dependency. Sam has benefited tremendously from the motivational therapy and understanding of a step-wise approach to recovery, is feeling much better about himself as a result of the antidepressant meds and group therapy, and feels he is ready once again to tackle a commitment to sobriety with new motivation. Both Sam and his parents recognize that they all need some help in getting beyond past problems and hurts and are willing to participate in treatment to support Sam's recovery.

Objective Worksheet #2

Created at review and update

This objective is related to which goal(s) or transition/discharge criteria (i.e. treatment goal) or barrier?
This objective relates immediately to Sam's life goal, the service/treatment goal, and his life enhancement goal
Is there more than one *active* objective that addresses this goal? ☐ Yes ☑ No

OBJECTIVE	*Using action words, describe the **specific changes expected** in measurable and behavioral terms. Include the target date for completion.*
# 2	Sam will maintain his living situation in his in-laws' unit, as reported by Sam and his parents.
TARGET DATE	6 months

INDIVIDUAL/ FAMILY STRENGTHS	*Identify the individual's and family's past accomplishments, current aspirations, motivations, personal attitudes, attributes, etc. which can be used to **help accomplish this objective**.*
Renewed family relationship, improved mood and functioning as a result of treatment, peer sponsor at Dual Recovery Anonymous (DRA)	

INTERVENTIONS	*Describe the specific activity, service, or treatment, the provider or other responsible person (including the individual and family), and the **intended purpose or impact as it relates to this objective**. The intensity, frequency, and duration should also be specified.*

- Psychiatrist to provide monthly ongoing pharmacotherapy management for 30 minutes each visit to include continued training on medication self-management.
- Case manager to coordinate and monitor for up to 2 hours weekly for 3 months Sam's attendance with his sponsor at 5 DRA weekly meeting.
- Occupational therapist to provide 4 1-hour sessions for the next 4 weeks at Sam's apartment to teach him how to use the kitchen and clean his apartment.
- Psychologist to provide weekly 1-hour family therapy for Sam, parents, and local siblings for 10 weeks to help family repair old wounds and support Sam and his mother at time of family crisis.
- Drug abuse counselor to meet with Sam 1 hour/week x 20 weeks to help Sam develop a relapse prevention plan including strategies for managing uncomfortable feelings without using drugs or EtOH.

APPENDIX D
PINE GROVE MENTAL HEALTH CLINIC
INTAKE ASSESSMENT
for
Carmen Suarez   DOB 10/24/87

Informants   ☒ **Individual**   ☒ **Family**   ☒ **Friends**   ☐ **Teacher**
☐ **Employer**   ☐ **Primary Care Provider**   ☐ **Other**

I. PRESENTING PROBLEM *Reason why individual is seeking services*

Carmen says: "I haven't been feeling well. I quit my part-time job, and don't feel like driving or going to school anymore." In addition, Carmen's parents express grave concern for her well-being. They are very worried about changes in her mood, behavior, and school performance over the past several months.

Carmen was referred to the mental health clinic by the social worker at the local hospital following an evaluation in the emergency room 2 weeks ago. Carmen was brought in by her parents because of an acute episode of chest pains and breathing difficulties that they thought was a heart attack. Her medical exam was normal and she was diagnosed with a panic/anxiety attack and was referred to the hospital's crisis evaluation team. Although Carmen had not been particularly forthcoming, their assessment was that Carmen was under intense emotional stress and this was the source of her physical symptoms as well as her difficulties attending school and keeping up with her job. The social worker at the hospital urged Carmen and her parents to seek mental health treatment.

During her initial assessment interview with Miriam Puentes (which was conducted in Spanish) at Pine Grove Mental Health Clinic, Carmen broke into tears and began to speak more freely about her problems. She revealed that she had an abortion over 1 year ago and has been feeling increasingly guilty and troubled about this decision/action. She stated that at times she feels so upset that she says she wants to die and join her baby. Her parents knew of the abortion, but they did not support her decision. Her father has dramatically withdrawn his love and support from her over the past year in what had been a previously close father–daughter relationship.

For several weeks now Carmen has been complaining of nausea, vomiting, dizziness, headaches, and difficulty sleeping, accompanied by anxiety, worry, and fearfulness. She is often tearful and has been avoiding both her friends and her family preferring to spend many hours alone in her room. These symptoms have caused her to miss most of her days at school for the past month and about half of her shifts at work at a local fast-food restaurant. Carmen and her family have tried to manage her physical health problems, school absences, and feelings concerning the abortion on their own. They have engaged the advice of friends and family members as well as the parish priest and have pursued traditional herbal remedies to try and help relieve her symptoms. Recently they took Carmen to see a "curandero" (folk healer) with the belief that she is suffering from "susto" (fearfulness and spirit possession).

Carmen's relationship with her parents has become increasingly conflictual and distant, particularly with her father. Carmen is bilingual and sees herself as part of the American culture and is embarrassed by her parents' inability to speak English and "campesino" (old-country) attitudes. Carmen says that she would like to have a better relationship with her parents but not at the price of her independence and freedom.

Past Psychiatric/Psychological History *include past medications*

None. This is the first experience of psychiatric problems for this young woman.

Current Medications
include psychotropic, over-the-counter, herbal remedies (all meds taken over past 6 months)

Current Medications	Dosage	Frequency	Prescribed By
None			

Past Medical History *include hospitalizations, surgeries, physical limitations*

None

Family/Social History *include minor children, associated needs and risk factors*

This is an intact family, with a mother, father, and 6 children, ages 10 to 19 years, with Carmen being the oldest female. Her one brother is 19 and living outside the home, and her two other brothers are 10 and 15. She has two younger sisters, ages 11 and 13. There are no reported difficulties with the other children. Both of her parents were born in Mexico and are monolingual Spanish-speaking. All of the children are bilingual, although the older children, some of whom were born in Mexico, are more comfortable with Spanish. They came to the U.S. from a small rural community and have been living in Texas for the past 15 years. They live in a predominantly Anglo-American neighborhood. The family is Catholic and attends church regularly.

No one in the family has ever sought mental health help in the past and both Carmen and her parents have a sense of shame and failure about this. However, they recognize that their own efforts to help have not worked. Carmen is the first child expected to graduate high school—her older brother left in 11th grade—and they want to make sure she completes school.

Current and Past Employment History *include past trainings*

Carmen works part-time after school at a local restaurant. Previously she did child care and baby-sitting.

Education *include highest grade completed, schools attended, special education, discipline problems, etc*

She is currently in the 12th grade at Radburn High School. She is an excellent student, receiving A and B grades, and hoping to go to college. She has had some recent problems with school attendance, and has missed so much work that she is worried that she may not be able to graduate in June as planned.

Current Legal Status	☒ No legal involvement	☐ Parole	☐ Probation
	☐ Charges Pending	☐ Previous jail	☐ Has guardian

II. DRUG/ALCOHOL ASSESSMENT

SUBSTANCE USE HISTORY *include experimentation & accidental ingestion; include alcohol, tobacco, and caffeine*										
Drug	**Method**	**Age 1st used**	**Age last used**	**Onset of heavy use**	**# Days used in last 30**	**Amt used in last 48 hrs.**	**1st as RX?**	**Last used when?**	**Amt used daily/ weekly?**	**Drug of choice?**
Alcohol	Oral	14	16		0	0				

Any changes in patterns of use over time?   No

Does individual ever drink or drug more than he/she intends? Rarely

Has individual experienced an increase in the amount he/she can use to get the same effect? No

Is there a history of overdose?   No   **If yes, describe:**

Is there a history of seizures?   No   **If yes, describe:**

Is there a history of blackouts?   No   **If yes, describe:**

Has individual ever used medications to either get high or come down from being high?   No

With whom does individual usually use?

Has individual had previous substance abuse treatment?   **If yes, where:**

Assessment of risk in this area: low

III.   HEALTH AND SAFETY

Identified Risk Factors

☒ Unsafe Sex Practices	☐ Physical Abuse	☐ Impulsivity
☒ Pregnancy	☐ Residential Safety	☐ Chronic Health Problems
☐ Sexual Abuse	☐ IV Drug Abuse	☐ Non-attentive to Need for Care
☐ Alcohol/Substance Abuse	☐ Diet/Nutrition	☐ Hygiene
☐ Self Harm	☐ Nicotine Use	☐ Household Management
☐ Aggression Toward Others	☐ Medication Interaction	☐ Physical Disability
☐ Verbal/Emotional Abuse	☐ Medication Management	☐ Recent Loss
☐ Children at risk	☐ Stress related to parenting	☐ Psychosis

Identified Needs

☐ Quarterly TD Screening	☐ Nutrition Assessment	☐ Dental Exam
☐ Vision Exam	☐ Labs—Frequency:	☐ Coordination of Care
☐ Assistance with children	☐ Health Care Assessment	
☐ Other:		

Unable to meet basic needs?

☐ Food	☐ Shelter	☐ Medical

Describe

Dangerousness

A. Suicide Risk   ☐ None

Describe history of suicidality   ☐ None

Ideation	☒ Yes	☐ No	Note	☐ Yes	☒ No
Chronic	☐ Yes	☒ No	Will	☐ Yes	☒ No
Acute	☐ Yes	☒ No	Give possessions away ☐ Yes		☒ No
Recent suicidal behavior ☐ Yes		☒ No	Other:		

Presence of Risk Factors   ☐ None

☒ Intent	☐ Plan	☐ Means to carry out plan
☐ Prior Attempts	☐ Likelihood of rescue	☐ Access to gun
☐ Lethality		

III. HEALTH AND SAFETY *(cont)*

B. Threat of Danger to Others

Thoughts of harm to others? ☐ Yes ☒ No

Recent threatening behavior?

☐ Identified Target   ☐ Intent   ☐ Access to gun

☐ Means to carry out   ☐ Lethality   ☐ Can thoughts
   plan   ☐ Plan   of harm be managed

☐ Prior aggression

C. Presence of Other High Risk Behaviors   ☒ None

☐ Cutting   ☐ Head banging   ☐ Risk-taking
☐ Anorexia/Bulimia   ☐ Poor or dangerous ☐ Other self-injurious
☐ Other: relationship   behavior

D. Presence of Deterrents   N/A

E. Other Safety Concerns   ☒ None

F. Assessment of Risk

IV. FUNCTIONAL SUMMARY

Clinician's view; check column as applicable

Function	N/A	Strength	Concern	Function	N/A	Strength	Concern
Daily Activities				Safety	X		
Family Relationships			X	Legal	X		
Social Relationships		X		Cognitive Functioning	X		
School			X	Housing	X		
Work	X			Social Skills			X
Finances	X			Impulse Control	X		
Physical Health	X			Responsibility			X

V. SUMMARY OF STRENGTHS, ABILITIES, NEEDS, AND PREFERENCES *clinician's view with client's input*

Carmen states her main interest at this time is graduating high school and furthering her education. She is a good student who is perfectly capable of going to college, if she feels better, stays in school and makes up for lost days of school. She participates actively in school, is on the cheerleading squad, and demonstrates good social relationships and comfort levels with her peers. She did have a boyfriend 2 years ago with whom she became sexually involved, but has not dated since the abortion.

Carmen has been able to maintain a part-time job so that she can have her own money for clothes and cosmetics that her parents do not approve of. She has a loving, intact family although her relationship with her parents is painful, distant, and conflictual at the moment. She would like to have a better relationship with her parents, but she realizes that may not be possible at this time.

Even though she speaks English fluently, her preference is for a Spanish-speaking counselor, who she feels will understand her better. Although she expresses pride in her cultural heritage and traditions, she states that she is sometimes embarrassed by her parents who seem very old-fashioned and out of touch with the world in which she lives—largely because of their unwillingness to learn and speak English.

VI. OBSTACLES/BARRIERS TO SUCCESSFUL OUTCOMES

Carmen is the first member of her family to ever seek mental health services and is embarrassed about being here. She does not think she is "crazy" and initially was very reticent during the intake process. However, once the assessment progressed she started crying, and then spoke more freely, describing the pregnancy and abortion she had a little over 1 year ago.

Her parents do not see the connection between her abortion last year and the subsequent change in her mood, affect, physical health, and family relationships. Although they helped her get an abortion, they did not support her decision, primarily due to their religious beliefs, and have simply tried to put it in the past and move on. Although her parents have lived in the U.S. for the past 15 years, they do not seem to have accepted the way of life in Texas, according to Carmen. Their beliefs, traditions, and attitudes are all steeped in the Mexican culture.

VII. MENTAL STATUS ASSESSMENT
describe any deviation from the norm in each category

Appearance
- ☒ Well groomed
- ☐ Disheveled
- ☐ Bizarre
- ☐ Other

Attitude
- ☒ Cooperative
- ☐ Uncooperative
- ☐ Suspicious

- ☒ Guarded
- ☐ Belligerent/hostile
- ☐ Other

Mood
- ☐ Normal
- ☒ Depressed
- ☒ Anxious

- ☐ Euphoric
- ☐ Irritable
- ☐ Other

Speech
- ☐ Normal
- ☒ Soft
- ☐ Loud

- ☐ Pressured
- ☐ Halting
- ☐ Incoherent

- ☐ Slurred
- ☐ Nonverbal
- ☐ Limited communication skills
- ☐ Uses yes/no only
- ☐ Uses a picture board
- ☐ Other

VII.   MENTAL STATUS ASSESSMENT (cont)

Motor Activity

☒ Calm
☐ Hyperactive
☐ Agitated
☐ Other
☐ Tremor/tics
☐ Lethargic

Thought Process

☒ Intact
☐ Tangential
☐ Circumstantial
☐ Loose association
☐ Flight of ideas
☐ Concrete thinking
☐ Inability to abstract
☐ Only follow 1 step directions

Affect

☐ Appropriate
☒ Sad
☐ Flat
☒ Anxious
☐ Other
☐ Inappropriate
☐ Angry
☐ Constricted
☐ Labile

Thought Content

☐ Normal
☒ Morbid
☒ Phobias
☐ Aggressive
☐ Other
☐ Paranoid
☒ Somatic complaints
☒ Obsessive

Orientation

☒ Person
☒ Place
☒ Time
☐ Responds to name
☐ Recognizes familiar faces
☐ Knows daily schedule

Psychosis

☒ Denies

Hallucinations

☒ Auditory
☐ Visual
☐ Other
☐ Denies
She says she has been hearing a baby
cry when she goes to school

Command Hallucinations

☐ Harm to self
☐ Harm to others
☐ Can resist commands
☒ Denies

Bizarre Delusions

☐ Thought broadcasting
☐ Thought insertion
☐ Thought withdrawal
☐ Ideas of reference
☐ Being controlled
☒ Denies

Delusional Belief

☒ Religious
☐ Somatic
☒ Persecutory
☐ Grandiosity
☐ Denies

VII.   MENTAL STATUS ASSESSMENT (cont)

Summary/Assessment of Mental Status Exam

Carmen is a well-dressed, soft-spoken, intelligent Mexican-American adolescent who appears her stated age of 17 years. She appears depressed with low mood, and notable anxiety and worry along with complaints of physical distress and social withdrawal. She seems to be preoccupied with traumatic events of the past and despondent over her father's apparent rejection of her. Her physical problems appear to be psychosomatic in origin and associated with her current difficulties at home and school, and are largely due to her feelings about her abortion last year. She reports hearing voices related to the abortion that is a source of tremendous internal conflict and family discord, although it is not clear if these are intrusive ruminative thoughts or actual hallucinations. Although her overall reality testing is intact, she reports fears that her problems are a result of possession by "bad spirits" as a result of her past wrongs and it is not clear whether or not these should be considered delusions or culturally derived religious beliefs. She has said she wants to die and join her baby, but she has no plan for suicide or previous attempts. There is no evidence of any significant cognitive impairment at this time, although she does complain of difficulty with concentration, memory, and clear thinking.

VIII.   CULTURAL FORMULATION

use the DSM-IV outline for cultural formulation

Cultural identity

Carmen readily identifies herself as Mexican-American and although she is bilingual, she has an expressed preference and increased comfort in speaking Spanish for her mental heath treatment. She and her family are practicing Catholics and the beliefs and teachings of the church play a significant role in her feelings of guilt about having had an abortion.

Cultural explanations of illness

Carmen's problems have up until now been understood by her family and community as the symptoms of *susto*, but with the inability to get relief from traditional healing methods, they are now open to considering a medical diagnosis.

Cultural factors related to psychosocial environment and levels of functioning

Although not born in the U.S., Carmen is culturally first generation and is struggling to find her own level of comfort in a transition between her parents link to the language, culture, and traditions of Mexico and her own desire to be "American." She expresses a desire to be more independent of family as well as pursue a college education and career beyond the traditional expectations of woman as a mother closely tied to and dependent on her family of origin.

Cultural elements in the client–provider relationship

Carmen has a clear preference for a Spanish-speaking female clinician and appears to be more comfortable with a Latina whom she feels can understand her, her family, and her conflicts about issues of culture and identity.

Implications for diagnosis and service plan

Issues of culture and identity are a major factor in understanding Carmen, her family, and their current needs. From language to attitudes and beliefs, as well as comfort with the entire mental health process, sensitivity to the role of culture will be critical in successfully helping Carmen to move beyond her current crisis. An important first step will be helping the family to resolve the question of *susto* and accept a diagnosis of depression and the implications for treatment. Even with this, any biological and psychosocial interventions will need to take into consideration the family's beliefs and traditions and comfort/discomfort with mental health treatment.

IX. DIAGNOSTIC INFORMATION

Code(s) & Nomenclature:

Axis I	Code 296.20	Major depression
Axis II	Code V71.09	No diagnosis on Axis II
Axis III	Code	Status post abortion
Axis IV	*Check all that are appropriate and specify the problem*	

✓ Problems with primary support group — Parents

Problems related to the social environment

✓ Educational problems — May not be able to graduate high school

Occupational problems

Housing problems

Economic problems

Problems with access to health care services

Problems related to interaction with the legal system/crime

Other psychosocial and environmental problems

None

Axis V	**Current GAF**	43

PINE GROVE MENTAL HEALTH CLINIC

Parent/Child Questionnaire
for
Carmen Suarez   DOB 10/24/87

The goal of the Pine Grove Mental Health Center is to provide the most appropriate services that we can for your current problem(s). With that in mind we are asking that you complete this form. We are aware that it asks some very personal questions and you may have concerns answering them at this time. Please be aware that we will use this information to best serve you, our customer, and we need this information to help determine how to best serve you. We will not release this information to anyone without your written consent. *Please put "N/A" in any section that doesn't apply.*

Informational Sources   *who is filling out this form*   Mother—Pilar

Do *you* have any trouble speaking, hearing, or writing?

No—we speak and write Spanish. My friend, Anna Patterson, is completing this form for me.

Referral source   *who referred you to us*   Hospital social worker

Is the child a ward of the court?   No

Does your child have a guardian?   No

Tell us about your family's current or past involvement with any community agencies

None

Tell us about your child's current or past legal involvements

☒ No legal involvements   ☐ Detained   ☐ Probation

☐ Charges pending   ☐ Not Sure

Ethnic-Cultural Origin Hispanic. We are from Mexico.

Racial Background

Is your church, religion or spiritual beliefs important to your family?

If so please explain to us

Yes, we are very religious and active in our church

What is your family's first language?

Spanish

Why are you seeking service for your child and family?

Our daughter is very sad and troubled. Last week she had breathing problems and chest pains and we took her to the emergency room. The lady at the hospital suggested she needs help.

What kind of help does your family need?

To make our daughter feel better

Does your child have any difficulty with personal self-care?	☒ No ☐ Yes

If yes, list difficulties:

Does your child have a physical limitation or problems walking?	☒ No ☐ Yes

Does your child have any communication problems?	☒ No ☐ Yes

If yes, list problems:

Does your family have access to public transportation/etc?	☐ No ☒ Yes

List any recreational/community activities *include hobbies, school activities, sports, etc.*

She is a cheerleader at school, member of several clubs, and has a part-time job after school.

Previous Mental Health Services	☒ None

☐ Inpatient, describe where and when

☐ Outpatient, describe where and when

Psychological evaluations

Psychological Testing

IQ (if known)

Developmental History

Did mother experience any of the following during pregnancy with this child?

Check all that apply

☐ Used prescribed medicine	☐ Smoked cigarettes	☐ Excessive tiredness
☐ Used street drugs	☐ Used alcohol	☐ Depression
☐ Premature labor	☐ Anxiety	☐ Hospitalization
☐ Morning sickness	☐ Anemia	☐ Mother beaten up
☐ Spotting	☐ Vomiting	☐ Ultra sound
☐ Excessive swelling	☐ High blood pressure	☐ X-ray
☐ Kidney infection	☐ Urinary infection	☐ Other special tests
☐ Malnutrition	☐ Hepatitis	☐ Nervousness
☐ Death in family	☐ Suicide Attempt	☐ Parents broke up
☐ HIV	☐ Diabetes	☐ Other

Please check if any of the following were experienced during delivery

Check all that apply

☐ Rh incompatibility	☐ Birth defects	☐ Transfusion	☐ Too slow
☐ Breech birth	☐ Anesthetic	☐ Jaundice	☐ Too fast
☐ Forceps	☐ Malformations	☐ Anoxia ('blue baby')	
☐ Caesarean section	☐ Birth injuries	☐ Convulsions	
☐ Cord wrapped around infant's neck		☐ Detached placenta	
☐ Other			

Did *mother* require: Oxygen? ☒ No ☐ Yes Blood transfusion? ☒ No ☐ Yes

How long was mother in the hospital?   2 days

Birth weight of child: 7   pounds   3   ounces

Did the baby go home from the hospital when the mother did?   ☐ No ☒ Yes

If not, how long was the baby in the hospital?

Reason for hospitalization?

Was the baby in Intensive Care after birth?   ☒ No ☐ Yes

Required incubation: ☒ No ☐ Yes

Please add anything else that you wish about the labor for and delivery of this child

Please describe your experience with the baby

☒ Cuddly	☐ Stiff	☐ Fussy	☒ Wonderful
☐ Colicky	☒ Easy	☐ Poor Sleeper	☒ Smart
☒ Good sleeper	☐ Hard to please	☒ Easy to please	☒ Attractive
☐ Fussy eater	☒ Good eater	☐ Too demanding	☐ Stubborn
☐ Other			

Please indicate at what age this child first did the following

Activity	Age	Activity	Age
Rolled over	3 mos.	**Smiled**	2 mos.
Sat up without help	7 mos.	**Slept all night**	8mos.
Crawled	9 mos.	**Ate solid food**	10 mos.
Took steps	10 mos.	**Spoke words**	18 mos.
Walked without assistance	1 year	**Spoke in sentences**	2 1/2 years
Bladder trained	2 years	**Bowel trained**	2 1/2 years
Regularly dry at night	3 years		

Did anyone think that this child had any problems between birth and beginning school? ☒ No ☐ Yes

If yes, what problems?

How old was your child when any close family members died? N/A

Who died? Under what circumstances? How did the child react?

Please note: According to state law, our staff *MUST* report current or unreported suspected child abuse or neglect to Protective Services.

Is your child sexually active? ☐ No ☒ Yes

What is your child's sexual history?

☐ **No sexual involvement**   ☐ **Practices Safe Sex**   ☒ **Not Sure**

Has your child ever had sexual contact with an adult or other child?

☒ **No**   ☐ **Yes**   ☐ **Not Sure**

If yes, with whom? Please describe the contact:
How old was your child at the time?

Has your child ever been physically or   ☐ **Yes** ☒ **No** ☐ **Not Sure**
sexually abused?

If so, please explain:

Was this contact/abuse reported to   ☐ **Yes** ☒ **No** ☐ **Not Sure**
Protective Services?

If yes, what happened as a result of report?

Substance Use History

To your knowledge, has your child ever used any of the following?

check all that apply

☐ Alcohol	☐ Heroin	☐ Codeine	☐ Morphine
☐ Dolantol	☐ T's –B's	☐ China White	☐ Little D-Lords
☐ Amphetamines	☐ Crank	☐ Ice-Speed	☐ Crystal Meth
☐ Phenmetrazine	☐ Uppers	☐ Peaches	☐ Hearts
☐ Caffeine	☐ Tranquilizers	☐ Sleeping Pills	☐ Muscle Relaxants
☐ Marijuana	☐ THC	☐ Hash	☐ Hash Oil
☐ Crack	☐ Barbiturates	☐ Methaqualone	☐ Quaalude
☐ Valium	☐ Downers	☐ Candy	☐ Ben-dia
☐ Mescaline	☐ Mushrooms	☐ Ecstasy	☐ LSD
☐ Steroids	☐ GHB	☐ Special K	☐ Roofies
☐ Opium	☐ Dollies	☐ Gack	☐ Nicotine
☐ Mickey Finn	☐ Cocaine	☐ Mandrex	☐ PCP
☐ Huffing	☒ Not Sure	☐ Others	

School History

Current school child attends Radburn High School

Previous schools attended

Highest grade completed   11   ☐ **Held back** *List grades*

Behavioral/emotional problems current or past   None

Average grades*(A, B, C, etc.)* B+   **Learning problems**   ☐ Yes ☒ No

Does your child attend *check all that apply*

☒ Public   ☐ Special Education   ☐ Private   ☐ Tutoring   ☐ Home Schooled
☒ Frequent Absences   ☐ Frequent Tardiness   ☐ Suspensions

III.   **Financial Status**

Current Employment/Education Status for Family

☒ **Father's Employer**   Burke Airframes   ☐ **Unemployed**

☒ Full-time   ☐ Retired   ☐ Enrolled in Training Program

☐ Part-time   ☐ Not Seeking   ☐ Enrolled in School
                          Employment

☐ Receives   ☐ SSI   ☐ SSDI   ☐ Other
   Support

☒ **Mother's Employer**   Merry Maids   ☐ **Unemployed**

☐ Full-time   ☐ Retired   ☐ Enrolled in Training Program

☒ Part-time   ☐ Not Seeking   ☐ Enrolled in School
                          Employment

☐ Receives   ☐ SSI   ☐ SSDI   ☐ Other
   Support

Tell us about the employment history of the family

We have been working since we came to the United States.

Family Situation

Describe the family's current living arrangements

We all live together: my husband, Carmen, her 3 brothers, and her 2 sisters.

Please describe who lives with your child, number of rooms, describe your home

There are 9 rooms in our house, 4 bedrooms. Carmen has her own room since she is the oldest girl.

Who else has the child lived with since birth?

Her grandmother when we first came to the U.S.

If child is adopted, please indicate and give family history here

Tell us about the child's extended family (aunts, uncles, etc.)

The rest of our family still lives in Mexico.

Please give any other information that you feel we should know

We love our daughter very much but we are very worried and frightened for her.

PINE GROVE MENTAL HEALTH CLINIC

Narrative Summary
for
Carmen Suarez   DOB 10/24/87

Carmen Suarez is a 17-year-old, Hispanic female, referred from the emergency room social worker. This summary is based on information provided via self-report from Carmen's mother and from a face-to-face interview with Carmen and her mother. Both she and her family have little understanding and insight into the relationship between her recent physical ailments and her grief over the decision to abort her pregnancy last year. There is no co-morbidity evident.

Carmen's strengths include her ability to get along well with others, her drive to further her education, her sense of responsibility, and her love for her family. She is free of medical and substance abuse problems, which is also considered a strength. Both she and her parents are willing to receive services, even though they have little knowledge of what that entails. They are all motivated by a desire for Carmen to "feel better" and complete high school so she can attend college. Understanding the role of culture, identity, and tradition for her and her family—as well as the conflicts around this sensitive issue—may be critical to a successful treatment outcome.

It appears that Carmen is suffering from an episode of major depression, single episode, largely precipitated by feelings of unresolved grief about an abortion 1 year ago that continues to be a source of conflict for her and tension between her and her parents—especially her father. There is some suggestion of low level psychotic symptoms associated with the depression, but it is not clear that they are of clinical significance. It is not known if the issues and conflicts about cultural identity are also a precipitating stressor or have been aggravated by the depression—both are possible. As a result of the depressive disorder, Carmen has suffered significant distress and impairment in her normal level of occupation and educational and social function that now threatens her ability to graduate high school and pursue future plans for education and independence.

Carmen and her family seem united in their focus/goal at this time; Carmen feels well enough to return to school and graduate. There appear to be no other priorities at this time.

Anticipated treatment issues to be addressed in the individual plan include the need for a psychiatric evaluation to determine if there is a need for any medications. There does not appear to be any immediate risk requiring 24-hour supervision or intensive day treatment. There also appears to be an immediate indication for outpatient mental health counseling to work on her unresolved feelings about the pregnancy/abortion, and a need to help her develop strategies for completing high school and going on to college. Family therapy may be indicated to help repair the relationships with her parents—particularly her father. Anticipated length of services is 3 to 6 months.

MENTAL HEALTH AND ADDICTION RECOVERY PLAN

for
Carmen Suarez   DOB 10/24/87

GOALS	*Goals should be stated in the **individual's or family's own words** and include statements of dreams, hopes, role functions and vision of life. For each individual and family and/or setting, completion of all three sub-goals may not be necessary or appropriate.*

Life Goals

"I want to graduate high school."

Service/Treatment Goals

Carmen will be able to resume her regular classroom attendance, after school employment and social involvement.

Life Enhancement Goals

"I want to have my old relationship back with my father."

ANTICIPATED DISCHARGE/TRANSITION SETTING AND CRITERIA	*Describe the setting in terms of location, level of care, length of stay and service needs. Describe changes in the individual's and family's current needs and circumstances that will need to occur in order to succeed in discharge or transition.*

Carmen is able to attend school regularly.

BARRIERS	*Describe the **challenges as a result of the mental illness or addictive disorder** that stand in the way of the individual and family meeting their goals and/or achieving the discharge/transition criteria. Identifying these barriers is critical to specifying the objectives as well as services and interventions in the following section of the plan.*

- Symptoms of depression.
- Social anxiety and fearfulness.
- Family conflict and anxiety.

Carmen Suarez

Objective Worksheet #1

This objective is related to which goal(s) or transition/discharge criteria (i.e., treatment goal) or barrier?
Inability to attend school because of her problems with depression
Is there more than one *active* objective that addresses this goal? ☐ Yes ☑ No

OBJECTIVE	*Using action words, describe the **specific changes expected** in measurable and behavioral terms. Include the target date for completion.*
#1	Carmen will attend school every day for a full day for 2 weeks without absences as reported by her parents.
TARGET DATE	90 days

INDIVIDUAL/ FAMILY STRENGTHS	*Identify the individual's and family's past accomplishments, current aspirations, motivations, personal attitudes, attributes, etc. which can be used to **help accomplish this objective**.*
Past performance, family support, motivation	

INTERVENTIONS	*Describe the specific activity, service or treatment, the provider or other responsible person (including the individual and family), and the **intended purpose or impact as it relates to this objective**. The intensity, frequency and duration should also be specified.*

- Psychiatrist to meet with Carmen every 1 to 2 weeks for the next 3 months to clarify diagnosis and prescribe medications to reduce acute symptoms of depression so that she can attend class.
- Social worker to provide 1 hour of psychotherapy twice a week for 4 weeks to help Carmen resolve feelings of guilt and loss.
- Case manager to meet with Carmen up to 3 hours/week for 4 weeks as required to coordinate return to school with school counselors and mental health team.
- Family therapy for 90 minutes every 2 weeks to resolve family conflicts that play a role in perpetuating/aggravating Carmen's problems of depression.
- Carmen to attend weekly peer group at Barrios Unidos community center for teens struggling with issues of identity and acculturation.

PINE GROVE MENTAL HEALTH CLINIC
Discharge/Transition
for
Carmen Suarez   DOB 10/24/87

☒ **Discharge** ☐ **Transfer Admission Date** 02/12/04 **Discharge Date** 04/10/04
Reason for seeking Services
Carmen had become extremely anxious, worried, fearful, and withdrawn. She has significant unresolved feeling of guilt and family tensions following an abortion approximately 1 year ago. Carmen and her family had attempted traditional healing without success and following an emergency room visit for an anxiety attack, was referred to Pine Grove for mental health treatment

Reason for Transfer or Discharge *check below the appropriate reason for termination*

☐ **Referral to AOD Treatment**   ☒ **Goals met, no additional services needed**

☐ **Referral to MH Treatment**   ☐ **Needed services not available**

☐ **Referral to AOD and MH Treatment**   ☐ **Client rejects continuation**

☒ **Referral to AOD Aftercare**   ☐ **Client did not return**

☐ **Referral to MH Aftercare**   ☐ **Client moved**

☐ **Increase/Decrease (circle) level of care**   ☒ **Other**
                                          Peer community services

---

Diagnosis At Admission			At Transfer/Discharge: ☐ No Change		
Check Primary	Code	Description	Check Primary	Code	Description
Axis I ☒	296.20	Major depression	☒	296.20	Major depression
☐			☐	305.00	Alcohol abuse
Axis II ☐	V71.09	No diagnosis	☐	V71.09	No diagnosis
Axis III		S/P abortion			S/P abortion
Axis IV	**Psychosocial/environmental problem(s)** Primary support, education			**Psychosocial/ environmental problem(s)** Primary support, education	
Axis V	**GAF** 43			**GAF** 75	

Indicate goal(s) addressed and progress made

☒ Life Goal	☒ Service Goal	☒ Life Enhancement Goal
☒ Met	☒ Met	☐ Met
☐ Partially met	☐ Partially met	☒ Partially met
☐ Not met	☐ Not met	☐ Not met
☐ Discontinued	☐ Discontinued	☐ Discontinued

Overall Progress In Treatment

☒ Much improved   ☐ Improved   ☐ No change   ☐ Worse

Comments

Carmen and her parents had much strength to build on, engaged actively in the process of meeting their goals, and made substantial progress in a relatively short period of time. However, in the course of treatment it became clear that Carmen had a hidden problem of binge alcohol use that was aggravating her problems with mood, school attendance, and work.

Level of Care/Services Provided

Carmen met with Dr. Harris for an initial assessment and follow-up pharmacotherapy, participated in weekly individual counseling, and attended peer groups at the local community resource center. The family also participated in 3 family therapy sessions. The case manager made several visits to Carmen's school to facilitate and support her classroom reentry.

Medication Summary

Carmen is now taking Effexor 150 mg q AM with substantial relief of her depressive and anxiety symptoms.

Client's Response to Treatment and Transfer/Discharge

Within one month Carmen reported feeling much better and with the support of her family and case manager was able to return to school full time after about 6 weeks. When her problems with alcohol became apparent Carmen began attending AA for teens 3 times a week and reports that it has been especially helpful. Her relationship with her father is improved, although there are some tensions that remain.

Continuity of Care Recommendations

Carmen will continue with her antidepressants with her family doctor and will also continue with AA and the peer group at Barrios Unidos. Carmen and her father may return at some point in the future to attempt to resolve issues between them.

Index